IО120З49

Advance Praise for *Remaking Islam in African Portugal*

"Resonant throughout *Remaking Islam in African Portugal*, the ethnographer's deeply informed voice is the one we ourselves need to hear, as we, too, face unprecedented, once hardly imaginable predicaments of closeness and distancing in our troubled times." —Richard Werbner, author of *Divination's Grasp: African Encounters with the Almost Said*

"The gripping narratives and nuanced interpretation found in Michelle Johnson's *Remaking Islam in African Portugal* demonstrates the considerable intellectual fruits of taking a slower more narratively contoured approach to ethnographic research and writing. . . . Given the depth of its analytical insights and the grace of its presentation, this is a work that will be read, savored, and debated for many years to come." —Paul Stoller, author of *Yaya's Story: The Quest for Well Being in the World*

"Written with great sensitivity and reflexivity, *Remaking Islam in African Portugal* . . . is a refreshing welcome addition to scholarly conversations on African diasporas and struggles over belonging." —Pamela Feldman-Savelsberg, Carleton College

"This insightful ethnographic narrative about the religious challenges of Muslim women from Guinea-Bissau in Lisbon deals with religion, gender and generations in a globalised world. While rooted in profound insights about the homeland, it spells out how Guinean women renegotiate ethnicity and religious identity." —Jónína Einarsdóttir, University of Iceland

REMAKING ISLAM IN
AFRICAN PORTUGAL

FRAMING THE GLOBAL SERIES

The Framing the Global project, an initiative of Indiana University Press and the Indiana University Center for the Study of Global Change, is funded by the Andrew W. Mellon Foundation.
Hilary E. Kahn and Deborah Piston-Hatlen, series editors

REMAKING ISLAM IN AFRICAN PORTUGAL

Lisbon · Mecca · Bissau

—◊—

MICHELLE C. JOHNSON

INDIANA UNIVERSITY PRESS

This book is a publication of

Indiana University Press
Office of Scholarly Publishing
Herman B. Wells Library 350
1320 East 10th Street
Bloomington, Indiana 47405 USA

iupress.indiana.edu

© 2020 by Michelle C. Johnson

All rights reserved
No part of this book may be reproduced or utilized in any form or by any means, electronic or mechanical, including photocopying and recording, or by any information storage and retrieval system, without permission in writing from the publisher. The paper used in this publication meets the minimum requirements of the American National Standard for Information Sciences—Permanence of Paper for Printed Library Materials, ANSI Z39.48–1992.

Manufactured in the United States of America

Library of Congress Cataloging-in-Publication Data

Names: Johnson, Michelle C., author.
Title: Remaking Islam in African Portugal : Lisbon-Mecca-Bissau / Michelle C. Johnson.
Description: Bloomington : Indiana University Press, 2020. | Series: Framing the global | Includes bibliographical references and index.
Identifiers: LCCN 2020000490 (print) | LCCN 2020000491 (ebook) | ISBN 9780253049766 (hardback) | ISBN 9780253049773 (paperback) | ISBN 9780253049780 (ebook)
Subjects: LCSH: Muslims—Portugal. | Islam—Portugal. | Muslims—Guinea-Bissau. | Islam—Guinea-Bissau. | Muslim women—Portugal. | Muslim women—Guinea-Bissau. | Guinea-Bissau—Relations—Portugal. | Portugal—Relations—Guinea-Bissau.
Classification: LCC BP65.P8 J64 2020 (print) | LCC BP65.P8 (ebook) | DDC 297.09469—dc23
LC record available at https://lccn.loc.gov/2020000490
LC ebook record available at https://lccn.loc.gov/2020000491

1 2 3 4 5   25 24 23 22 21 20

To Badim Clubo members, past, present, and future

CONTENTS

ACKNOWLEDGMENTS

THIS BOOK TOOK ME A decade to finish, and so many people have contributed to it in multiple ways that it is nearly impossible to remember and acknowledge them all. Since I work at a liberal arts university where I spend much of my time working with students, it feels right to begin with my own teachers. When I was an undergraduate at the University of Washington, Clarke Speed, the late Edgar "Bud" Winans, and Simon Ottenberg introduced me to anthropology and African studies, gave me an extraordinary amount of time and attention, and encouraged me to go to graduate school. When I told Clarke that I wanted to become a professor of anthropology, he helped me believe that it was possible. As a graduate student at the University of Illinois, I had the privilege of working with Alma Gottlieb, an outstanding teacher, scholar, and mentor. It took reading only one of her books to know that I wanted to work with her. Her influence on my thinking and writing is still evident so many years later, on every page of this book, and I am thankful for the wisdom, advice, and friendship that she and Philip Graham have offered over the years. I also benefited greatly from my other teachers at Illinois, Ed Bruner, Alejandro Lugo, and especially Valerie Hoffman and Mahir Şaul, who taught me what I needed to know about Islam in and beyond Africa.

Scholars of lusophone Africa are a small, tight-knit group, and those who work in Guinea-Bissau have been an invaluable sounding board. Eric Gable was the first of this group whom I met, and he gave me the advice, wisdom, and support that I needed to start my research in Guinea-Bissau. I have benefited greatly from his friendship and careful reading of my work since then. This book has also been enriched greatly by the work of and scholarly dialogue with Maria Abranches, Lorenzo Bordonaro, Clara Carvalho, Joanna Davidson, Jónína Einarsdóttir, Joshua Forrest, Brandon Lundy, Henrik Vigh, and Walter Hawthorne.

My earliest fieldwork in Guinea-Bissau and Portugal, which I conducted in the late 1990s and early 2000s in graduate school, provided the foundation for the future research out of which this book emerged. Research in Guinea-Bissau was funded by a Social Science Research Council International Predissertation Fellowship. While this preliminary fieldwork was intended to prepare me for an additional year of research, Guinea-Bissau's 1998 civil war prevented me from returning until 2003. That initial year was a gift and became more important than I ever imagined. I was affiliated with the Instituto Nacional de Estudos e Pesquisa (INEP) while in Bissau and am grateful for the support and mentorship of Peter Mendy, INEP's director at the time.

Fieldwork in Portugal was supported by a Social Science Research Council International Dissertation Research Fellowship, a Department of Education Fulbright-Hays Fellowship, and a Marianne A. Ferber Graduate Scholarship in Women's Studies from the University of Illinois at Urbana-Champaign. As these fellowships were intended for research in Guinea-Bissau, I will never forget the granting officers' flexibility and willingness to work with me as I scrambled to move my research to Portugal. JoAnn D'Alisera encouraged me to work in Lisbon, and she opened my eyes to the importance of transnational research and assured me that this radical move at the time would eventually be fruitful. I am eternally grateful for her confidence, support, and friendship over the years. In Lisbon, Paula Zagallo e Mello and Rita Bacelar from the Luso-American Educational Commission and Maria João Santos Silva from the US Embassy provided the logistical support that made moving my research from Bissau to Lisbon possible.

Bucknell University generously funded my later fieldwork periods. Start-up research money allowed me to return to both Portugal and Guinea-Bissau in 2003, and a 75 percent sabbatical grant, a Dean's Fellowship, an International Research Travel Grant, and a grant from the Center for the Study of Race, Gender, and Ethnicity funded my 2011 and 2017 fieldwork in Portugal.

I owe the book's real beginning, however, to a 2010 Social Science Research Council (SSRC) Book Fellowship. I am indebted to my (now retired) colleague and friend, Marc Schloss, for his insightful comments on my proposal draft and for his encouragement during the writing period. The SSRC workshop in Brooklyn was one of the most intellectually stimulating experiences of my academic career, and conversing and receiving feedback from other fellows and participating editors was incredibly helpful and humbling. My SSRC fellowship editor, Bud Bynack, had a sharp vision for the book from the very beginning and knew exactly the direction in which I needed to move to realize it. He pushed me to think in nuanced and creative ways, and when life intervened (I was seven months pregnant at the time of the workshop), he agreed to work with me well beyond the official fellowship period, as I struggled to complete chapters while teaching and parenting. I can only hope that the finished product meets his high standards.

I wrote half of the book, chapters 2, 3, and 4, during my first sabbatical from Bucknell when I was a visiting researcher in the Department of Cultural Anthropology and Ethnology at Uppsala University. I would like to thank Hugh Beach for this exciting opportunity, as well as Sten Hagberg and the late Jan Ovesen for their hospitality and support that year. Beyond being invited to participate in a vibrant research community in Uppsala, I also benefited from office space, free daycare and schooling for my children, the best health care system I have ever experienced (including on-site massages for faculty every semester), and a daily *fika* (afternoon coffee break), which I continue to practice in the United States.

I would never have completed the rest of the book, chapters 1, 5, and 6, without support from two other extraordinary research communities. I drafted each of these chapters at Bucknell University's Faculty Writer's Boot Camp, where I benefited from the energy and conversations with the other participants and the brilliant writer-proctors, who kept us on track and conferenced with us when we got stuck: Peg Cronin, Loren Gustafson, Sabrina Kirby, and Deirdre O'Conner. I then presented these drafts at the Sattherthwaite Colloquium for African Ritual and Religion, where I received invaluable feedback from the various participants. Julie Archambault, Christopher Annear, Aurelien Baroiller, André Chappatte, Diane Ciekawy, Deborah Durham, Marloes Janson, Tim Landry, Adeline Masquelier, Inês Ponte, Katrien Pype, Robert Thornton, Richard Werbner, and Pnina Werbner provided particularly helpful suggestions. I am forever indebted to Dick and Pnina for their friendship and hospitality and for the opportunity to engage with such a vibrant group of scholars of ritual and religion in Africa.

I also had the opportunity to present a draft of chapter 6 at an invited workshop, "Being Muslim: How Local Islam Overturns Narratives of Exceptionalism, IV: Transnational and Local Networks of Pilgrimage," at Vanderbilt University's Department of Religious Studies in 2015. I would like to thank Tony Stewart for the invitation, as well as Tal Tamari, Jocelyn Hendrickson, Daniel Birchok, and Richard McGregor for their helpful comments. Sections of chapter 2 appeared in "'The Proof Is on My Palm': Debating Islam and Ritual in a New African Diaspora," *The Journal of Religion in Africa* 36, no. 1 (2006): 50–77. An earlier, slightly different version of chapter 4 appeared as "Death and the Left Hand: Islam, Gender, and 'Proper' Mandinga Funerary Custom in Guinea-Bissau and Portugal," *African Studies Review* 52, no. 2 (2009): 93–117. I am grateful for the editors' permission to reprint this material in the book.

Insightful comments and helpful suggestions from two reviewers challenged me and made for a much better book. My editors at Indiana University Press were with me every step of the way. Jennika Baines believed in the book from the very beginning, and I am grateful for her encouragement, advice, and enthusiasm. I also wish to thank Allison Chaplin, who handled the photographs, and my project manager, Pete Feely, for putting everything together for the final push. A subvention grant from Bucknell University provided me with the funds to hire Martin White, who expertly compiled the index.

I would also like to thank my colleagues in the Department of Sociology and Anthropology and other colleagues and friends at Bucknell University, who encouraged me by commenting on early drafts of chapters, helping me with title options and which photographs to include, and asking me how the project was coming along: Debby Abowitz, Debbie Baney, Chris Boyatzis, Coralynn Davis, Elizabeth Durden, Cymone Fourshey, Michael James, Linden Lewis, Carl Milofsky, Karen Morin, Sue Reed, Clare Sammells, Ned Searles, Tristan Riley, Jennifer Silva, Paul Susman, Allen Tran, and Richard Waller. The students in my Religions in Africa seminars also commented on drafts of several chapters, and my former honors thesis student, Vikram Shenoy, assisted with editing and references.

My parents, Nancy Johnson and the late Ron Johnson, never questioned my desire to go to college and study anthropology, even as most people in my hometown, Yakima, Washington, pursued work in offices, factories, and agriculture. My mother accompanied my husband, my children, and me for the year in Sweden, and she made it possible for me to work on the book and conduct my 2011 fieldwork. I would like to thank my sisters, Kim and Jackie, for their support of a career that has taken me so far away from home. Kim and her husband, Dave, provided feedback on potential titles; I can only hope that they are satisfied with the current one. Ned Searles, my colleague, fellow anthropologist, and beloved life partner and friend, was by my side (or at the very least, only a phone call or text away) during fieldwork in Guinea-Bissau and Portugal and was incredibly supportive during the long write-up period. I am a better anthropologist and person because of him. I hope that while our daughter, Nora, and son, Wyatt, might agree that being the children of parent-anthropologists is not easy, it is rarely, if ever, boring. Nora and Wyatt have endured a lot, but hopefully not too much, accompanying their parents to various countries or getting by while I (or my husband) traveled. Their courage, resilience, openness, and curiosity about the world are inspiring and make me proud.

My heaviest debt, of course, lies with the Guinean Muslims I have had the pleasure of working with in Guinea-Bissau and Portugal, who never seemed to grow tired of my questions and have so graciously shared their lives with me for two decades. In Bissau and Bafata-Oio, I would like to acknowledge especially the late Al-Hajj Fodimaye Turé, Karamadu and Fatumata Turé, Numoo Turé, Saajo Daabo, and Musukeba Mané. Arafam Kamara, Idrissa Seydi, and Ansu Mané were outstanding research assistants and warm friends. In Lisbon, I would like to thank Aminata and Demba Baldé; Mansata Djassi and Alaaji Suané; my Qur'anic teacher, Al-Hajj Daramé; Rosa Djassi; Chembo Djassi; Odette Djau; Kadi Keita; Muna Ali; the Rossio merchants; and Maternal Kin Club members. Several close friends in both sites died before this book was published, and I will always remember them: Al-Hajj Fodimaye Turé, Bacar Djana, Tunbulo Faati, and Senhora Mané. I have tried my best to balance meeting people's desires for their names to appear in the book and my own responsibility to protect people's identities when necessary. In some cases, I have been able to do both simultaneously (I know dozens of people named Fatumata and Aminata in both sites), and at other times I used nicknames, clan names, or initials. At those times when I (or the reviewers) felt I needed to use pseudonyms, I can only hope that people will understand and forgive me.

NOTE ON TRANSCRIPTION

SPELLINGS OF MANDINGA LANGUAGE TERMS follow those in the *Mandinka English Dictionary* (Banjul, the Gambia: W.E.C. International, 1995), except for the following simplifications:

-*s* instead of -*lu* for pluralizing words
ng in place of *η*
ny rather than *ñ*

On occasion, I have used slightly different translations than the ones suggested by this dictionary.

REMAKING ISLAM IN
AFRICAN PORTUGAL

ONE

FAITH AND FIELDWORK IN AFRICAN LISBON

ONE AFTERNOON DURING MY FIELDWORK in Lisbon, my husband and I joined Amadi; her fiancé, Laalo; and her mother, Aja, to celebrate the Muslim feast day of Tabaski, the West African name for *Eid al-Adha*, the Festival of Sacrifice, which takes place annually during the time of the hajj, the pilgrimage to Mecca. On this day, Muslims throughout the world slaughter a sheep or goat and hold a feast to commemorate Abraham's sacrifice of a ram in place of his son, Ishmael, according to God's command. When we arrived at their apartment in Cacém, Aja was sitting in her favorite chair, dressed in her finest "big" (Muslim) clothing. We handed her a small offering to mark the occasion: a bag of fresh okra and five kola nuts, which we had bought from the Guinean merchants at Rossio in central Lisbon. We greeted Aja in Mandinga, saying, "Mother, is there peace?" to which she responded, "Peace only, my children," as she wiped the tears streaming down her face with a white handkerchief. Fearing the worst, such as the death of a close relative or community member, I quickly went into the kitchen to join Amadi, who was grilling meat for the afternoon meal. As she handed me a bag of roselle leaves to clean and sort, she sighed and said, "My poor mother. She missed prayer at the mosque on Tabaski because I couldn't find her a ride. This morning she asked me if we were going to kill a sheep. How can I kill a sheep in my tiny kitchen? If we kill one on the street, the police will surely arrest us. I went to the grocery store and bought some lamb. They gave me the head, so at least it looks like we killed it ourselves."

I could hear Aja talking to my husband in the living room: "Son, I killed *two* goats in my compound last year in Bissau, not one, *two* goats!" Amadi explained that her mother had not been sleeping well since she arrived in Lisbon after the 1998 coup and start of the civil war in Guinea-Bissau. "She suffers from the cold and jumps at the slightest sound. I hoped to get her to the mosque today, but she will have to suffer it." Amadi put another piece of meat on the grill and said, "Ah, Fatumata, Africa and Europe are not the same."

This book is about the religious lives of Muslim immigrants from Guinea-Bissau living in and around Lisbon, Portugal. I focus on what being Muslim means for Guinean immigrants in the context of diaspora, as well as their changing relationship to their ritual practices as they remake themselves and their religion in a new locale. In exploring immigrants' religious lives in Lisbon, I draw from and build on two related fields: the anthropology of Islam and religion and migration. Since the publication of Clifford Geertz's (1968) seminal book *Islam Observed*, anthropologists of Islam have concerned themselves with the challenge of representing the diversity of Muslim communities worldwide while at the same time acknowledging Islam's universal features. More often than not, this challenge has become an either/or matter. As John Bowen (2012, 1) explains, scholarship and popular discourse often reveal the tendency to consider Islam as "only a matter of culture" or "only a matter of religion."

In an attempt to reconcile the problem of the "one and the many" in the anthropology of Islam, some scholars have asked, given the diversity of Muslims worldwide, if it even makes sense to talk about Islam in the singular, or if there are instead multiple Islams. But as Robert Launay (2004, 5) writes, such a notion is "theologically unacceptable to most Muslims, who assert that there is, and can only be, one Islam."[1] Here, I join Edward Simpson and Kai Kresse (2008, 24), who critique the universalist-particularist dichotomy in the study of Islam and acknowledge that most Muslims oscillate between these two positions, or even embody both simultaneously, in their daily lives. Anthropologists of Islam have examined this complex dynamic, highlighting debates sparked by religious conversion, change, and Islamic reform movements (e.g., Janson 2013; Launay 2004; Masquelier 2001, 2009; McIntosh 2009; Soares 2005; Schulz 2012) in African societies. They focus on conflicts that emerge, for example, between various types of Muslims that can be characterized loosely as "traditionalist" and "reformist." While the former commonly conflate Islam with ethnicity, customary practices, or belonging in a Sufi order, the latter stress the importance of Islam's central texts (the Qur'an and hadith) and the five pillars: the declaration of faith, prayer, almsgiving, fasting during the holy month of Ramadan, and the pilgrimage to Mecca. Islamic reformists—for example, Wahabbis in Côte d'Ivoire as described by Launay (2004) and the

Tablighi Jama'at in the Gambia as described by Marloes Janson (2013)—seek to "purify" local versions of Islam and divide communities by introducing new ways of being Muslim.

These works have provided considerable insight into the complex relationship between Islam and local cultures on the continent. We know much less, however, about how these processes play out in contemporary diaspora settings, where their contours are different and the stakes far higher. As the various case studies and ethnographic vignettes throughout this book demonstrate, being Muslim in African Lisbon is fraught with ambiguities and contradictions that extend beyond the traditionalist-reformist dichotomy. There are no names for the various groups or positions, and the usual oppositions of global/ local, one/many, and orthodox Islam / popular Islam do not hold. Rather, the orientations of "African custom" and "global Islam" appear more as points along a continuum, between which people move back and forth at certain times or even during fleeting moments throughout their daily lives.

This book also draws inspiration from scholarly works in the field of religion and migration (e.g., D'Alisera 2004; Daswani 2015; Fesenmyer 2016; Leichtman 2016; Selby 2012; van Dijk 1997; P. Werbner 1990). These scholars ask, as Mara Leichtman (2016, 2) puts it, "What is at stake for religion in a globalized world unchained yet bounded by processes of migration [and] cosmopolitanism?" JoAnn D'Alisera (2004, 9) explains that for Sierra Leonean immigrants in Washington, DC, religion has become "a focal point of transnational identity." In providing new ideas about faith and proper practice, members of a culturally diverse community of Muslims inspire Sierra Leonean immigrants to reflect more deeply on what it means to be Muslim in Africa, America, and beyond. In a similar fashion, I argue that when Guinean Muslims leave their homeland and make their way to the European metropolis and the land of their former colonizer, they encounter a new version of Islam and a novel approach to religion more generally.

Like members of other Muslim ethnic groups in West Africa, such as Mende (Ferme 1994) and Kuranko (Jackson 1977) peoples in Sierra Leone and Dyula peoples (Launay 2004) in Côte d'Ivoire, Mandinga and Fula in Guinea-Bissau have conflated ethnicity and religious identity since Islam arrived in West Africa centuries ago: to be Mandinga or Fula was to naturally be Muslim. But as they come into increased contact with Muslims from outside Africa and encounter other ways of being Muslim, they are coming to see these identities as increasingly distinct. This heightened consciousness has also sparked a broader shift in how Guinean Muslims understand religion more generally. In his insightful volume, Hent de Vries (2008, 10) argues that "the study of 'religion' . . . depends upon a rigorous alternation between the 'universal' and 'essential' and the 'singular' or exemplary 'instant,' 'instance,' and 'instantiation.'" Religion is what people do on a daily basis; it is, as de Vries (2008, 14) puts it, the "words, things, gestures, powers, sounds, silences, smells, sensations, shapes, colors, affects, and effects" of everyday life. At the same time, however, religion is bigger than this. Abstracted from taken-for-granted experience, it is a frame that connects practitioners to a new, unfolding present and imagined future, full of possibilities. I argue that in African Lisbon, these two experiences of religion are sometimes congruent and other times conflictual.

For Guinean Muslim immigrants in Portugal, new encounters with Islam and religion are sparking debates focused on customary aspects of life-course rituals and other ritual practices. Like Pakistani Muslims in England as described by Pnina Werbner (1990), for whom migration inspires reflection on taken-for-granted aspects of ritual, Guinean immigrants are also examining, questioning, and revising their own ritual practices as they encounter Muslims from outside Africa and other, more universalistic ways of being Muslim. Many claim, for example, that aspects of the rituals they have long practiced—name-giving rituals, writing-on-the-hand rituals to initiate Qur'anic study, initiation rituals, funerals and postburial sacrifices, and healing-divining—are really African customs that should be updated or replaced altogether by a more cosmopolitan practice of Islam focused on the five pillars of faith that unite Muslims everywhere. At the same time, however, I show that these same people continue to draw on customary beliefs and practices as they remake themselves and their religion in Lisbon.

In the chapters that follow, I reveal the complex gender, class, and generational dynamics at play as Guinean Muslims remake Islam in African Portugal. Specifically, I consider what is at stake as men and women in the colonial metropolis grapple with dissonant visions of what previously they had taken for granted as Islam and religion in their homeland. For example, while Guinean Muslim women believe that in order for them to be truly Muslim they must be circumcised, their husbands insist that female circumcision is an African custom that has nothing to do with Islam, a debate I explore more fully in chapter 3. I argue that as Guinean Muslim immigrants confront various groups of others in Lisbon and as they move in and between different types of religious and cultural spaces, they forge new accommodations between ethnic and religious identity, new ways of being simultaneously Mandinga and Muslim, national and transnational, local and global, in a new diaspora where secularism, racism, and anti-Muslim sentiment abound.

Before I explore the contours and details of these accommodations and debates, it is first necessary to say something about the research and the people who have informed it.

BETWEEN AFRICA AND EUROPE:
GUINEAN MUSLIMS IN LISBON

My experience with Guinean Muslims in Portugal spans two decades, but it has an even longer history than that. In fact, I never intended to work in Lisbon. I conducted my predissertation fieldwork in 1996–97 in Guinea-Bissau both in the capital city, Bissau, and in Bafata-Oio, a Mandinga village in the country's northern Oio region. In 1998, shortly before I was planning to return to the village to conduct my dissertation fieldwork, a civil war broke out in the country. A coup attempt led by rebel leader Ansumane Mané to oust the country's president João Bernardo ("Nino") Vieira divided the country and sparked an eleven-month political conflict. The War of June 7, as some call it today, resulted in widespread death, destruction, and displacement as refugees fled to neighboring countries and to Portugal. I spent one year working with established Mandinga immigrants in Lisbon, as well as the refugees who were pouring into the city. This resulted in my dissertation, a transnational study of debates about personhood, religious identity, and ritual practices.

I returned to Lisbon in 2001 for new fieldwork and again in 2003 (as well as to Guinea-Bissau) and went back to Lisbon in 2011 and 2017. It was during these subsequent periods of fieldwork in Lisbon that the focus of this book took shape. While it draws on my previous fieldwork in both sites, unlike my dissertation, it focuses on the religious lives of Guinean Muslims living in Lisbon and its many exurbs. Although the Guinean Muslim community in Lisbon is ethnically diverse, consisting of Mandinga and Fula peoples, I chose to work primarily with Mandinga immigrants. Having worked previously with Mandinga in Guinea-Bissau, I was familiar with their culture and ritual practices and proficient in their language.

In West Africa, Mandinga are part of the Mande diaspora, which comprises a variety of ethnic groups whose members speak related languages and trace their origins to the Mande heartland, located in present-day Mali. This unified, diasporic identity is exemplified by the common Mande proverb "We are all one." Mande peoples live in many countries throughout West Africa, where they make their living primarily as farmers, merchants, or Qur'anic scholars and healer-diviners. Mandinga are the fourth-largest ethnic group in Guinea-Bissau and make up about 15 percent of the country's total population of 1.4 million (Mendy and Lobban 2013, 3). Because their origins lie elsewhere, they are considered outsiders even though Guinea-Bissau has been their home for centuries. They differentiate themselves from Guinea-Bissau's egalitarian ethnic groups who live on the coast and practice indigenous African religions, Christianity, or both, and they identify with other socially stratified Mande and Fula peoples throughout West Africa who inhabit the interior regions and practice Islam (see Brooks 1993; Lopes 1987).

For most Guinean Muslims, Islam is as much an ethnic identity as it is a religion: to be Mandinga or Fula is to be Muslim, and the fusion of ethnicity and religion shapes their identity and infuses their ritual practices. A common response to the question "What is your ethnicity?" is "I am a Muslim" or "I am a Christian," with the term *Christian* denoting a non-Muslim, either a Christian, a practitioner of an indigenous African religion, or both simultaneously. Increasingly, these religious identities are becoming racialized, in that people term others *Musulmanu* ("Muslim") or *Kriston* ("non-Muslim") and generalize about their beliefs and practices irrespective of their actual ethnicity and religious identity. Although Mandinga and Fula historically consider themselves rival ethnic groups, Islam has brought them together to some extent in Guinea-Bissau and even more so in Lisbon, where they often live side by side, worship together at the same mosques, and, on some occasions, even attend each other's life-course rituals and other cultural events. Many Mandinga in Lisbon also speak Fula and vice versa.[2]

Although it is often assumed that ethnicity is replaced by a more unified, national identity in diaspora contexts, in this book I show that ethnicity remains key for Guinean immigrants in Lisbon. During my fieldwork, Fula immigrants would often joke with me as Fula in Guinea-Bissau often did, asking me why I was studying Mandinga rather than them. When I explained I did not understand or speak Fula, they told me that this did not matter, since Fula is "lighter" (by which they meant easier to learn) than Mandinga, they are good teachers, and as many Fula as Mandinga in Lisbon speak Kriolu, Guinea-Bissau's lingua franca. Intermarriage between these two ethnic groups is still rare, even in Lisbon. Indeed, I knew of only one case in Lisbon, and the couple faced much criticism in the Guinean Muslim immigrant community.

Migration from Guinea-Bissau to Portugal is a relatively recent phenomenon. As Clara Carvalho (2012, 19–20) explains, elites of mixed African and Portuguese descent first migrated to Portugal from Guinea-Bissau in the 1950s to study. A larger wave of migration followed Guinea-Bissau's independence from Portugal in 1974. Guinean Muslims, including the Mandinga and Fula immigrants I came to know, were part of the largest wave of immigration to

Portugal, which occurred in the 1980s and 1990s. Guinea-Bissau's 1998–99 civil war sparked another wave of immigration, which continued as conditions in the country deteriorated through the early 2000s. Fernando Machado (1998, 49) points out that Muslim immigrants to Portugal were distinct from earlier groups in that most came to Lisbon directly from villages rather than from the capital, Bissau. As such, they remain rooted in *ado*, or "custom," which they imagined as originating in rural Guinea-Bissau and representing the most traditional or authentic aspects of their cultures. I show that it is precisely such custom that is being destabilized and remade as Guinean immigrants engage new models of Islam in the diaspora, and the chapters that follow demonstrate that ritual practices are the principal sites of argument and debate. Talal Asad (2009, 22) asserts that conflict and argument over the meaning and form of ritual and other religious practices are "a natural part of any Islamic tradition." In exploring such debates among Muslims worldwide, however, scholars have privileged text and discourse over the body. In this book, I focus on embodied ritual practices as forms of argument and, in so doing, join Rudolph Ware (2014) in the attempt to recapture the primacy of the body in the making and remaking of Islam.

The Guinean Muslims I met lived either in apartments in central Lisbon or in the city's many exurbs. Some exurban neighborhoods were inhabited almost entirely by African immigrants from Portugal's former African colonies, who at the time of my fieldwork organized themselves by country of origin, ethnic group, or religion. Some of these neighborhoods were known locally as *barracas*, which referred to the small, shack-like structures that were common in some areas. This term also described large, unfinished apartment complexes—many of which lacked internal plumbing, electricity, and even doors and windows—into which African immigrants moved and lived rent-free, a phenomenon referred to in Kriolu as *salta parediu*, or "building jumping."[3]

The men I knew earned their living primarily as construction workers, tailors, or street merchants who sold "things from the homeland," such as kola nuts, local tobacco, tea, and fruits and vegetables, to fellow Guinean immigrants. While the most prosperous of these men owned shops in commercial centers in central Lisbon, most of them sold their goods on the streets near train stations or the central mosque. Others worked as healer-diviners, treating African and Portuguese clients alike for problems concerning work, health, or personal relationships. I explore these healer-diviners in detail in chapter 5 (see also Abranches 2014; Carvalho 2012). The women I came to know worked primarily as wives and mothers or as clothing merchants or house

Figure 1.1. A tailor at work in Monte Abraão, 2017. Photograph by the author.

Figure 1.2. Rossio merchants, 2017. Photograph by the author.

and office cleaners. Others sold things from the homeland at Rossio, owned or worked in Guinean restaurants (see Johnson 2016), or assisted their healer-diviner husbands by booking appointments or translating for clients who did not understand or speak Kriolu or Mandinga.

In Portugal, Guinean Muslims' diasporic identity is affirmed and remade as they encounter two new diasporas: immigrants from Portugal's other colonies—Angola, Mozambique, Cape Verde (see Fikes 2009), and São Tomé—and a transnational community of Muslims from North Africa and the Middle East, whom my interlocutors called "Arabs," and from South Asia, whom they termed "Indians." Throughout my fieldwork in Lisbon, I observed Guinean Muslims continually negotiating their simultaneous inclusion in and exclusion from these new diasporas.

My husband, Ned, an anthropologist who works with Inuit in the Eastern Canadian Arctic, was with me for my fieldwork in Guinea-Bissau and for much of my fieldwork in Portugal. We were thrust directly into debates about Islam as an ethnic affiliation and Islam as a global religious identity, the contours of which shifted considerably as we moved from Guinea-Bissau to Portugal. In the village, our Mandinga hosts gave us Muslim names, Lamini and Fatumata, urged us to wear "big clothing," and assumed we would—even expected us to—attend life-course rituals and Muslim holiday celebrations. While people never pressured us to attend Friday prayer at the village mosque, we went occasionally, and our attendance delighted them. Our own religious identities—I was raised Roman Catholic and Ned Episcopalian, though we were both nonpracticing at the time—did not matter much to people. They simply put us in the category of "believers" and never raised the issue of our conversion to Islam, a detail they deemed unimportant.

The situation was a bit different in the capital city, Bissau, where we lived for several months before moving to the village. In the evenings, we spent our free time with Mandinga friends in the neighborhood of Pilon, several of whom were merchants from the Gambia. They were critical of what they described as Guinean Muslims' apathy toward Islam. They complained that unlike Gambians, who were good (observant and pious) Muslims who could read Arabic, Muslims in Guinea-Bissau could hardly be considered Muslims at all: they did not pray, they had very little (if any) knowledge of Arabic, and their rituals had an "animist" (their term) flavor to them. Indeed, at the time, boys' initiation was in full swing in Bissau, and Muslims and non-Muslims participated side by side in the festivities, dancing and running from *Kankurang*, the masquerade figure thought to protect the initiates from witchcraft (see de Jong 2007).

Two of our Gambian friends, Boubakar and Baba, worried that we would return to America with the "wrong message" about Islam and sought to rectify this. As a start, they insisted on escorting us to the neighborhood mosque. Boubakar loaned us "proper" Muslim attire from his shop, including Saudi-style robes, a hijab for me, and a Muslim hat for Ned, and before we left for the mosque, Boubakar photographed us on our prayer mats. At the mosque, people welcomed us enthusiastically. I remember the event vividly, as if it happened yesterday. Bending, sitting, and touching my head to my prayer mat provided me with one of my first and most memorable embodied experiences of Islam. Ned and I left the mosque invigorated.

Later that evening, a boy from Pilon arrived at our compound in Sintra with a message: an *omi garandi* (elder holy man) wanted to see us. We immediately thought the worst: in praying at the mosque as non-Muslim foreigners, we had crossed a line and in doing so may have jeopardized my fieldwork. On the way to Pilon, we stopped at a shop to purchase some white things: tinned milk, sugar, and kola nuts, customary offerings that we hoped might clarify our intentions and appease the holy man. We arrived at the compound and exchanged greetings, and the holy man reprimanded us, but for a different reason than we had imagined. He explained that as guests in Guinea-Bissau, we should have attended mosque with elder Guinean escorts, not young foreign (Gambian) ones. Indeed, Guinean Muslims contend that one earns special favor from God by bringing foreigners to Islam, and the points were in danger of going to the wrong team.

In Portugal, the situation was completely different. Many people, especially men who studied the Qur'an or had made the hajj, often asked Ned and me if we were Muslims and inquired about the details of our conversion. On one occasion as I was carefully gathering my thoughts to answer, several people asserted that we were "Al-Hajj Fodimaye's people" and that the holy man himself had converted us in the village. Feeling compelled to set the record straight, I explained that although we had participated fully in Muslim life in the village and even considered ourselves "Muslims of the heart," we had never officially converted. On learning this, a few men wanted to plan a conversion ceremony for us, which would provide us with official Muslim status and grant us full access to Lisbon's central mosque. I got around this by explaining that my (very pious, practicing) Roman Catholic parents might consider my conversion to Islam as a rebellious, even disrespectful, act. In short, I did not want religion to divide my family. They agreed wholeheartedly and told me that the conversion ceremony could wait until my parents' deaths. When I accompanied people to the mosque on Fridays in Lisbon, I usually remained outside and chatted with the merchants.

These vignettes illuminate the shifts in how Guinean Muslims think about Islam and religion more generally as they move from the village to the city in Guinea-Bissau, and especially from Africa to Europe. In Guinea-Bissau, being Muslim means being a member of a Muslim ethnic group, being born of Muslim parents, possessing a Muslim name, and participating in three rituals: the name-giving ritual, the writing-on-the-hand ritual, and initiation, which includes circumcision for boys and girls (see Johnson 2000). Living with Muslims, participating in their daily lives, and attending their most cherished rituals rendered the visiting anthropologists Muslim enough. In Bissau, participation in Islam engaged tensions between elders and youth, locals and foreigners, as well as between competing ideas about belonging and salvation. In Portugal, however, being Muslim was something altogether different: it meant inclusion in a community of believers beyond Africa and embracing the five pillars of faith, which unite Muslims worldwide. Rather than acquiring Muslim identity at birth and solidifying this identity through embodied ritual practices, it comprised, at least for some, embracing the beliefs and practices of global Islam. In short, this change underscored the difference between Islam as an ethnic affiliation and Islam as a world religion. In rural Guinea-Bissau, my husband's and my conversion to Islam was unimportant because according to our Mandinga hosts, being Muslim was never really a possibility for us: we were not ethnically Mandinga or Fula and never could be, and we had not experienced the essential rituals. In Portugal, however, these were African customs that had nothing to do with Islam, a world religion to which anyone could convert and become a true believer.

METROPOLITAN METHODS

My previous research in Guinea-Bissau greatly facilitated my fieldwork in Lisbon; in fact, I doubt that it would have been possible without it. I was familiar with the country, its various ethnic groups and their cultures. I spoke Kriolu and Mandinga and had spent a considerable amount of time both in the capital city, Bissau, and in Bafata-Oio, a village known for its elaborate annual celebration of *Gammo*, the Prophet's birthday. Ned's and my Muslim names and Mandinga clan names, which we had acquired several years before arriving in Portugal, anchored us in the home country and shaped our interactions with our interlocutors in Lisbon. People described us as "Fodimaye's people from

Bafata-Oio," and many claimed they had heard about us. To everyone's delight, we could identify our "joking cousins," how to ritually insult them, and what we could expect or even steal from them. We also spoke Kriolu and Mandinga and understood the importance of diaspora for Mandinga identity. In the late 1990s, we journeyed overland from Guinea-Bissau to Mali with the explicit goal of experiencing firsthand the Mande heartland, which impressed people and gave us considerable legitimacy. In their eyes, we had gone deep in our exploration of Mandinga culture.

Having Ned with me in Lisbon provided me even more legitimacy, especially for men, who praised me for being a good (devoted) wife. For the first decade of our marriage, however, we had no children, and people worried that our relationship would not survive. When midway through my fieldwork Ned accepted a postdoctoral fellowship and moved to Quebec City, women warned me that he would surely take another wife. On one occasion when I was visiting a family in the neighborhood of Damaia, a five-year-old girl who adored Ned asked me where "Uncle" had gone. When I told her that he was in Canada, she asked me, "He trusts you?" Even though I had told people that Ned and I were waiting to have children, they always showered us with blessings for many children, and some encouraged me to consult a healer-diviner for fertility medicine. Everyone was delighted when we finally became parents, gave our children Mandinga names, and brought them to Lisbon.

Beyond an anchoring in the homeland, I shared with my interlocutors the experience of displacement, because, like them, I was unable to return to Guinea-Bissau (as initially planned) during the war. Much like the famous Polish anthropologist Bronislaw Malinowski, who waited out World War I for two years by conducting research in the Trobriand Islands, my research in Lisbon was fieldwork in exile. The experience of transnationalism during this period was not at all what I had imagined it to be, the relatively easy flow between sending and receiving countries. For several months, flights between Lisbon and Bissau were suspended, and communication was extremely difficult. I sat with community members in their homes or in Guinean restaurants, watching the news reports about war-torn Guinea-Bissau and worrying about their relatives and friends. Like them, I had been unable to contact anyone I knew in Bissau or Bafata-Oio, and I felt guilty being in Europe. These shared experiences and emotions provided Guinean immigrants and me concrete ways of relating to each other in Lisbon.[4]

My fieldwork involved constant movement between established centers of community life—public squares near train stations and stops, Guinean restaurants, Lisbon's central mosque, and various "culture clubs" (Gable 2000,

2011)—and people's private homes, workplaces, and life-course rituals that united members of the dispersed Guinean Muslim community. I hung out regularly at Rossio in central Lisbon, where people went to catch up on the latest news in the community, to leave packages for people on their way to Bissau to take to relatives or friends, or to purchase things from the homeland. As soon as I heard that Aja—who appears in the opening vignette—had fled the war in Guinea-Bissau and was living with her daughter in Lisbon, I showed the Rossio merchants her photograph. They confirmed the news and told me where I could find her in Cacém.

I had initially hoped to live with a host family in Lisbon. I quickly learned, however, that the success of my fieldwork depended on establishing a neutral and central home space. I rented a room in downtown Lisbon a short walk from Rossio. I spent my days traveling—by metro, bus, train, and ferry—mobile phone in hand (Johnson 2013), to visit community members in central Lisbon and the various exurbs, all of which were (relatively) easily accessible from my central location. I accompanied those community members I came to know best to their places of work, to Friday prayer at the mosque, and to life-course rituals and other cultural events. In order to better understand and experience embodied ways of being Muslim, my husband and I took weekly Qur'anic lessons with a Qur'anic master and healer-diviner in the neighborhood of Bairro Santos in Lisbon. In these sessions, we sat on the floor, writing and reciting Qur'anic verses until we had fully memorized them, as Qur'anic students in West Africa do.

When the war ended and the political situation improved in Guinea-Bissau, I interviewed people about their experiences of return or how they felt when they were unable or chose not to return. During my 2003 fieldwork in Lisbon, Ned and I returned to Guinea-Bissau, to which people responded ambivalently. Some worried about our safety and tried to convince us not to go. Others were excited that we were returning but encouraged us to consult a healer-diviner to ensure our safety (which we did). For many, our return to Guinea-Bissau engaged feelings of guilt for not returning or shame knowing that whatever they sent home would probably fall short of their relatives' unrealistically high expectations. Our own return thrust us into transnational networks of exchange. Several people in Lisbon asked us to take money, clothing, and other items to their relatives in Bissau. We visited them, also bringing them news of their relatives in Lisbon. We then brought back to people in Lisbon gifts from their relatives in Bissau or things they had specifically requested from home.

In conducting my fieldwork in Lisbon, I remained committed to a model of ethnography that sees knowledge as produced in the relationship between

Figure 1.3. The view from the Queluz-Belas train stop, 2017.
Photograph by the author.

Figure 1.4. Preparing *bajiki* (roselle leaves with okra) in Queluz with the mortar and pestle that I brought from my 2003 fieldwork in Bissau, 2017. Photograph by the author.

anthropologists and their interlocutors over time. I used some formal methods, such as semistructured interviews, focus groups, and life histories, but participant-observation was (and remains) my most valuable fieldwork method. While I met and talked to hundreds of people in Lisbon, I came to know members of about a dozen families very well and spent much of my days in Lisbon with them. Our relationships have evolved considerably over two decades, as have our strategies for staying in touch, which have moved from letters and phone calls to mobile phone conversations to WhatsApp text and video chats. Maria Abranches (2013a, 340) writes that "'traditional' anthropological matters such as family and kinship do not disappear in transnational contexts." Indeed, I remained committed to grounded fieldwork in Lisbon and even to some of the more "traditional" methods I used in Guinea-Bissau, such as making kinship or household charts, which were invaluable to understanding the complexity of immigrant life. For example, early on in my fieldwork in Lisbon when I began visiting people in their homes in the exurbs, I noticed that the polygynous family arrangements that were so common in Guinea-Bissau seemed to have been replaced by more monogamous, nuclear family ones. As I began to formally chart who was related to whom, however, I quickly realized that the situation was more complicated than it seemed. In many cases, men had other wives back in Guinea-Bissau in addition to their wife in Lisbon and were raising one or more of their other wives' children.

My commitment to grounded, subject-centered ethnography is also evident in my approach to writing. Throughout this book, I highlight through narrative the experiences of named individuals as they refashion themselves, their religion, and their ritual practices to a wider world. I draw inspiration from the Manchester School's extended-case method. This approach highlighted individuals' histories and lives and the complex choices they faced. In short, it revealed a "concern for the immediacy of everyday social life and real-world agency" (Kempny 2005, 160). I also employ contemporary humanistic approaches to ethnographic writing. Scholars such as Ruth Behar (1996), Michael Jackson (2011), Kirin Narayan (2012), and Paul Stoller (2014) explore the boundaries between anthropology and other genres of writing, such as creative nonfiction, poetry, memoir, and fiction, and urge anthropologists to include themselves in their ethnographies, to incorporate detailed descriptions of named people and places, and to pay attention to voice and characterization. In both fieldwork and writing stages, I attempted to highlight what Narayan (2012, 58), building on Victor Turner's work, terms "inner biography," or the "central imaginative project in another person's life." For those I came to know in Lisbon, ritual was the activity through which people found the deepest satisfaction and what most provided meaning in their lives. Following Jackson (2011, xiii), I believe that ethnography involves the quest for human understanding as "an emergent and perpetually renegotiated outcome of social interaction, dialogue, and engagement." Most important, I have tried to "write subjectivity into anthropology" (Behar 1996, 6) by acknowledging that what I learned in the field and present in this book were shaped in large part by my own life history and the unique relationships I have developed with Guinean Muslims in Lisbon. These approaches and orientations were particularly helpful to me as I struggled to interpret and write lived religiosity in African Portugal.

MOSQUES, CULTURE CLUBS, AND GENDERED COSMOPOLITANISMS

Kirsten Hastrup and Karen Olwig (1997, 11) define *cultural sites* as "focal points of identification for people who, in their daily lives, are involved in a complex of relations of global as well as local dimension." Mosques and culture clubs are two cultural sites that Guinean Muslims frequent and imagine themselves in relation (or opposition) to in Lisbon. While they might seem like mutually exclusive spaces at first glance, they are actually overlapping, mutually constitutive ones, within or against which Guinean Muslims move as they remake themselves, their religion, and their ritual practices in Portugal.

Lisbon's central mosque was inaugurated in 1985 and is a focal point for members of the city's diverse Muslim community. My Guinean Muslim interlocutors were proud of the mosque's size and prominent location and often invoked it in response to growing anti-Islamic sentiment in Lisbon, saying, "People may insist that Portugal is a Christian country, but if you go to a church on Sunday, you'll find it empty. If you go to the mosque on Friday, you'll find more Muslims than you can count." Many Guinean men I met in Lisbon, especially more pious men who made the hajj, regularly attended Friday prayer and Muslim holiday celebrations at the mosque.

But the mosque was more than a place of worship for Guinean Muslims: whether one prayed there or not, it had symbolic importance and was a principal force shaping their daily lives and identities. Like public squares in central Lisbon, such as Rossio, and Guinean restaurants (see Johnson 2016), the mosque was a landmark where community members gathered to catch up on the latest news or gossip from home, to find out who was on their way to Bissau and who had recently returned, and to engage in commerce. On Fridays, Mandinga and Fula merchants from Guinea-Bissau transformed the space outside the mosque into a bustling open-air market, where vendors sold things from

Figure 1.5. Lisbon's central mosque, 2017. Photograph by the author.

the homeland, such as food and kola nuts, as well as Muslim religious parapher-
nalia, including prayer beads, head scarves, and wall hangings of the Kaaba.

Despite the importance of the mosque for Muslim identity in Lisbon, the
Guinean Muslims I came to know were acutely aware of their minority status
there. During my early fieldwork, Muslims from the Middle East and South
Asia dominated the mosque and held positions of power there. For Guinean Muslim men, the mosque's multiculturalism was central to its appeal:
the presence of Arabs and Indians highlighted their own participation in the
umma, the global Muslim community. It engaged their imagination and represented a direction in which they desired to turn in their own identity and faith.
In short, it made them feel cosmopolitan.

Much like the one-and-the-many debate in Islam, scholarly works on cosmopolitanism commonly reveal a binary between the global and the local.
Cosmopolitanism is often imagined and portrayed, as Mamadou Diouf (2000,
683) explains, as an entirely novel configuration that is uninfluenced by local
religion and customs. But scholars do speak of vernacular cosmopolitanisms,
which they situate somewhere between the local and the global. For Senegalese

Figure 1.6. Women at Friday prayer at Lisbon's central mosque, 2017.
Photograph by the author.

Shi'a converts in Senegal as described by Leichtman (2016, 5), cosmopolitanism
is "a specific cultural and social condition that allows Muslims to inhabit the
contemporary world." As part of the work of imagination, it incorporates both
the past and the future and is at once rooted in local cultures and universalism.
P. Werbner (2008, 1) describes a *situated* cosmopolitanism," "an aspirational
outlook and mode of practice" that "juggle[s] particular and transcendent loyal-
ties." For Guinean Muslims in Portugal, cosmopolitan sensibilities also oscillate between the global and the local, and the experience of them is deeply
gendered.

While men saw their involvement in the mosque as proof of their status
as global Muslims, for example, women—especially those with little formal
Qur'anic education or knowledge of Arabic—felt excluded from the mosque
and global Islam more generally. They were intimidated by Indian and Arab
Muslims, whose cosmopolitan religious sensibilities seemed beyond their
immediate reach. One Fula woman explained that Indians often refused African women entry into the mosque on Fridays and Muslim holy days:

You wouldn't believe it; sometimes there are fights at the door. The Indians think they own the mosque, but the mosque is for all of us, not just for them. They stand at the entrance, and if they don't recognize you, they'll stop you and ask for ID. If you're an African woman, you'll surely be asked. Once an Indian asked me to show him [documented] proof of my conversion to Islam. I told him that my ancestors converted to Islam centuries ago and that they didn't keep records back then. He told me to recite the Al-Fatiha instead. I was so angry that I forgot the words.

Racist encounters such as this intensified women's insecurity regarding the formal aspects of their religious practice, especially Arabic literacy and knowledge of the Qur'an. Guinean Muslim women studied the Qur'an less intensely than their male counterparts did, and their responsibilities as wives and mothers left them with less time to devote to prayer, Qur'anic study, and pilgrimage. When men went to the mosque on Fridays, for example, women stayed home to prepare the afternoon meal for their husbands and their husbands' friends when they returned. The majority of the women I knew prayed at home, if they prayed at all, and many confessed to me that they simply did not have time to pray. Some women viewed such gender inequality as particular to Guinea-Bissau, which they described as "backward" when compared to neighboring Gambia and Senegal. Muslim women in these countries, they claimed, were pious Muslims who were as knowledgeable as men were about Islam—they studied the Qur'an and made the hajj, and some were even respected Qur'anic scholars and healer-diviners. While Guinean Muslim men in Lisbon often looked to the Middle East, especially to Saudi Arabia, for a truer model of Islam, women tended to look closer to home, to other West African countries.

One's ability to frequent the mosque was also complicated by distance, which revealed further gender and class dynamics. Most Guinean Muslims lived in Lisbon's many exurbs, and effectively navigating the city's transportation system demanded map-reading abilities, proficiency in Portuguese, and money. Many women claimed they could not afford to travel to visit community members or attend the mosque. Others felt intimidated by Lisbon's vastness and worried about getting lost. I was astonished to learn that some Guinean Muslim immigrants I knew had not been to central Lisbon since they arrived at the airport twenty or more years ago. Community members marveled at how I made my way around the city, often alone, visiting multiple households separated by dozens of kilometers in a single day. "You travel like a Fula [referring to this ethnic group's nomadic roots]," they would remark. Things were different for the wealthier, mostly male, Guineans I knew who owned cars. Owning a car or having access to one through a relative enabled movement throughout the city, facilitated mosque attendance, and carried considerable social prestige.[5]

On Fridays during my fieldwork, I always rode with Bacar to the mosque. After prayer, young Guinean Muslim men would gather around his sparkling-clean Ford (he always ran it through the automatic wash beforehand, which he called "car ablutions"), take photographs, and vie for a place inside. Bacar would take as many people as could fit—what he called "*kandonga*-style" after Guinea-Bissau's infamous bush taxis—back to Queluz for the afternoon meal, tea, and conversation. Many women told me that they would go to mosque if only they could be driven there, but they rarely got rides over men. When I asked Bacar's wife, Aminata, about this, she claimed she did not mind staying home on Fridays to cook for her husband and his friends, as long as they brought back the latest gossip from the mosque. But the situation was different for older women, like Aja, from the opening vignette. Women who were past their childbearing years, who prayed five times daily, and who had made the hajj were not intimidated by Arab and Indian mosque-goers and felt that their elder status entitled them to rides over younger men and women who had not yet been to Mecca.

In response to the exclusion from Lisbon's central mosque that Guinean Muslim women felt, they created the culture club, an alternative space in which they could fashion their own cosmopolitan model of Islam. At the time of my fieldwork, there were several clubs in Lisbon, including the Saabo Nyima (Sweetness), the Gente Rica (Rich People), and the club whose members I came to know best, the Badim Clubo (Maternal Kin Club). Tunbulo the Maternal Kin Club's "mother," explained that she and three of her friends had founded the club in 1989 so that Mandinga immigrant women could "live together," or form a community in Lisbon: "When we [Mandinga women] first started arriving in Portugal, we were all spread out. Our husbands saw each other at Rossio, but we women stayed at home. Most of us didn't know each other well, and we rarely saw each other because Lisbon is so big. After some time, a few of us decided that we shouldn't remain isolated any longer. We said, 'We are all in a foreign land now, so we should find a way to live together as we did back home.' And so, we formed the club."

In addition to its social dimension, the Maternal Kin Club, like the other culture clubs in Lisbon, acted as a rotating credit association, providing funds to assist Mandinga immigrant women in a variety of endeavors, such as starting a business, returning home to attend a funeral or postburial sacrifice, or helping members make the hajj. The club's name underscores one of the most quintessential of Mande cultural themes: the importance of maternal kinship.

Badim is an orthographic variation of the Mandinga term *baadingo*, which refers to siblings of the same mother or children who nursed from the same breast. As Charles Bird and Martha Kendall (1980, 14–15) assert, maternal kinship among Mande peoples is a powerful symbol of "oneness"—of equality, loyalty, and affection—in contrast to paternal kinship, which fosters difference and competition. When I asked Tunbulo about the club's name, she evoked this powerful symbolic construct, which she claimed shaped how club members both understood and interacted with one another: "Club members are all the same, all equal, because the club is like a breast from which we all nurse," she told me.[6]

Although Mandinga immigrant women started the Maternal Kin Club for Mandinga immigrant women, members explained to me that women cannot work alone. As Tunbulo put it, "We need men by our side." At the time of my fieldwork, the club had four male members who held leadership positions—the father, the president, the vice president, and the president's counselor—who supported the women, helping them with those activities that women could not do or preferred not to do, such as bookkeeping (while the women were actually capable, shrewd businesswomen, they insisted that money only caused problems in Portugal), driving, and slaughtering animals for life-course rituals and Muslim holy days. Male club members provided significant financial support to the club, and their dues were double those of the women. In addition to official, card-holding members, the club had several hundred supporters—male and female alike—who regularly attended club-sponsored life-course rituals and cultural events. While supporters did not pay dues, they contributed money, usually in the form of entry fees, to help defray costs associated with hosting events.

Male members described the club as being "good for women." Ibrahim, the club's president at the time of my fieldwork, complained that before the club, their wives would go to malls, cinemas, or even *discotecas* with their non-Muslim friends and begin replacing their "big clothing" with tight jeans or miniskirts. With the creation of the club, men could rest assured that their wives were spending their time in the company of other Muslims. Female members took pride in the club's Muslim character, which they understood more in ethnic or cultural than religious terms: only people from Guinea-Bissau's Muslim ethnic groups could join the club, and alcohol and pork were taboo at events. As Tunbulo explained, "Other ethnic groups have their different traditions, like drinking. Club money only pays for juice. Muslims don't have much contact with non-Muslims back home or in Portugal. We can't have a strong relationship because our paths are different. If you're part of the club, you won't fall from Islam because you know your place, where you've chosen to put yourself, and you'll never forget who you are."

Club events were organized primarily around life-course rituals, including name-giving rituals, writing-on-the-hand rituals to initiate children into Qur'anic study, coming-out ceremonies following boys' circumcision, weddings, ceremonies marking Mecca pilgrims' return, and funerals and postburial sacrifices. The club also occasionally held its own Muslim holiday celebrations, such as Tabaski and the Prophet's birthday. Finally, it also sponsored secular cultural events, such as African fashion shows and music concerts, featuring well-known artists, such as Gambian kora sensation Jaliba Kuyateh.

People celebrated at large because, as they asserted, "this is Europe": events were held in enormous rented ballrooms in central Lisbon. Women changed into three or four different outfits in a single evening (I never felt appropriately dressed no matter what I wore). Women prepared more elaborate versions of traditional Mandinga dishes with halal meat and vegetable oil—two of the most coveted luxuries back home—and served them in portion sizes that were practically unheard of in Guinea-Bissau. The club created an alternative Muslim space (B. Metcalf 1996), a vernacular cosmopolitanism that rivaled Lisbon's central mosque. In this alternative space, ethnicity and Islamic piety coexisted rather than conflicted, and women could be both Mandinga and Muslim in ways they found most meaningful.

Once I had been attending club meetings and events and visiting members in their homes for several months during my initial fieldwork, I presented five kola nuts to Tunbulo and became a card-holding, dues-paying member, which altered my status from guest to participant. At the time I joined the club had seventy-five members, and membership remained steady. In 2011 in the wake of the economic crisis, club members told me that they had lots of people but no money for parties. In 2017, I learned that membership had declined significantly after many members died, returned to Guinea-Bissau, or emigrated to England or Germany.

As I stated earlier, the mosque and the culture club are not mutually exclusive cultural spaces but rather mutually constitutive, overlapping ones. Many people I met in Lisbon frequented both, and during my 2011 fieldwork in Lisbon, I learned that members of the Guinean Muslim community had established a third space, a mosque at Rossio in central Lisbon. In 2017, I returned to Lisbon to investigate it more formally. The mosque, which more closely resembles a prayer space, is located in the basement of a Fula-owned shop. It consists of one large room with white walls, and the floor is covered with Middle Eastern–style red carpets on which people sit, study, and pray. The mosque was created to serve primarily the Guinean Muslim merchants at Rossio, who needed a convenient place to pray during their long workdays. It was not, people insisted, meant to discourage people from attending Friday prayer at the central mosque. The Rossio mosque doubles as a school, where Guinean Muslim children study the Qur'an and healer-diviners gather to work, writing Qur'anic verses that leatherworkers sew into amulets for clients. Unlike the central mosque, which is frequented by Muslims from throughout the Muslim world, only West African Muslims pray at the Rossio mosque. And unlike most of the culture clubs, which remain specific to a single ethnic group, the Rossio mosque is multiethnic: Fula and Mandinga Muslims pray together, and not all of them are even from Guinea-Bissau. Muslims from other countries in the Senegambia—such as Guinea-Conakry, the Gambia, and Senegal—who own or work in African shops and restaurants at Rossio also frequent it. Thus, the Rossio mosque signals the possible emergence of not a national Guinean Muslim identity but rather a regional diasporic (i.e., Senegambian) Muslim identity in African Lisbon.

Whether they preferred to frequent mosques or culture clubs, Guinean Muslims were united by their minority racial and religious status (as *pretos*, or blacks, and as Muslims) in a predominantly white, secularizing (cultural) Roman Catholic country. Although I did not directly focus on this topic (a subject for another book), my interlocutors often mentioned these experiences to me. A few told me that although they always knew that they were Africans, being Mandinga or Fula (ethnicity) had always been key for them, and they had never actually thought of themselves as *black people* until they came to Europe and were referred to by this phrase. The development of racial consciousness was often connected to the experience of racism in their daily lives in Lisbon, which was painful for them. Some told me, for example, that Portuguese dogs only bark at black people. Others claimed that grocery store clerks preferred to put their change on the counter rather than directly in their hands, so as to avoid touching them. Still others complained that people on the streets stared at them, especially when they wore African clothing, and avoided sitting next to them on buses or the metro.

At the same time, however, many Guinean immigrants shared with me personal stories in which Portuguese neighbors or friends, or even complete strangers, showed them extraordinary kindness at crucial moments in their lives. Through these and other experiences, they learned that they shared more with their Portuguese hosts than they had previously thought. For example, many immigrants told me that before migrating, they had imagined the Portuguese as strong and powerful people. They were thus surprised to learn on arriving in Lisbon that many Portuguese struggled economically and even migrated to other European countries or the United States in search of work. Many of my Guinean interlocutors in Lisbon also dreamed of migrating to England or Germany, where they thought they had a better chance at getting ahead in life and where they believed the locals were more open to marrying and raising a family with them.

My interlocutors' experience of being part of a religious minority was complex. Some complained that being Muslim was difficult in Lisbon and felt that the Portuguese did not really want Muslims in their country. A few men told me that TAP, Portugal's national airline, slipped pork into its onboard meals labeled "halal" in an attempt to "ruin" Muslims. Others, however, described the Portuguese as not afraid of religion, by which they meant that they were more accepting of openly religious people than citizens of other European countries, such as France, where, they explained, Muslims could not even wear head scarves.[7] During my 2017 fieldwork, a Fula mother described Portugal as a Muslim-friendly country and told me that the school provided her children a halal lunch option, for which she was very grateful.

Despite differing views concerning Portugal's acceptance of them, Guinean Muslims shared a fear of falling from Islam as a result of living in Portugal. When I began my fieldwork, Amadi had been living in Lisbon for seven years and was doing well compared to many Mandinga immigrant women I knew. She managed a group of house and office cleaners, and her fiancé, Laalo, managed a group of construction workers. As a result of their combined income, they were able to purchase their apartment in Cacém, which they outfitted with stylish furniture, modern appliances, and a Portuguese-style bar. Amadi's mother, Aja, disapproved not only of the bar but also of the relationship. Laalo was of mixed Muslim (Mandinga) and non-Muslim ancestry and did not practice any religion. He also ate pork and drank alcohol. The couple had not yet officially tied their marriage—kola nuts had not been exchanged, and their parents had not officially agreed to their union—but they were living together nevertheless. Aja was convinced that her daughter had forgotten Islam: she did not pray and replaced her big clothing indoors with European styles whenever she left the house. Amadi was one of the few Mandinga women I met in Lisbon who did not affiliate with either the mosque or the culture club. She knew that her mother disapproved of her lifestyle and explained to me that her lack of piety couldn't be helped: her demanding work schedule left her too busy and too exhausted to attend mosque, or pray at all, or to participate in a culture club. But her lack of engagement was about more than logistics; it was also about class conflict and failed aspirations, which have intensified since Portugal joined the

European Union (see Fikes 2009) and economic conditions for the Portuguese and African immigrants alike have steadily worsened.

Indeed, Amadi told me that she was a member of the Maternal Kin Club shortly after she arrived in Lisbon. This changed, however, when she received her first promotion and club members grew jealous of her success. "Some people wouldn't speak to me, and others spoke badly of me to try to ruin me," she said. In Amadi's view, mosques and culture clubs were both really just fashion shows where Guinean Muslims—men and women alike—flaunted their wealth and status by donning the latest clothing styles from Dakar or Mecca and "filling their wrists with gold," as she put it. Furthermore, Amadi claimed she did not feel at ease taking public transportation to the mosque or club events dressed in her big clothing. She attributed this to racism and anti-Islamic sentiment in Lisbon: "[Portuguese] people stare at me like they've just seen something from the bush. They don't know that I probably make more money than they do and that I even own my house. If I had a car, I would go to mosque every Friday. People would see me in my car and say, 'Hey, that woman has money!'"

Movement in and between (and sometimes against) the cultural spaces of mosques and culture clubs demonstrates that ethnicity, religious identity, and national and regional identities coexist in Lisbon. It also highlights Guinean Muslims' gendered experiences of African custom, global Islam, and cosmopolitanism as they strive to build their name in Lisbon's wider immigrant community and to imagine themselves as Africans and as cosmopolitan Muslims between and beyond Africa and Europe.

ORGANIZATION OF THE BOOK

In the chapters that follow, I explore how my interlocutors remake Islam through their ritual practices. Part 1 focuses on life-course rituals, which have long shaped how Mandinga understand themselves both as members of an ethnic group and as practitioners of the world religion of Islam. Chapter 2 explores two childhood rituals. In the name-giving ritual, which takes place one week after birth, Guinean children receive a Muslim name. In the writing-on-the-hand ritual, which occurs seven years later, they are initiated into Qur'anic education. I highlight the transformations these two rituals undergo as Guineans Muslims move from Guinea-Bissau to Portugal. For example, some believe that the writing-on-the-hand ritual inscribes Islam onto the body, preparing children's hearts and minds to study the Qur'an. Others, however, contend that since the

Prophet Mohammed never had his hand written on, Guinean Muslims should dispense with the African custom of writing on their children's hands.

Chapter 3 explores the rituals of initiation and circumcision for both boys and girls. Like the name-giving ritual and the writing-on-the-hand ritual, initiation and circumcision shape ethnicity and Islam and inscribe these onto bodies. I show that as Guinean Muslims remake Islam in Lisbon, and as they confront stereotypical, even racist media images of "female genital mutilation," they are arguing about the consequences, meanings, and futures of these rituals for both boys and girls. The ensuing debate reveals tensions along gender, generational, and class lines. Chapter 4 examines funerals and postburial sacrifices in a transnational era. It highlights the rupture between place and identity as Guinean Muslim immigrants hold rituals for people who died in Guinea-Bissau or for fellow immigrants who are buried away from home, in Lisbon. As Guinean Muslims remake themselves and their religion in the contemporary diaspora, such distant departures and the rituals that mark them are currently altering how people see themselves as Africans, as members of a specific ethnic group, and as Muslims in a changing world.

The second part of the book explores ritual practices beyond the life course. By their very nature, these rituals have the potential to connect Mandinga more intensely with the *umma*. I show, however, that these rituals engage feelings of estrangement from, as much as inclusion into, this community. Chapter 5 looks at Muslim healer-diviners in Lisbon as they negotiate a space between custom and innovation and as they struggle to both meet the demands of their cosmopolitan clients and make a living in Lisbon. I demonstrate the importance of gender and generation as healer-diviners remake Islam and as tensions emerge between old and young healers and male and female healers in Lisbon.

Chapter 6 explores Mandinga experiences of the hajj, the pilgrimage to Mecca, and welcome-back-from-Mecca ceremonies marking the immigrants' safe return. As one of Islam's most essential ritual practices, the hajj is a dramatic symbol of inclusion in the *umma*, but I argue that it also engages profound feelings of estrangement—based primarily on race and gender—from it. I examine the hajj as a site of tension and ambivalence as Mandinga remake Islam in African Portugal and as they reimagine the pilgrimage (and its consequences), themselves, and their religion. This chapter tells the story of Aja Fatima, whose untimely pilgrimage to Mecca (before many of her aunts and even her own mother had gone) sparked a community-wide debate about how old one should be before making the hajj and who should be allowed to go to Mecca before whom within a family.

NOTES

1. See also Mommersteeg (2012, 25). According to Asad (2009, 20), the Islams perspective fails to acknowledge that Islam is first and foremost a "discursive tradition that includes and relates itself to the founding texts of the Qu'ran and Hadith." See Ware (2014, 19–23) for a thorough discussion of the racism inherent in scholarly discussions about "Islam in Africa," "African Islam," and "Islams."

2. Fula, also known as Fulani, Peul, or Fulbe peoples, live in an east-west savanna belt at the southern edge of the Sahara Desert in many countries, including Chad, Mauritania, Senegal, Burkina Faso, Gambia, and Guinea. In Guinea-Bissau, they are the second-largest ethnic group and make up 20 percent of the country's total population (Mendy and Lobban 2013, 3). Fula, along with non-Muslim Manjaco, constitute the majority of Guinean immigrants in Portugal (Abranches 2014, 263).

3. Many of the *barracas* I frequented during my earlier periods of research were torn down in subsequent years, and unfinished apartment complexes that African immigrants had "jumped into" were completed and transformed into public housing. Many Guineans who had been living rent-free were forced to pay subsidized rent, which some resented or found difficult.

4. See Abranches (2013b) for a compelling study of items that are sent and received by migrants and their kin between the airports of Bissau and Lisbon. She demonstrates how social, transnational networks are maintained over time without corporal travel between Guinea-Bissau and Portugal.

5. Transportation passes, which came in various types and allowed unlimited monthly access to different combinations of the metro, trains, buses, ferries, and cable cars, were status symbols during my early fieldwork. Children wore their passes around their necks outside of their clothing, and people commented on how beautiful they were, referring to the color, photograph, or number (which indicated the type and price). After dressing her three-year-old daughter to attend a name-giving ritual, one woman exclaimed, "The only thing she lacks is a [transportation] pass!"

6. While most described the Maternal Kin Club as ethnically Mandinga, others preferred to think of it as a multiethnic Guinean Muslim association. Some members, they explained, were "really" Fula, Jakanka, or Beafada, even though they spoke Mandinga.

7. See Bowen (2007, 2010) and Selby (2012) for discussions of Islam and Muslims in France.

PART I

REMAKING ISLAM THROUGH LIFE-COURSE RITUALS

TWO

—⚋—

NAME-GIVING AND HAND-WRITING

Childhood Rituals and Embodying Islam

ONE AFTERNOON IN LISBON, MEMBERS of the Maternal Kin Club invited me to attend a name-giving ritual where, they claimed, God willing, six children would be "shaved and named." I met Bacar and Aminata the next morning at their apartment in Queluz, located twenty minutes by commuter train from central Lisbon. Together, we traveled to Rio de Mouro for the ritual. As we navigated traffic on our way to the community hall, Aminata told us that she is not fond of holding life-course rituals in public spaces rather than in people's homes. "I don't care how many people are invited," she explained. "The blessings aren't captured by anyone; they just stay in the public space." As we entered the hall, Aminata and I sat in the plastic chairs that had been set out for the event. Bacar took his place at the front table with the elders and other *alhaajis,* who would oversee the ritual.

Guests were slow to arrive, and people complained that the place was far and difficult to find. Kadi and Jenaba said they had been cooking for two days and had not slept. "We've never seen more food in our lives," they exclaimed. The children, who ranged in age from one week to seven years old, sat alone or in their mothers' laps in a row of chairs. They wore European clothes, but just before the ritual began at two o'clock, an elder woman draped colorful African cloths over their shoulders or heads. An elder man removed a bit of each child's hair with a disposable razor; then the praise-singers announced each name aloud while the guests showered the children with money and new African-print fabric. An elder man blessed the children, rubbing their heads as he prayed, and the praise-singers danced, sang, and shouted the children's names. Kadi was elated, since one of the babies was named Malam, her older brother's name. She would call him "older brother," and she would have a special relationship with him forever. Once all the children were named, the women began serving the guests the afternoon meal.

After the ritual, I asked Bacar why so many of the children were older as opposed to infants. All the name-giving rituals I had attended in the past in both Guinea-Bissau and Portugal had taken place one week after birth, the customary age. "Life is more complicated in Lisbon; it has to do with work, school, and money," Bacar explained. He confessed that he had not yet held a name-giving ritual for his own daughter. He planned to wait until Aminata had another baby, at which point they would name both of the children in a single ritual, since, as he claimed, "it's more beautiful that way." As we drove back to Queluz, Bacar told me that when my husband, Ned, and I had children, we should name them after him and Aminata to "make their names go far."

In this chapter, I discuss two childhood rituals in the lives of Muslim Guineans: the name-giving ritual and the writing-on-the-hand ritual. These are the first rituals that infants or young children undergo on the path to becoming full-fledged Muslims. Both rituals are deemed essential for the construction of ethnic and religious identity at home in Guinea-Bissau and in the contemporary diaspora in Lisbon. Like the other Guinean Muslim life-course rituals I address in this book, both rituals inscribe Islam onto living bodies. Africanist anthropologists have addressed at length the relationship between the body and identity. They have shown, for example, that bodily substances such as blood, bone, and breast milk (e.g., Bird and Kendall 1980; Boddy 1989; Gottlieb 1992; Jackson 1989; Lambek and Strathern 1998) shape different forms of relatedness and belonging. I build here on the work of scholars who have explored how various forms of embodiment and their implications for identity making articulate with migration and globalization. Sharon Hutchinson (2000), for example, shows how Nuer in Sudan liken the new substances of money, guns, and paper to blood. For his part, Brad Weiss (2009) explores the links between hair, fantasy, and globalization in Tanzania. He argues that fantasy, embodied in different hairstyles, helps young men "inhabit . . . their own displacement" and "live through rupture" in contemporary Arusha, a place ravaged by neoliberal reform (Weiss 2009, 94). Although these works explore how local people evoke the body to understand wider social and economic transformations, we know less about the role of the body in reconfiguring identity and religious practices in diaspora settings. In this chapter, I show how embodied ritual practices create community in a new locale and become the primary way in which immigrants remake themselves and their relationship to others they encounter in Lisbon. Indeed, I contend that Guinean Muslims are arguing with (and through)

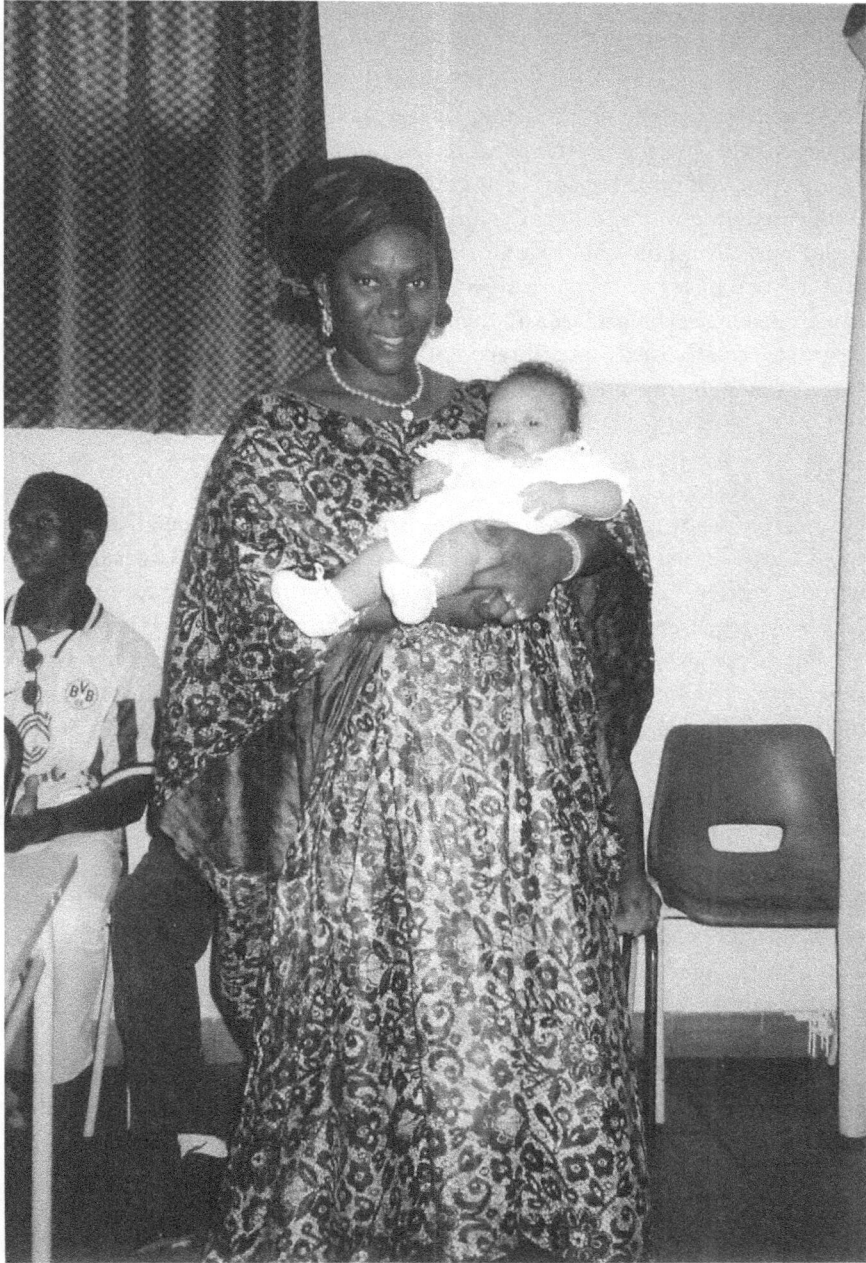

Figure 2.1. Kadi and baby Malam at his name-giving ritual, 1999.
Photograph by the author.

ritual and that innovations in embodied ritual practices themselves become, as M. E. Combs-Schilling (1989, 36) suggests, "forms of argument."[1]

In the name-giving ritual, a child's head is shaved, and he or she receives a Muslim name and is invited to "take up the path" that God has chosen for him or her. In the writing-on-the-hand ritual, Guinean Muslim parents actively "place the child on this path," and children literally ingest the word of God. Both rituals, like all rituals, are dynamic and are undergoing considerable innovation and change both at home and in the diaspora. Some of these innovations and changes have become the subject of community-wide debates as Guinean Muslims remake themselves and their religion in Lisbon. These debates reveal migrants' creative attempts to reconcile African custom and global Islam as they make their way in Portugal.

A FATHER'S DEBT: THE NAME-GIVING RITUAL

Guinean Muslim men and women are said to become full social adults only when they become parents. The attainment of social adulthood does not come without a price. For women, the price is obvious: they must endure the challenges of pregnancy and the pain of childbirth. The price for men is less obvious but equally important. Guinean Muslims believe that babies are born with a debt owed to them by their fathers, a debt that must be repaid one week after birth in a *kulliyo*, or name-giving ritual, in which an infant receives a Muslim name. In the Muslim world, this ritual is commonly referred to as the naming ceremony. I have chosen instead to refer to it as the name-giving ritual, following Victor Turner's (1967, 95) classic distinction between ritual and ceremony: the former transforms while the latter merely confirms a status or identity.[2] The Mandinga term *kulliyo* literally means "head-shaving," referring to the fact that either infants' heads are completely shaved or a bit of hair is removed during the ritual.[3] Although both parents take part in the name-giving ritual, the primary responsibilities fall on the father, who must schedule and finance the ritual, hire praise-singers and holy men, and invite relatives and guests to attend.

On the day of the ritual, people gather around midmorning in the couple's home or, as in the opening vignette, in a public space where the ritual will be held. Before the ritual begins, guests congregate in groups according to their gender and age and drink tea and visit. A holy man then shaves the infant's head with a disposable razor. Boys' heads are fully shaved while girls' heads are only partially shaved, leaving a small tuft of hair at the crown of the head. Alternatively, a small lock of hair is removed in symbolic fashion, which is often the case in Lisbon, especially if the child is older and is a girl. At the same time that

Figure 2.2. Blessing baby Malam at his name-giving ritual, 1999. Photograph by the author.

Figure 2.3. Offering blessings before the meal at a name-giving ritual, 1999. Photograph by the author.

the infant's head is shaved, a man slaughters a goat in accordance with Islam, cutting the animal's throat while uttering the proper Qur'anic verses. The holy man then pronounces the child's name out loud, at which point the father's debt is considered officially paid. The holy man next whispers the name in the child's right ear, telling the child who he or she is. He then whispers "God is great" three times and reminds the child to take up the path that God has chosen for him or her. Finally, the holy man bestows blessings on the child for a long and prosperous life. At that point, an elder distributes kola nuts and meat, and the women serve the afternoon meal.

"THE PROOF IS ON MY PALM": THE WRITING-ON-THE-HAND RITUAL

After completing our weekly Qur'anic lesson with Alaaji, Ned and I stopped for dinner at Morabeza, one of the most popular Guinean restaurants in central Lisbon during the time of my early fieldwork. We ordered chicken and peanut sauce with okra, one of Guinea-Bissau's national dishes, served with rice. As usual, we specified to Muna, the restaurant's owner, that we would like it "Guinean-style," served in a common bowl with two spoons and lots of hot pepper. We reviewed our most recent Qur'anic lesson as we waited for our food. Basiro, a Mandinga man in his early twenties at the time and one of Morabeza's regular customers, joined us at our table. Exhausted from a day's work of hauling bricks and buckets of cement at his construction job, Basiro ordered a plate of chicken and peanut sauce with okra and glanced at our open Qur'anic notebooks. I asked him, half jokingly, if he could read the verses. "Of course I can!" he exclaimed. "When I was a boy back home in Guinea-Bissau, my father used to meet me on the soccer field every day and bring me home for prayer. After we prayed together, he would let me go. Now I no longer have the time to practice my religion." Like many Muslim immigrants I met in Lisbon, Basiro complained that the anxieties and stresses of immigrant life prevented him from studying the Qur'an, praying five times a day, and attending Friday prayer at Lisbon's central mosque. Basiro confessed that he no longer fasted during Ramadan and that he had even started eating pork. "What doesn't kill the Portuguese won't kill me," he laughed. Returning to a more serious tone, he added, "When I go back home to Guinea-Bissau, my mother cries and cries. She tells me that it's because my father is dead that I've stopped practicing my religion."

"Are you still a Muslim?" I asked Basiro.

He extended his open hand across the table and said, "The proof is on my palm."

"Yoo," I responded in approval as I examined Basiro's hand. Beyond the rough and callused skin of an immigrant laborer, and irrespective of his recent suspension of Islamic practice, Basiro's Muslim identity remained permanently inscribed on his body in the form of Qur'anic verses that, no longer visible, were ritually written on his hand when he was a child.

When Basiro showed me his palm as proof of his Muslim identity, he was referring to his experience of the *bulosafewo*, the "writing-on-the-hand" ritual, which Muslim children in Guinea-Bissau and elsewhere in West Africa undergo before beginning Qur'anic study. For Basiro, as for many Mandinga I came to know in Guinea-Bissau and Portugal, the Qur'anic verses written in ink on the hand during this ritual, though they eventually fade away and become invisible to the naked eye, are a permanent mark of both one's ethnicity (Mandinga or Fula) and one's religious identity (Muslim). But others, challenging the once taken-for-granted relationship between ethnicity and Islam, contend that the writing-on-the-hand ritual is an African custom that, like other African customs, should be abandoned for a more cosmopolitan model of Islam, practiced by "Arabs"—one grounded in the five pillars of faith. Before exploring this debate, I begin with an ethnographic description of the writing-on-the-hand ritual.

The writing-on-the-hand ritual is the next milestone in Mandinga children's religious development after the name-giving ritual. It is performed ideally at age seven, when children throughout the Muslim world usually begin studying the Qur'an (Denny 2016, 265; Ware 2014, 43).[4] During the ritual, a holy man dips a fountain pen into black ink and writes the opening verse of the Qur'an on a child's palm. He then adds a pinch of salt to the ink and instructs the child to lick the mixture from his or her hand with three strokes of the tongue. After the child has literally ingested the word of God, the holy man points to each letter of the Arabic alphabet, written on a wooden slate used in traditional village Qur'anic schools. He utters the name of each letter and instructs the child to repeat it. Relatives and friends join in the recitation and make offerings of money and kola nuts, often placing these directly on the child's head. Finally, women give rice flour to all relatives and guests present, officially marking the end of the ritual. Everyone celebrates the child's new status by sharing a meal.

The writing-on-the-hand ritual operates on metonymic logic, meaning that it treats an object or body part in a ritual manner in an attempt to mimic—and eventually produce—broader effects. This logic is operative throughout West Africa in both ritual and mundane contexts. Songhay sorcerers in Niger, for example, ingest a heavy paste made from magical powder and water to fill them, both physically and metaphorically, with knowledge and power (Stoller and

Olkes 1987, 55). Similarly, when Qur'anic students in West Africa erase their lessons written with ink onto wooden slates, they collect the mixture of ink and water, thought to be "charged with the spiritual power of the Qur'an" (Ware 2014, 57), and drink it or use it as medicine. Jack Goody (1968, 230) explains that in "drinking the word," people internalize and embody the otherwise external power of the written text (see also Goody 2000). Rudolph Ware (2014, 57–58) explains that scholars have often cited these practices as examples of the Africanization of Islam, but he contends that they are actually ancient Muslim practices that are "probably as old as Islam itself."[5]

Salt and pounded rice flour sweetened with honey (*munkoo*) are two crucial substances in the writing-on-the-hand ritual and might be considered "key symbols" (Ortner 1973). Both fall into the category of "white things," which Guinean Muslims deem sacred. Although the association of the color white with goodness and purity is found in indigenous African religions (see Turner 1967; Jacobson-Widding 1979), it is also common in Islam. White is thought to be pleasing to God and the Prophet Mohammed, and Muslim healers encourage clients to give white things as ritual offerings (deemed necessary through divination) or as charity.

Both practical and symbolic properties of salt contribute to its importance. First and foremost, Guinean Muslims acknowledge that people and animals depend on salt for daily life. In Bafata-Oio, the village where I conducted my fieldwork in Guinea-Bissau, salt production is central to the village economy. In the dry season, women strain the mud of the lowlands and collect the brackish water, which they distill into salt and sell in the nearby town of Farim or at regional markets. Local salt is thought to be superior to the imported Portuguese salt sold in shops and is preferable both for cooking and for use in rituals. Guinean Muslims also recognize the practical cleansing properties of salt, and they use it (along with sand) to polish silver bracelets and rings, especially those worn for protective purposes.

Mandinga also consider salt to be a "strong" substance that is "good for the head." When I asked one man in Bafata-Oio about the use of salt in the writing-on-the-hand ritual, he made an analogy to the tape recorder I used in conducting my interviews: salt's strength (power) literally records the Qur'anic verses into children's heads so that they will always remember them. In an interview I conducted with Ibrahim, who was the president of the Maternal Kin Club when I met him in Lisbon in 1999, he described salt as offering an important moral lesson for human beings.

> MJ: Why do you put salt on a child's hand during the writing-on-the-hand
> ritual, and why is salt good for the head?

Ibrahim: We put salt on the hand because salt is in everything. It's good for
the head because a little bit goes a long way. How much salt is in the ocean?
MJ: A lot.
Ibrahim: That's right. There's a lot of salt in the ocean because God put it
there. Now, when you cook rice, how much salt do you add to the water?
MJ: Just a little bit.
Ibrahim: That's right. You add a little bit because you're a human being, not
God.

Ibrahim's explanation defines salt as a part of God's creation that is essential
to human life. Placing salt on a child's hand during the writing-on-the-hand
ritual is a reminder of God's creative powers and the responsibility of humans
to respect them. More important, placing a bit of salt on a child's hand is a
reminder of the limits of human agency and, thus, of the importance of humility. God acts on an awesome scale, one that humans could never approximate
without "spoiling" their endeavors, as my interlocutors would say. But what
humans do—albeit small or insignificant—is important in God's eyes. Salt
is good for the head, then, in that it reminds children that their efforts in
Qur'anic school—sacrifice, patience, and hard work—although small when
compared to God's work, are important nonetheless. Like salt in rice water, a
little goes a long way.[6]

Like salt, rice flour is also said to be good for the head. Specifically, rice
flour contains honey, which is thought to open the head. Because Guinean
Muslims consider honey to be effective in aiding students with their studies, it
is used in a variety of local medicines for success in school examinations or for
rapid acquisition of foreign languages. When I consulted a Mandinga healer
in Bissau to help me learn the Mandinga language, which I studied early in my
fieldwork with a private tutor, he supplied me with "language medicine"—a
concoction of water, herbs, and wild honey. He assured me that drinking one
spoonful daily would open my head, allowing me to learn Mandinga quickly
and effortlessly. The rice flour sweetened with honey that children eat during
the writing-on-the-hand ritual is said to be particularly effective in facilitating
the memorization of Qur'anic verses.[7]

While Guinean Muslims distribute rice flour at other life-course rituals,
such as funerals, my interlocutors claimed that *bulusafe munkoo* (the rice flour
used in the writing-on-the-hand ritual), is the "strongest" (i.e., most powerful) type of rice flour and is thought to possess healing properties. Considering this, guests commonly take some rice flour to relatives or friends who are
unable to attend the writing-on-the-hand ritual, especially if they are suffering
from an illness or facing difficulties in their work or study (e.g., examinations).

In Guinea-Bissau, Mandinga acknowledge another magical use for *bulusafe munkoo*. A bit of the substance placed secretly in the rafters of one's house is said to offer protection from fire. One man explained that even if the entire village were to burn, a house protected with *bulusafe munkoo* would not catch fire.

INTERPRETING THE WRITING-ON-THE-HAND RITUAL

When I inquired about the purpose of the writing-on-the-hand ritual, my interlocutors in both field sites explained that it initiates children into Qur'anic study. As one Mandinga woman in Lisbon put it, "When Europeans enroll their children in school, they write on papers. We write on our children's hands." In preparing children for the difficult pursuit of Qur'anic study, which involves the memorization of texts over a number of years, the writing-on-the-hand ritual is thought to produce physical transformations in the body: it purifies the child by opening the mind, cooling the heart, and steadying the spirit. Furthermore, it pardons the child's social transgressions, providing a clean start as he or she begins Qur'anic study. Such transformations of body, mind, and spirit are thought to be necessary for success not only in studying Islam's sacred texts but also more generally in living one's life as a Muslim. The child is not the only one to benefit from the purifying effects of the writing-on-the-hand ritual. People told me that when a holy man writes the first half of the Al-Fatiha (the opening verses of the Qur'an) on a child's palm, God pardons the sins of one hundred of his or her maternal relatives. When he writes the second half on the child's hand, God pardons the sins of one hundred of his or her paternal relatives.

The writing-on-the-hand ritual also marks a fundamental cosmological transformation: it initiates children into a lifelong relationship with angels (*malayikoo*), who become their spiritual and moral counselors. Although the Qur'anic verses written in ink on a child's palm gradually fade and disappear altogether, they are thought to remain forever visible to angels. Acting as one's witnesses in the afterlife, these beings are said to record a child's lifetime actions and intentions, both good and bad, and to report them to God on Judgment Day. People explained that angels ultimately determine whether or not a person should be allowed to pass through the gates of heaven. As one Mandinga man told me,

> Angels are beings in the service of God. Their job is to deliver messages to people and to act as intermediaries between God and humans. Every person has two angels that guide and protect him or her. The angels record the actions and intentions of humans during their lives on earth. The *malayika*

bulubaa ["right angel"] sits at a person's right side and records his or her good deeds. The *malayika maraa* ["left angel"] sits at a person's left side and records his or her bad deeds. When you are about to do something bad, the angel reminds you that if you do that thing, it will be recorded, so that you will reconsider it. The angels record everything on giant wooden tablets and report it to God upon one's entrance to the next world.

On the day of a writing-on-the-hand ritual, angels are said to descend from heaven, filling the room in which it takes place. Despite their presence, they remain completely invisible to their human counterparts. Until children have their hands written on, they are said to have little contact with angels, since they are deemed too young to know the difference between right and wrong. The new relationship between children and angels instigated by the writing-on-the-hand ritual brings with it new responsibilities not only to the children but also to their parents. Parents must work to keep the channels of communication open between children and angels, avoiding those situations or activities that are said to threaten or completely block this communication. For example, Mandinga believe that angels fear dogs and refrain from delivering messages to humans whenever and wherever dogs are present. For this reason, Mandinga are reluctant to keep dogs in their houses. When I inquired about the origin of this belief, one man in Bissau explained,

> A long time ago, the [Mandinga] people realized that for an entire week no one had received a message from an angel. The people didn't understand why the angels had refused to bring them messages, and so they began to worry. One day, Fatumata, the Prophet Mohammed's first daughter, was sweeping her house when she ran into a dog. She decided to put the dog outside, and that night the angels returned and spoke with the people in their dreams. That's when the people realized that angels fear dogs. From that day on, the people refused to let dogs into their houses and refrained from eating their meat.

As angels are also thought to fear female nudity, Mandinga discourage female nudity (especially below the waist) around the house so as not to deter angels further from delivering God's messages to human beings. Once children have had their hands written on, people must refrain from waking them, since this is thought to interrupt any messages that angels might be transmitting to them, messages offering advice or commentary on past or future actions and intentions. Before the relationship with angels is established, Mandinga commonly wake sleeping children, indeed, even newborns, to greet guests or to do chores.[8]

REMAKING CHILDHOOD RITUALS IN LISBON

When I was conducting my first fieldwork in Lisbon in 1999, I noticed that the writing-on-the-hand rituals I attended were especially elaborate, with normative aspects of the ritual—such as dress, food, and capturing the moment through photography or film—often taking on an exaggerated importance. Pnina Werbner (1990, 335) writes that when immigrants perform rituals outside of their "natural" contexts, they reinvent cultural categories and extend symbolic meanings, aligning them with novel experiences and predicaments in the new setting. Such is the case when Guinean Muslims confront the challenge of religious education and its consequences for identity in Portugal.

In Guinea-Bissau, Muslims value religious over secular education, and all Muslim children, whether they live in remote villages or in the capital city of Bissau, attend Qur'anic school. Few Guineans (and even fewer Guinean Muslims) have much confidence in the formal educational system in Guinea-Bissau, especially given that teachers sometimes go months without being paid and often hold strikes and cancel classes as a result. The Mandinga I came to know in Guinea-Bissau never expressed concern to me that their children were forgoing opportunities by attending Qur'anic school rather than the official Portuguese school.[9]

The situation is markedly different in Portugal, however, where educational opportunities far exceed those in Guinea-Bissau. All of the Guinean Muslim parents I met in Lisbon sent their children to Portuguese schools, and they took pride in their ability to provide their children with the benefits of a European education. New educational opportunities bring with them, however, some unintended consequences. Due to demanding school schedules, Guinean Muslim children in Lisbon spend the majority of their days in the company of non-Muslims, such as increasingly secularized Roman Catholics, who hold different values and orientations. As a result of long hours of instruction in Portuguese, children often refuse to speak Mandinga or Fula (or even Kriolu) at home, preferring to speak Portuguese even with their parents, many of whom do not speak the language. As visiting anthropologists who had lived in Guinea-Bissau, my husband and I were often implicated, much to our dismay, in this struggle. Mandinga parents would tease or insult their children, saying, "You should be ashamed of yourselves; these white people speak Mandinga and Kriolu better than you do!"

Demanding schedules also leave Guinean Muslim children with little free time to study the Qur'an in Lisbon, and attending Qur'anic school is further complicated by socioeconomic factors. While the mosque is located in central

Lisbon, most immigrants live in the city's exurbs, situated anywhere from twenty minutes to an hour away by bus, commuter train, or ferry. Parents are often too afraid to allow their children to make the journey on their own, and transportation is costly. Guinean Muslim parents in Lisbon often expressed concern that their children were losing their language and culture—in their words, "forgetting where they're from" (see Johnson 2017)—as a result of the new challenges of life in Europe. For many disillusioned immigrants, a continued or renewed emphasis on African custom—exemplified by life-course rituals and other traditional ritual practices—offers a potential solution to this problem and becomes key to the creation and maintenance of community in Lisbon. Indeed, the cultural elaboration of the writing-on-the-hand ritual in Lisbon can be interpreted as a creative response to the challenges that migration and transnationalism pose for Guinean Muslims.

Rather than seeking out formal Qur'anic educational opportunities for their children as they would in Guinea-Bissau, immigrant parents rely on informal instruction—that is, the daily experience of being raised in a Muslim household and participating in life-course rituals and other cultural events in the immigrant community, all of which retain a distinctively African flavor. Indeed, as they struggle to integrate into Lisbon's transnational Muslim community and become cosmopolitan Muslims, they also emphasize the importance of remembering where they are from. This takes the form of embracing their ethnic identity by strengthening their allegiance to *ado*, or "custom," exemplified by life-course rituals. They contend that these rituals are crucial for shaping both ethnic and religious identities, two identities that many people continue to conflate in Lisbon. In their view, the writing-on-the-hand ritual is at once African and Muslim and should continue to be practiced both back home and in the diaspora.

But some Guinean Muslim immigrants contend that African custom conflicts with their desire for integration in Lisbon's transnational Muslim community. For those who have studied the Qur'an formally for many years, have attained some degree of Arabic literacy, and have made the hajj (mostly men, Qur'anic teachers, and Muslim healer-diviners), the quest to become cosmopolitan Muslims is a continuous source of personal empowerment. More specifically, increased contact with non-African Muslims and the knowledge of Islam as practiced beyond Guinea-Bissau have increased their awareness of the *umma*, the global Muslim community, and their desire to belong to it. This experience has profoundly altered the way they imagine themselves both as members of a distinct ethnic group (Mandinga or Fula) and as practitioners of the world religion of Islam.

According to these people, Muslim identity is not acquired "naturally" simply by being born Muslim or Fula; it is not transmitted through a mother's breast milk or a father's name, nor is it conferred through participation in life-course rituals, such as the name-giving ritual or the writing-on-the-hand ritual. Rather, it is contingent on living one's life according to the doctrines and practices of Islam. This includes, most importantly, praying five times daily, attending Friday prayer at the mosque, upholding the taboos on pork and alcohol, fasting during Ramadan, and, if possible, making the hajj. This new model also emphasizes the meaning of the written word (i.e., Arabic literacy to ensure the accuracy of Qur'anic interpretation) over its more magical properties, such as sewing Qur'anic verses into protective amulets or ingesting God's word by licking Qur'anic verses written in ink from one's hand. In short, there is no room for such customary practices in this model of Islam, which instead emphasizes the five pillars of faith that unite Muslims throughout the world.

Thus, both the relationship between ethnicity and Islam and the role of embodied ritual practices shaping these two aspects of identity have been profoundly unsettled as Guinean Muslim immigrants remake Islam in African Portugal. In this process, they are beginning to understand religion not as something that one acquires passively at birth but as something that one consciously adopts, even strives to achieve. The result is a heightened awareness and an elaborate debate about the nature of culture and religion, African custom and global Islam. Since this complicated situation is best captured in moments of lived religiosity and actual voices from the field, I now present case studies of two Guinean Muslim healer-diviners in Lisbon. In teasing out these specialists' complex and contradictory viewpoints on the writing-on-the-hand ritual, I expose the creativity and ambiguity involved as Guinean Muslims remake themselves as ethnic and religious subjects in contemporary Europe.

IS THE WRITING-ON-THE-HAND RITUAL ISLAMIC?: CONFLICTING VOICES IN LISBON

Aside from serving as the president of the Maternal Kin Club during the time of my early fieldwork, Ibrahim worked as a Muslim healer-diviner, treating clients—African and Portuguese alike—for a variety of problems, including barrenness, unsuccessful employment, and drug and alcohol abuse. He told me that he was from a long line of especially powerful healer-diviners in Guinea-Bissau, of Jakanka origin. But unlike many of his relatives, whose training centered on the simple memorization of Qur'anic verses, Ibrahim prided himself in his ability to read and write Arabic and, more important, to translate Qur'anic verses into Mandinga so that he could explain their deep meanings to others. Ibrahim was in his midthirties at the time and felt he was too young to make the hajj, though he looked forward to making it one day. Although he regularly attended Friday prayer at Lisbon's central mosque, he spent most of his free time planning and attending events with his fellow club members. Indeed, despite Ibrahim's outward dedication to Islam and his knowledge of Arabic, he advocated the continued importance of African custom in Lisbon and emphasized its complementary, rather than contradictory, relationship to global Islam.

Ibrahim explained that life-course rituals are essential for making people both Mandinga persons and true Muslims. When I asked him to comment specifically on the role of the writing-on-the-hand ritual in configuring these identities, he defined it as an "obligatory rite." Specifically, he contended that it is the responsibility of all Mandinga parents to hold three rituals for their children in order to ensure that they grow up to be true Muslims—the name-giving ritual, the writing-on-the-hand ritual, and circumcision (the subject of the next chapter). Ibrahim, like many other Guinean Muslims I met in both Guinea-Bissau and Portugal, claimed that these rituals were mentioned in the Qur'an, the holy book of Muslims.

For Ibrahim, living in Lisbon has strengthened his belief that customary ritual practices, such as life-course rituals, confer both ethnic identity and religious identity. He explained that the writing-on-the-hand ritual in particular transmits "Mandinga-ness" (Mandinga identity) primarily by socializing children into their own educational system, their indigenous ways of knowing. This is especially important in Portugal, he claimed, where Guinean Muslim children attend the "white people's school," rather than Qur'anic school. He explained, "In the white people's school, you dress up in a suit, tie, and jacket, and you sit at a desk. When the teacher says, 'It's one,' you stand up and say, 'No, teacher, it's two.' In our school [Qur'anic school], we sit on the ground. If your teacher is sitting here, you take your shoes off over there before you come and sit down. You light a fire, and you learn to write verses from memory onto wooden slates, while mosquitoes bite you." Ibrahim's comparison of these two educational systems underscores the problematic nature for Guinean Muslims of challenging or questioning elders and other authority figures. Indeed, many immigrants I met in Lisbon complained that their children who were born and raised in Lisbon did not respect their elders and refused to take orders from them. Such behavior is practically unimaginable in Guinea-Bissau and is highly reprimanded when it occurs. Frustrated and ashamed immigrant parents are quick to blame their children's obstinate behavior on the European educational system, which emphasizes critical and independent thought over deference and humility.[10]

Ibrahim's comparison also highlights the cultural significance attributed to *sabaroo* ("suffering") in Mandinga society, a theme that I take up more extensively in chapter 3. For Mandinga, suffering a difficult situation—enduring it with a calm and patient spirit—is a sign of social maturity and is linked to the enhancement of self. Before Qur'anic students can recite by heart the sacred texts of Islam, they must suffer through hours of memorization in difficult circumstances, without the comforts of chairs and electricity. Ibrahim told me that he was planning to hold writing-on-the-hand rituals for his two young daughters. In emphasizing the continued importance of this African custom in Lisbon, Ibrahim removed his passport from his front shirt pocket and said, "When you travel to another place, you need a passport, don't you? Well, the writing-on-the-hand ritual is like a Mandinga child's passport to the next world."

During my fieldwork in Lisbon, I got very close to Bacar and his family. Like Ibrahim, Bacar made his living as a Muslim healer-diviner and ran his own business out of his home in Queluz. Bacar attended weekly Friday prayer at Lisbon's central mosque. Although he belonged to the Sweetness Club—the Maternal Kin Club's rival culture club—Bacar felt that his time was better spent at the mosque, associating with Muslims from all over the world. Bacar had traveled to Saudi Arabia several times to study Arabic and to make the hajj. During my 2003 fieldwork in Lisbon, he was leading the group of Guinean Muslim pilgrims to Mecca, which he had done several times previously. As a result of his firsthand experience of Islam as practiced by Arabs, Bacar was confident of his knowledge of true Islam, and he often criticized his rival healer-diviners in Lisbon—including his colleague, Ibrahim—for their ignorance of Arabic and of what he called the Qur'an's "deep" meanings.

When I asked Bacar why Mandinga practice the writing-on-the-hand ritual, he explained that the elders invented the tradition a long time ago as a form of "Muslim propaganda." That is, it sparks young children's interest in Islam by encouraging them to study the Qur'an. In filling young children with pride in their religion, Bacar explained, the writing-on-the-hand ritual "gives Islam power in Africa." But Bacar explained that the writing-on-the-hand ritual is an African custom, not a Muslim one. Indeed, he claimed that the Qur'an makes no mention of the ritual:

> Deep in the Qur'an, the writing-on-the-hand ritual isn't there. As Muslims, we should do those things that the Prophet Mohammed did. This is what we must follow. Those things that he didn't do, we shouldn't follow them. The writing-on-the-hand ritual isn't in the Qur'an. The Prophet Mohammed

never did it. It was the angel—the one you call Gabriel—who taught the Prophet Mohammed to read. But he never wrote on the Prophet's hand! If the Prophet's hand was never written on, then why do we insist on writing on our children's hands? You won't find the writing-on-the-hand ritual practiced in any Arab country because the Prophet Mohammed never did it.

Bacar's reformist views, his desire to distinguish between African custom and true Islam as practiced by Arabs, were shaped by his newfound participation in the *umma*. According to Bacar, there are many ways to ensure that Mandinga children in Portugal become good Muslims, but African custom should not be one of them. Bacar contended that the writing-on-the-hand ritual, like other Mandinga life-course rituals practiced in Lisbon, is simply a way in which Mandinga immigrants can build their name in Lisbon's immigrant community by publicly displaying their fame, financial success, and (false) allegiance to Islam. In Bacar's view, this behavior merely conceals deeper shortcomings in Muslim piety—one's ignorance of the Qur'an and one's refusal to follow God's laws.

When I asked Bacar if he felt that Mandinga in Lisbon should stop practicing the writing-on-the-hand ritual, however, his views became more complex, even contradictory. He explained that just because people say that the ritual is unimportant or even un-Islamic does not mean that they should or will stop practicing it. "Many people continue to hold African rituals because they fear criticism from the elders," Bacar asserted. "If you don't hold a writing-on-the-hand ritual for your children, the elders will accuse you of being a bad parent." But according to Bacar, the ritual itself is less important than the idea behind it—the responsibility of Guinean Muslim parents to enroll their children in Qur'anic school. "My children haven't had their hands written on," Bacar told me, "but they go to Qur'anic school and are learning about their religion just the same."

Bacar then told me about a deep and much-debated reason to continue the writing-on-the-hand ritual, despite its un-Islamic nature, in Portugal. It is said to instill a fear in children of "falling from Islam," of suspending one's dedication to the religion, exemplified by Basiro in a vignette earlier in this chapter. The temptation of falling from Islam is intensified in Portugal, where Guinean Muslim immigrants are surrounded by non-Muslims and separated from a Muslim way of life. Specifically, the salt and ink that children lick from their palms during the writing-on-the-hand ritual are said to safeguard against the breach of the Muslim taboo on alcohol consumption. Bacar explained, "It's nearly impossible for people who have had their hands written on to develop an alcohol problem during their lifetime. If they begin to experiment with alcohol out of curiosity, once they get to a certain age they will stop drinking once and for all. If you see someone who develops a drinking problem, you will know that this person never had his or her hand written on."

Some of my Guinean Muslim interlocutors in Lisbon took this philosophy one step further, stating that even a sip of alcohol subsequent to the writing-on-the-hand ritual would be "too strong" for a person's head and would lead to insanity. This magical safeguard that some believe the writing-on-the-hand ritual provides takes on a renewed importance in Lisbon, where the constant pressures of immigrant life and encounters with many forms of otherness, such as Roman Catholics and other non-Muslims, often compel Guinean Muslim immigrants to experiment with alcohol for the first time. As one young Fula man told me, "Many Guinean Muslims in Lisbon start drinking alcohol because of worry or stress, but most of the time it's just influence from non-Muslims. Once you come to Portugal you start hanging out with non-Muslims who drink all of the time. You resist and resist, insisting that you are a Muslim and that Muslims don't drink, until one day you decide to have just one or two beers. Then you suddenly change your opinion on the matter." But despite the allure of this ritual safeguard against falling from Islam, Bacar believed that refusing to drink alcohol—whether in Africa or Europe—should reflect a deep and conscientious allegiance to Islam, rather than a fear, created magically through an African ritual, of losing one's mind. That being said, the stakes are high enough in Portugal that when I visited Bacar in 2003, he still had not completely ruled out the possibility of holding writing-on-the-hand rituals for his own children. His wife, Aminata, had just given birth to a son, whom they named Abudu. Bacar told me that he was considering having all three of his children's hands written on at the same time when Abudu turns seven.

"BIG-PARTY-STYLE" RITUALS IN LISBON

Name-giving rituals are more variable in Portugal than in Guinea-Bissau. Like writing-on-the-hand rituals and other life-course rituals, variations and contrasting ideas about what constitutes proper practice in name-giving rituals are the subject of lively debate among Guinean Muslims in Lisbon. The name-giving ritual I describe in the opening vignette of this chapter is the most common form in both locales. This type has a distinctive Muslim flavor and highlights the religious elements of the ritual, such as shaving the baby's head, slaughtering a goat or sheep, pronouncing the baby's name, bestowing blessings, and partaking in a modest communal meal. But some name-giving rituals in Lisbon vary considerably from this form. Often referred to as "Muslim baptisms" in the community, they draw from and incorporate hybrid cultural and religious traditions and typically occur in two parts. The religious part takes place first in the morning or early afternoon and is often a private affair, with only the baby's close relatives and friends attending.

Later in the afternoon or evening, a larger, mixed-faith group of Muslim and non-Muslim guests attend the "big party," featuring large quantities of food beyond rice and sauce—such as grilled meats, corn on the cob, and soda—and live music and dancing. For this part of the ritual, the baby's parents often hire either traditional kora musicians and drummers or popular bands (or sometimes even both) from Guinea-Bissau. They also commonly hire someone from the community to film the event and to later edit and transform the footage into a DVD that the family can watch and show to others. Because of the ethnic and religious diversity of this form of name-giving ritual, alcohol and pork may be served for non-Muslim guests and for those Muslims who do not uphold these taboos. Some of the guests who attended the religious portion of a name-giving ritual in the morning or early afternoon wearing "big clothing" (modest, Muslim-style dress) return later for the big party dressed in European-style clothing.

One of the most striking differences in name-giving rituals in Portugal when compared to those in Guinea-Bissau is the flexibility surrounding their scheduling. Whereas in Guinea-Bissau parents usually hold a name-giving ritual one week after their baby's birth, Guinean Muslim immigrants place much less importance on the timing of the ritual. Indeed, many of the name-giving rituals I was invited to attend in Lisbon were postponed not once but multiple times, with some parents waiting several months or even years to officially name their children. In many cases, this was due to the challenge of school and work schedules. In others, it had to do with economic factors. Many Guinean Muslims I met in Lisbon saw name-giving rituals, like other life-course rituals, as opportunities to "build their names" in the wider immigrant community. As such, they wanted to invite as many people as possible, which made the rituals more expensive. On one occasion as my husband and I prepared to attend our first name-giving ritual in Lisbon, one of the baby's relatives called me on my mobile phone, informing us that the ritual, which was scheduled to take place one week after the baby's birth, had been postponed. She explained that the baby's father had recently started a new job as a bricklayer on a construction site and his first paycheck was delayed. As a result, he had postponed the ritual for the following week, at which point I received another call, informing us that the ritual was postponed again for the same reason. When the baby's father finally received his first paycheck nearly two months later, the ritual was finally held.[11]

My interlocutors had much to say on the subject of postponing name-giving rituals and other life-course rituals in Lisbon, but their opinions varied considerably. Some merely shrugged their shoulders, claiming that postponing rituals "can't be helped; Portugal is not the same as Guinea-Bissau." They claimed that one's intent to hold a particular life-course ritual was more important than the actual timing of the ritual. In their minds, as long as people did their best to hold the ritual on time, it did not matter if they actually managed to do so or not. "God is understanding," they insisted. Older men who worked as healer-diviners, devoted considerable time to Qur'anic study, and had made the hajj, however, were more critical of this practice. While postponing a ritual due to sincere financial hardship was acceptable in their minds, postponing one in order to give the parents the time to save up enough money to hold a big-party-style ritual with the goal of building their names in Lisbon was problematic. As one healer-diviner put it, "God doesn't want this." Another healer-diviner explained,

> When you have a baby, you must give him or her a good Muslim name. You must shave your children's heads and give them names like Ibrahim, Aliu, Hawa, or Fatumata. This is how we know that our children are Muslims. If you have the means to kill a chicken, then kill a chicken. If you can kill a sheep, then kill a sheep so that Muslims can come and eat. But name-giving rituals are not about drumming, dancing, and killing more animals than you can afford or eat. The Qur'an doesn't tell us to do that, nor do God and the Prophet approve of that.[12]

Healer-diviners emphasized the importance of remembering why Muslims practice the name-giving ritual in the first place: to give their children an identity before God. Like other West African Muslims, Guinean Muslims believe that infants who have not yet been named in a ritual are not complete human persons and their future is uncertain. In Guinea-Bissau, a baby who dies before his or her name-giving ritual is buried quickly, without the proper accompanying funerary rites or postburial sacrifices, rituals I address fully in chapter 4. In holding a name-giving ritual for their children and giving them a "good Muslim name," parents take the first step in securing their children a place in the afterlife. As one man explained, "When your child's name is pronounced during the name-giving ritual, the angels hear it and record it on God's wooden tablet. At the end of the world, God calls out all of the names on his tablet. If your children were properly named, then they will be on the list. When God calls out their names, they will hear them and rise to join their companions in the next world." Unnamed children have no possibility of rebirth, since they have no identity before God. In Guinea-Bissau, where infant mortality is high, postponing name-giving rituals is risky. But in Lisbon, Guinean Muslim immigrants do not feel this risk as acutely as they do back home. While they acknowledge that human beings, no matter where they happen to live, are always powerless against death, which can strike at any time without warning, they are also well aware of the fact that fewer infants die in Europe than they do in Africa.

Immigrant parents are familiar with the critical views of elders and healer-diviners concerning big-party-style name-giving rituals, and they had their own response to them. In Lisbon, hard work is ideally supposed to equate to financial success, and people feel the pressure to be recognized as having money. People's desires and standards for life-course rituals also tend to be higher in Portugal than in Guinea-Bissau, which puts considerable stress on immigrants who are struggling to get ahead in Lisbon while also sending remittances to relatives back home, most of whom have little to no understanding of the challenges of life in Europe. As one woman put it, "Back home, guests are just happy that a child is being named and are content with one or two handfuls of rice. But not in Portugal: here they expect ten handfuls!" Many people told me that if they fail to provide guests with enough food and drink at life-course rituals, people "talk" (gossip) and "spoil their names" (destroy their reputation) in the immigrant community.

MAGICALITY AND TRUE ISLAM

Guinean Muslim immigrants confront multiple forms of otherness in Lisbon: their Portuguese "hosts," other Luso-African immigrants from Portugal's former colonies in Africa and Asia, and Muslims from outside of Africa ("Arabs" and "Indians"). As a result, they are coming to understand religion as something different from—something beyond—their own cultural practices. Their identities—once rooted in a comfortable convergence of ethnic identity, African custom, and Muslim identity—are therefore becoming increasingly unsettled. As the above case studies of the early childhood rituals of name-giving and hand-writing reveal, this process, intensified by the twin experiences of migration and globalization, is fraught with ambiguities and contradictions. It also extends beyond the conventional dichotomies of traditionalist/reformist positions and African custom/global Islam.

In the case of the name-giving ritual, the very healer-diviners who criticized parents for postponing name-giving rituals or holding them in big-party style attended these very rituals, defended them, and even postponed their own children's rituals. The situation is even more complex in the case of the writing-on-the-hand ritual. Ibrahim's allegiance to Mandinga custom and his belief in the substantive power of ritual seem to identify him as a traditionalist. Yet he turned to the Qur'an to legitimate the writing-on-the-hand ritual, convincing himself and others that there is a place for African custom in the holy book of Islam. Likewise, Bacar's cosmopolitan desire to be a true Muslim—more specifically, his need to separate African customs from Muslim ones—seems to mark him as a reformist. Yet he was unable to relinquish completely the efficacy and importance of the writing-on-the-hand ritual, its magical power to prevent Guinean Muslims in Portugal from falling from Islam by protecting them from alcohol addiction. Ibrahim was willing to remain traditional only to the extent that this stance did not exclude him completely from participation in the *umma*. For his part, Bacar was prepared to embrace true Islam only to the point that his Mandinga ethnicity remained firmly in place.

The above exchange challenges one of Max Weber's most widely accepted claims: as religions "rationalize"—in this case, as they become more systematic and closely aligned with text-based doctrine—they are supposed to become less magical. But as the above case studies demonstrate, many Guinean Muslims who profess adherence to a more cosmopolitan version of Islam still acknowledge the magical efficacy of African custom and often expand its influence to fit their changing circumstances. As Guinean Muslims remake themselves and their religion in Lisbon, African custom and global Islam are not mutually exclusive categories but rather complementary and overlapping ones, and the creative tension that exists between them is central to Guinean Muslim identity and religious practice in Africa, Europe, and beyond.

NOTES

1. In an earlier work, Weiss (1992) showed how Haya in Tanzania attempted to understand and control global processes by grounding them in bodily experience. Haya children who developed "plastic teeth"—a new disease that appeared around the same time as AIDS and symbolically parallels it—believed that they must have these teeth surgically removed or they would die.

2. Gluckman's (1965, 285) distinction between ritual and ceremony differed from Turner's. For Gluckman, participants believed that a ritual worked by mystical means, whereas "the mystical" was absent in ceremonial contexts.

3. Van Gennep (1960, 166–67) suggested that shaving the head or cutting the hair in a ritual marks a person's separation from a previous state. In the case of the name-giving ritual, shaving or removing some hair symbolically might mark the severing of the infant from the spirit world (see Rasmussen 1997, 94). When I

asked my interlocutors about this, however, they claimed they did not share this interpretation of the shaving.

4. The writing-on-the-hand ritual might mark the development of "social sense," the point at which Guinean Muslim children are considered capable of making moral decisions and are held accountable for their actions. The development of this awareness continues during initiation, when it is more actively cultivated and refined. See Riesman (1998, 127–29), Richards (1982, 123), and Boddy (1989, 57) for discussions of social sense in other African societies. For similar descriptions of the writing-on-the-hand ritual in other West African countries, see Mommersteeg (2012, 39–40), Sanneh (1979, 187), and Ware (2014, 50).

5. Trachtenberg (2004, 122–23) describes similar methods of "transferring the word to the body" among medieval Jews. Scholars and students ate cakes and eggs inscribed with biblical verses and incantations to promote success, and schoolchildren consumed these foods before their studies to "open their minds." Medieval Jews also applied magically charged liquids to their hands and faces for a variety of purposes. Marcus (1996, 36–37) writes that the medieval initiation ceremony prescribed that Jewish school students "read and symbolically eat three sacred texts that were written on the writing tablet and smeared with honey." He compares this to the contemporary practices of feeding school-aged children "edible alphabets" (1996, 18) in the form of noodles or cereal.

6. The ritual importance of salt is ancient and widespread and has been documented both in indigenous religions in Africa and elsewhere and in the monotheistic religious traditions. Granqvist (1975, 98) addresses the link between salt and modesty among Muslim Palestinians. It is common to say to a disobedient child, for example, "Be ashamed of thyself and put a little salt in thy eye." Furthermore, babies are rubbed with a mixture of salt and oil for seven days after they are born to "make them modest." Among Semitic peoples, salt was a sign of purity and incorruptibility, owing to its preservative qualities. The ancient Romans placed a few grains of salt on the lips of an infant on the eighth day after birth to chase away demons (Livingstone 1997, 1447–48). Contemporary Christians use salt to make holy water, but in this case salt's link to wisdom is emphasized over its antidemonic qualities (see Latham 1982, 169–73 for an interesting discussion of salt and wisdom). The Ehing of Senegal equate salt with semen, and salt plays an important ritual role in curing a child who has been made chronically ill by adulterous parents (see Schloss 1988, 106). The connections between salt and "blood" (semen) made by the Ehing as described by Schloss point to a possible pre-Islamic symbolism of salt (i.e., fertility and health) as used in the writing-on-the-hand ritual among Guinean Muslims.

7. Honey was also an important substance used in medieval Jewish initiation ceremonies for young students. Students were commonly given honey cakes as a reward for recitation, and the teacher would smear honey over the letters of a

tablet onto which the Hebrew alphabet had been written, instructing the child to lick it off (see Marcus 1996, 1). Marcus further notes that the ancient Greeks associated honey with preserving memory (1996, 145n30).

8. See Gottlieb (2004, 176–77) for a discussion of waking sleeping Beng babies in Côte d'Ivoire.

9. This is a significant problem, considering the country's already dismal educational system. Forrest (1992, 136) estimated that in 1990 only 36 percent of Guinea-Bissau's children between the ages of seven and fourteen were enrolled in school full-time and only 21 percent were considered literate. See Forrest (1992, 134–38) for a discussion of education in Guinea-Bissau.

10. See Launay (2016) for a collection of essays comparing "writing boards and blackboards," embodiments of the two distinct educational systems in Africa: Qur'anic education and the colonial institutions of state (secular) and mission schools.

11. In Guinea-Bissau, name-giving rituals may be postponed in situations of economic hardship, when parents cannot afford to hold one and cannot find anyone to loan them money or an animal. In this case, they hold a replacement ritual in which the father shows a chicken or some halal meat to the baby and promises to hold a proper ritual at a later time. This replacement ritual does not cancel but rather postpones a father's debt to his child (see Johnson 2017, 59–60, for a more complete description of this replacement ritual).

12. See D'Alisera (2004, 55–57) for parallel debates about the timing of naming ceremonies and "big parties" among Sierra Leonean Muslim immigrants in Washington, DC.

THREE

—ɯ—

MAKING MANDINGA, MAKING MUSLIMS

Initiation, Circumcision, and Ritual Uncertainty

ONE MORNING DURING MY FIELDWORK in Lisbon, I put on my best *den-dikooba* (matching pants and long shirt) sewed by a tailor in Guinea-Bissau and caught the metro to Anjos. I rang the bell at Tunbulo's apartment, and she let me in. Jakumba was still getting ready, and Tunbulo's husband had just finished praying. He sat on his prayer rug behind a lit candle, fingering his prayer beads. Tunbulo's mobile phone rang several times as people called for details or how to meet up with us along the way. The ceremony would take place around noon in Setúbal, about an hour-long bus ride from central Lisbon.

We walked to the end of the street, where we waited for several Maternal Kin Club members. "If they don't show up," Tunbulo said, "we'll take a taxi to the bus station." Just then a car pulled up, and two women greeted us and told us to get in the car. We squeezed in, letting Tunbulo ride up front. The driver told us that although she was not going to Setúbal, she could give the five of us a ride to the bus station.

When we arrived in Setúbal, the women realized that no one had brought Mariama's contact information, and no one knew how to get to her house. Luckily, I had her mobile number and home address listed in my contact book. I called her, but there was no answer, so we took a taxi to her address. "This is the place; I remember it now," Tunbulo said as we arrived. We greeted everyone there, especially Mariama, the mother of the initiates, who carried her infant daughter tied to her back with a colorful wrap from Guinea-Bissau. Some women were gathered in the kitchen, cooking and visiting. Most of the guests, however, were crammed into the living room, watching a videotape of the most recent Maternal Kin Club *spectáculo*, featuring Gambian kora master Jaliba

Figure 3.1. Posing for the camera at a coming-out
ceremony, 1999. Photograph by the author.

Kuyateh. People pointed at the screen, laughing at how "So-and-So" danced and at how much money a group of men managed to stuff into Jaliba's mouth.

Soon the praise-singers arrived. One played an acoustic guitar plugged into an amplifier kora-style, while others simply sang, trying desperately to extract money from people at the back of the room, their eyes glued to the video. The women served a fabulous lunch of rice and goat meat with Portuguese-style salad. We all made donations of money, which the club president presented to the father of the initiates.

After lunch, the women congregated in the kitchen, and one woman began to drum on a plastic bowl turned upside down over a basin of couscous. The women formed a circle, clapping their hands and singing initiation songs interspersed with Muslim chants. Mariama entered the circle, little Fatu still tied to her back, and "danced" her boys, both born in Portugal, into their new status as initiated persons. The boys, ages eight and ten, had been circumcised recently in the hospital. They came out of their rooms dressed in stunning *dendikoobas* complete with Saudi-style hats and brand-new Nike Air Jordan shoes. As they passed by, the women clapped and cheered. Then the initiates stood in the hallway as people snapped photographs. At one point, the club's president brought over a houseplant, a perfect centerpiece, around which he carefully positioned the initiates. People snapped more photographs until the boys yelled in Portuguese, "*Ja cheiga!*" ("That's enough!"). The men distributed kola nuts, marking the end of the ceremony. Frantically, people attempted to secure rides back to Lisbon. Tunbulo grabbed my arm, pulled me outside, and shouted, "Come on, get in!" Ten of us rode home, squished in a minivan, *kandonga* ("bush taxi")-style. People talked about the political situation in Guinea-Bissau and how the water in Mecca makes one cough. When we arrived at Rossio, we gave each other blessings for a safe trip home and for a peaceful night.

MANDINGA INITIATION: "SMALL" AND "BIG" RITES

Initiation is the next ritual that Mandinga experience as they make their way through the life course. Like the writing-on-the-hand ritual, it shapes ethnicity and Muslim identity and inscribes these onto bodies. But unlike the writing-on-the-hand ritual, whose permanent marks cannot be seen by the naked eye, Mandinga initiation, which involves circumcision for both sexes, permanently alters bodies. As Mandinga remake Islam in Portugal, they have come to disagree about both the consequences and the meanings of this alteration for both boys and girls.[1]

As I have argued previously (Johnson 2000, 2007), it is impossible to address circumcision among Mandinga without also addressing initiation rituals, to which circumcision is linked. Traditionally, circumcision for Mandinga boys and girls took place in the context of initiation rituals. In everyday speech, Mandinga use the single term *kwiong* to refer to both circumcision (the physical act of genital cutting) and the initiation rituals that have traditionally accompanied it. When people want to specify further, they simply add the ending "big" or "small" (e.g., *kwiongba*, or "big initiation"). The small initiation refers specifically to circumcision, and the big initiation refers to initiation rituals.[2]

For boys, small initiation, or circumcision, entails the removal of the foreskin of the penis. The situation is a bit more complicated for girls, in that there are at least two types of female circumcision practiced in Guinea-Bissau. Furthermore, due to the multiethnic nature of initiation rituals, which type is practiced varies across and even within ethnic groups. The majority of my Mandinga interlocutors stated confidently that the traditional, most common type is partial clitoridectomy, which involves the removal of the prepuce or part of the clitoris or both.[3] Over the years, as I have continued to conduct research on this topic, I have encountered several variations of this traditional type. Several Mandinga women with whom I worked closely in Lisbon, for example, claimed that the circumciser "took it all," removing the entire clitoris. A few others told me that their genitals were "totally cleaned." When I asked them what they meant by this, they explained that the circumciser removed the entire clitoris and part or all of the labia minora. Anthropologists commonly refer to this latter practice as excision, and some men and women in both Guinea-Bissau and Portugal used the Portuguese word *excisão* as a general term for female circumcision, irrespective of the type practiced.[4]

What I found most intriguing about the Mandinga women who told me they had experienced more severe forms of female circumcision is that they attended Fula, rather than Mandinga, initiation rituals. It is common in Guinea-Bissau, especially for boys, to attend another ethnic group's initiation rituals. Since Muslim initiations for boys had the best reputation during my fieldwork in Guinea-Bissau and still do today, I met many non-Muslim parents who chose to send their sons to Fula or Mandinga rituals. This was not an option for non-Muslim parents of girls, of course, since they would not want their daughters to be circumcised. I did, however, meet many Mandinga women who had attended a different Muslim ethnic group's ritual, such as Fula or Beafada initiation (and many Fula or Beafada women who went to Mandinga initiations, for that matter). As my Muslim interlocutors put it, "As long as the rituals are Muslim, they're acceptable."[5]

Many of my Mandinga interlocutors in Lisbon claimed that Fula practice a different form of female circumcision than do Mandinga (excision rather than partial clitoridectomy). When I asked Fula women in Lisbon about this claim, however, they denied any difference in cutting between the two ethnic groups. Furthermore, they claimed that the Mandinga women who made this claim were simply "trying to make themselves look better" than Fula women. In attempting to make sense of this conflicting information, I can only reiterate that the type or degree of cutting varies and that it is difficult to accurately ascertain what female circumcision is for Guinean Muslim women, at least in the physical sense.

What is most intriguing about the Fula women's comments is that they highlight the role of the media in global discourses and debates surrounding female, and I would add male, circumcision. The women were concerned about the image Mandinga were painting of one of their ethnic group's traditional practices, and they were fully aware of the fact that Westerners consider more severe forms of female circumcision "worse" than less severe forms. They did not want me, a white American "scientist," to think poorly about all Fula people because they might practice a more severe form of female circumcision than Mandinga people, their rival ethnic group. This reflexivity and heightened concern about one's reputation in the world were very common during my fieldwork in Lisbon, and I discuss them later in more detail.

In Guinea-Bissau, the big initiation encompasses a variety of practices. First, the elders build a thatched structure in the bush where the initiates stay for a period of time. Indeed, the Mandinga word for initiation, *kwiong*, is actually the word for this structure. Although children used to stay in the bush for three to six months, nowadays this period has been reduced to one to two weeks or even less. During this time, the initiates learn initiation songs and important rules of etiquette. After circumcision and a brief period of healing, a coming-out ceremony marks the changed status of the initiates—from uninitiated to initiated persons.

Today Mandinga coming-out ceremonies are often held in front of the local mosque and are often elaborate. In the case of boys, the initiates' sponsors, usually their maternal uncles, carry the initiates from the bush to the mosque. The mothers then dance their newly initiated sons while people throw money onto the boys' heads and *Kankurang*, the boys' masquerade figure, chases spectators with his rice cutlasses and safeguards the initiates. The ceremony ends with a shared meal.

Traditionally, Mandinga boys and girls experienced the big and small rituals simultaneously around puberty, and initiation was associated with marriage. Nowadays, however, most children are circumcised at a much younger age (from infancy to six years old), and boys are frequently circumcised in the hospital. Due to the government's official condemnation of female circumcision in Guinea-Bissau during my early fieldwork (the practice was subsequently made illegal in 2011), as well as in Portugal, hospital circumcisions are not an option for girls, who are circumcised by a traditional circumciser either in the bush (in a big initiation) or at home. While some children attend a big initiation when they are older, some never do. Indeed, there has been a recent separation between the small and big rituals, and details of initiation rituals have become highly variable.

I learned quite early in my fieldwork that when it comes to initiation, things are not always what they seem. On one particularly memorable occasion in Bissau in 1997, Ned and I were invited to attend what everyone described as a traditional boys' initiation in Pilon, a multiethnic Muslim neighborhood that at the time of my research was famous for its elaborate initiation rituals. The rituals went on for weeks. The sponsors carried the young boys, who were wrapped in traditional funerary cloth and hunched over to resemble corpses. Kankurang, with his highly unpredictable movements, engaged in crowd control, chasing away curious spectators (including the two foreign anthropologists) and women who, in typical fashion, tried to discover his identity. Later, mothers, dressed in their finest outfits, complete with hats and umbrellas, danced their initiated sons in front of the mosque, while people placed offerings of money on their heads. At one point during the festivities, I turned to one of the initiate's sponsors and asked, "How long did the boys spend in the bush?" He responded, "These boys were circumcised in the hospital; they're just doing the cultural part now."

INTERPRETING INITIATION: THE ENTANGLEMENT OF ETHNICITY AND ISLAM

In contrast to initiation rites in many African societies, Mandinga initiation does not mark the attainment of adulthood (cf. Turner 1967; Ottenberg 1989; MacCormack 1979; Prazak 2016). Rather, Mandinga adults of both sexes attain adult status only after the birth of their first child in the final stage of marriage, when husband and wife reside together. Initiation is loosely associated with adult status, however, in that it is considered one step in the process of becoming fully adult. Indeed, my Mandinga interlocutors could not imagine getting married or having children without being initiated (circumcised) first.[6]

Nor is Mandinga initiation explicitly associated with the cultivation of gender identity. In those African societies where initiation rituals are thought to transform gender-ambiguous children into gender-unambiguous adults, circumcision accomplishes this most explicitly. Cutting the clitoris (a woman's "male" part) and the foreskin (a man's "female" part) is thought to remove sexual ambiguity, creating men and women (see Beidelman 1997; Boone 1986; Boddy 1988).

The meaning of Mandinga initiation is rather found in the entanglement of ethnicity and Islam. The link between initiation and ethnicity is complex, however, and requires some explanation. It is through initiation that Mandinga believe that children learn to "know the eye" (*nya lon*). Knowing the eye is a type of moral education that, although lifelong, is cultivated most explicitly during the big initiation. Specifically, it defines how one should behave in different social situations and in the presence of elders and people of the opposite sex. It encompasses an awareness of one's place and role in society according to ethnicity, age, sex, and caste.[7] Initiates learn this in part by mastering the deep meaning of a number of signs or gestures they will encounter throughout their lives. As one example (and there are dozens of them), if a person sees shoes stacked on top of one another outside a house or door, he or she should not enter, because this signals that a couple is having sex inside.

My Mandinga interlocutors described people who know the eye as socially refined and perceptive. They are able to sense the emotions and thus anticipate the needs of others before they are expressed. Juditi, a Mandinga woman I worked with closely in Guinea-Bissau in 1996–97 and later in Lisbon in 2003, explained this clearly: "After I was initiated, I could sense what the elders were thinking before they said anything. On one occasion, I knew I was supposed to leave my mother with her guests. She didn't have to tell me; I knew by the expression on her face."

In contrast to initiated people, who know the eye, uninitiated people, or *solimaa*, are disrespectful, simpleminded, and aloof. My Mandinga interlocutors often described these people to me through their eating habits. For example, they eat more sauce than rice from their side of the bowl. Although it may sound trivial, this impolite behavior actually has a deeper significance: it signals an unbridled desire for life's "sweetness" (symbolized by sauce) and a rejection of things essential to life (symbolized by rice). Those who know the eye demonstrate their respect for essential things by eating the rice grains that have fallen out of the food bowl onto the sitting mat. *Solimaa*, in contrast, do not even notice these grains, or, even worse, they refuse to eat them. Beyond their eating habits, uninitiated people are said to have no shame: they run around naked with playmates of the opposite sex and bathe in open spaces without covering their bodies. They are also stubborn and disobedient, evidenced in their refusal to run errands for adults who send them.[8]

Further complicating the relationship between initiation and Mandinga ethnicity is the concept of *sabaroo*, or "suffering." Knowing the eye does not come without hardship, and many of my interlocutors, especially men, told me how difficult their initiations were. They complained of hunger and of being forced to eat less-than-desirable food. Kankurang beat them, and the elders deprived them of sleep, making them sing and dance endlessly in the rain. Many of my Mandinga interlocutors, however, described these hardships as an essential part of initiation. During my fieldwork in both Guinea-Bissau and Portugal, I heard the common Mandinga phrases *duniyaa man diyaa* ("life is not sweet") and *i sabiri* ("suffer it") daily. These are two common responses to difficult situations, such as an illness or death of a loved one. These were the second group of phrases I mastered in the Mandinga language (after the extensive traditional greetings), and people delighted whenever I used them correctly.

My Mandinga interlocutors linked suffering to perseverance, growth, and self-enhancement. Before villagers can feel the strength provided by a hardy breakfast of millet porridge, they must endure an entire season of the back-breaking labor of planting, weeding, and harvesting. Before becoming respected Qur'anic scholars, students must spend years engaged in the arduous memorization of Qur'anic verses in Arabic, a language they do not speak or understand. Before a woman becomes a mother, her initiation into adulthood, she must endure the exhaustion of pregnancy and the pain of childbirth. It is only after knowing suffering, Mandinga claim, that people can truly appreciate life's sweetness.

Although they may not appear to be at first glance, knowing the eye and suffering are ethnic categories. Indeed, they define the values and behaviors that all adult Mandinga people should ideally possess. I did not understand this fully until I returned to Bafata-Oio in 2003, six years after my first fieldwork in Guinea-Bissau. Fatumata, my namesake and one of my closest friends, invited me to join a group of women who were pounding rice to make funerary *munkoo* (rice flour). There was a lot of rice to pound, and the work was lengthy and intense. My neck and shoulders ached as I struggled to thrust the pestle into the mortar with enough force to turn rice into flour. I did my best to hide my pain until one woman asked me how it was going. I couldn't help but respond, "My hands are killing me." "Show us," the women said in unison. The blisters on my palms had now opened, exposing raw, bleeding flesh. "Suffer it," several women told me as they resumed pounding. Fatumata smiled at me and said, "Now you are truly Mandinga!"

While the big initiation (initiation rituals) is linked to knowing the eye and suffering, two essential components of Mandinga ethnicity, the small initiation (the physical act of circumcision), is linked to Islam. Mandinga claim that circumcision makes boys clean, enabling them to pray, slaughter animals in the proper fashion, and fast during Ramadan. My Mandinga interlocutors explained that the Prophet Mohammed was circumcised as a rite of purification, and in order to be good Muslims, they must follow his example. Most Mandinga I met in both Guinea-Bissau and Portugal were also very aware of the fact that boys in other parts of the Muslim world are circumcised like them.

Female circumcision, as both imagined and practiced by Mandinga men and women, is more complicated and controversial. Mandinga women link the practice explicitly to Islam. In their view, female circumcision simply parallels male circumcision: it makes women clean and allows them to pray, rendering them full, proper Muslims. The accepted scholarly view is that female circumcision did not originate in Islam but that Islam later accepted it (Kouba and Muasher 1985, 104). Nowhere is it found in the Qur'an, and the hadith—reports of what the Prophet Mohammed said and did—dedicates one sentence to it (see Winkel 1995; Gruenbaum 2001, 64), a sentence that is interpreted differently by different people. Ellen Gruenbaum (2001, 56–57) explains that while most Muslim theologians view female circumcision as an optional practice, a few consider it contradictory to Islam. The relationship between Islam and female circumcision is equally tenuous in the realm of practice: many Muslim women do not practice female circumcision, and many non-Muslim women do.

None of the Mandinga women I worked with in Guinea-Bissau or Portugal are familiar with these scholarly views, however, and the overwhelming majority of them are convinced that female circumcision is an Islamic practice that is crucial to their Muslim identity. Because it is the job of the anthropologist to identify and document reality as fashioned and lived on the ground by local people, the link that Mandinga women make between female circumcision and Islam cannot be dismissed or even taken lightly. Instead, it must be fully understood and "thickly described" (Geertz 1973).

Mandinga women claim that uncircumcised women's genitals produce an odor that renders them unclean and spoils their prayers. Corinne Kratz (1994, 341) argues that discourses about circumcision "are located more generally within histories of the body and understandings of the body as a site of signification." Along these lines, Muslim beliefs about gender and the life course shed light on the meaning of female circumcision according to Mandinga. Like Muslims elsewhere, Mandinga believe that children are born pure but become progressively more impure as their bodies and minds mature, as they come in contact with polluting bodily substances (such as menstrual blood and the blood of childbirth), and as they discover they have free will (the freedom to choose to do right or wrong). My Mandinga interlocutors often explained this to me by saying, "Babies' mouths don't smell." Babies' mouths begin to produce an odor, they explained, only after they get teeth, a sign that they have heard an adult tell a lie.

Mandinga women are more at risk for impurity in their daily lives than are men. As girls mature, they come in contact with the polluting substances of menstrual blood, the blood of childbirth, and bodily emissions of young children, which limit their involvement in religious activities, such as prayer and fasting. Mandinga women believe that female circumcision neutralizes this impurity. In scholarly terms and in contrast to prevailing popular views and media portrayals, therefore, it might be considered a feminist religious practice in that it allows women to participate as fully as their male counterparts in Islam.[9]

Further emphasizing the link between female circumcision and Islam, most of the Mandinga men and women I worked with in Guinea-Bissau and Portugal believe that the Qur'an prescribes female circumcision. In 1997 in Bissau, I recorded the first version of a story I rerecorded several times in subsequent visits to both field sites. In this version, female circumcision began with a conflict between the Prophet Mohammed's wives.

The Prophet Mohammed married a woman who was so old she couldn't get pregnant. The couple wanted a child very badly, so Mohammed took a younger wife who could give them one. Time went on, and Mohammed's first wife noticed that her husband was beginning to favor his new wife over her. She grew so jealous that when Mohammed went on a trip she pierced her cowife's ears. In those days, only slaves had pierced ears, so she hoped that when Mohammed returned he would reject his young wife.

Mohammed was a very powerful man who had many advisors who received messages from God. One heard about the incident and approached Mohammed. "Don't be angry," he said. "Soon all the village women will pierce their ears." So Mohammed bought his wife a pair of gold earrings, and she looked more beautiful than ever. All of the village women admired her beauty and pierced their own ears.

Mohammed went on another trip. His first wife, even more jealous than before, took her cowife into the courtyard and cut her clitoris. The old woman was sure that Mohammed would reject her now. He returned and wanted to sleep with his young wife, but she refused him. "What is it?" Mohammed asked her. "My genitals hurt," she replied. One of Mohammed's advisors approached him again. "Don't be angry," he said. "God has spoken to me, and your wife is now purer and more beautiful than ever." God was content that the young girl was circumcised, and that's why Mandinga practice female circumcision today.[10]

Although people often argued over the details of the story, nearly everyone I spoke with claimed that the story is in the Qur'an. Many Muslim healer-diviners in Bissau and Lisbon, however, told me that the passage was secret and that only elders and learned scholars could see it. One healer-diviner told me that the passage about female circumcision, like other secret Qur'anic passages, was very powerful: reading it before the age of forty could render a person blind or insane. Some versions of the story I collected confound time and space and thus further emphasize the entanglement of Mandinga ethnicity and Muslim identity. They describe, for example, the Mande heartland (present-day Mali) and Saudi Arabia as one and the same, or African fauna, such as lions and hyenas, as roaming the streets of Mecca. Several people even concluded from the story that God sent female circumcision to the Mandinga people.

I argue throughout this book that remaking Islam in African Portugal is a highly contradictory experience that at times affords Mandinga women, somewhat ironically, more exclusion from than inclusion in global Islam. If this is the case, then why do Mandinga women continue to affirm the link between female circumcision and Islam, a link that, as I show below, is becoming increasingly more tenuous in Lisbon? The answer to this question is found, once again, in the entanglement of Mandinga ethnicity and Muslim identity. Mandinga men and women believe that in order to be full Mandinga persons, they must be full Muslims, and in order to be full Muslims, they must pray and fast. These important activities require that one be clean, and Mandinga believe that only circumcision accomplishes this.

Considering the enduring link between circumcision and Islam, it is perhaps no surprise that nearly all Mandinga I spoke with, both men and women, placed more importance on the small initiation than the big initiation. Although many were convinced that the big rituals would eventually come to an end, they stated confidently that they would never stop circumcising their children. But as more and more Mandinga study Arabic and make the hajj, and as they come into increased contact with Muslims from other parts of the Islamic world, as well as media condemnations of female circumcision as a human rights violation, some Mandinga, especially men, are questioning the once taken-for-granted link between female circumcision and Islam. Furthermore, they are insisting on a more complete separation between the big initiation, which they associate with African custom, and the small initiation, which they associate with Islam. Indeed, some Mandinga men in Portugal condemn the link between female circumcision and Islam altogether and refuse to allow their daughters to be circumcised. Mandinga women, whose inclusion in global Islam remains tenuous at best, find these views unconvincing and thus face some very difficult choices.

FROM THE BUSH TO THE HOSPITAL: MEN'S VIEWS

One day at Morabeza restaurant, over heaping portions of rice and palm nut sauce, Braima asked me how my research was going. I told him about the coming-out ceremony I had just attended in Setúbal, which made him recall his own initiation. "I will never have my sons circumcised in the bush," he told me. "I will send them all to the hospital. [The big] initiation is about nothing more than hardship." Braima recounted his initiation story:

> A young boy, the Italian missionary's son, kept inviting me over to his house to eat. One day, he invited me to attend his father's school. It was initiation season, and all of my friends were preparing to enter the bush. I wanted so badly to join them. I didn't want to be a *solimaa* [an uncircumcised person], someone different. My father knew that I wanted to go, but he reminded me of the missionary's son's invitation. "Don't go to the initiation bush and miss that opportunity," he pleaded with me. My paternal grandfather, who was a traditional circumciser, insisted that I be initiated and pressured my father and me.
>
> The day the initiates were to enter the bush, I couldn't even eat. At the edge of the bush, my father and the missionary's son both begged me not to enter. My mother sensed that I would go. My grandfather warned me that once I passed the cord, I couldn't turn back; I would have to be initiated. When I passed the cord, my father cried.
>
> After that, all I remember was hardship. They made us walk on our knees from here [Martim Moniz] to Restauradores [one-quarter of a mile]. Then we had to kneel down while Kankurang hit us on our backs with his rice cutlasses. The rain soaked our bodies, and we didn't sleep or bathe for weeks. Our mothers brought us food every day, but the elders mixed it all together in one big calabash. Could you imagine eating palm oil mixed with peanut sauce? We only ate it because we had to, but we never felt satiated.
>
> Deep cultural practices like initiation are slow to change, but they will soon come to an end. If you aren't circumcised, you aren't clean and you can't pray, but I will have my sons circumcised in the hospital.

Braima's story raises several issues that are central to my discussion of men's views on initiation and circumcision. One intriguing aspect of his experience is that his family was divided on the issue of his being initiated. Although Braima's grandfather wanted him to enter the bush, Braima's own father clearly preferred missionary school over a more traditional bush education for his son. Conflicts such as these appear quite frequently in the initiation stories I collected during my fieldwork. Furthermore, Braima's story challenges conventional media portrayals of initiation and circumcision as acts performed by parents on children, who are powerless victims of these acts. Indeed, Braima decided to be initiated against his father's wishes.[11]

Although I hesitate to describe Braima's story as typical, I encountered many similar scenarios during my fieldwork. I documented stories of children who begged their parents to let them be initiated before their parents were ready, whether emotionally or financially. I recorded examples of children's agency in the initiation bush, especially vis-à-vis traditional circumcisers. In several accounts, children "with a head" (possessing mystical powers) playfully make their genitals disappear when the traditional circumciser tries to cut them. In other accounts, children demonstrate extraordinary bravery and strength in the initiation bush by demanding that the traditional circumciser "cut more" (of their genitals) or cut off a finger or toe because they "didn't feel anything" and they wanted the opportunity to demonstrate their ability to suffer. Interestingly, such stories were more common among women than men.[12]

Despite the cultural importance that Mandinga place on suffering and knowing the eye, however, many men I worked with in Portugal, especially Muslim healer-diviners and men who had made the hajj, believed that these are lessons that parents, not rituals, should teach their children. Consider the following views:

> When I was initiated, I was the youngest boy in the bush. All I remember was suffering. People say that if you don't suffer, you'll never learn to respect your elders. But you can learn this from a good upbringing, too. For Muslim men, the important thing is that you're circumcised. It doesn't matter if you're circumcised in the bush or in the hospital. (Yaya, a Mandinga man in his midthirties)
>
> When I was circumcised, I spent six months in the bush, and I didn't learn anything. Initiation has nothing do with education; it's only about suffering. Knowing the eye is something you learn from your parents, not the bush. No ritual can teach you that. (Arafam, a Mandinga man in his early forties)

Although all Mandinga boys in Guinea-Bissau are circumcised, how, when, and where they are circumcised is becoming increasingly variable. While some boys are still circumcised in traditional initiation rituals, others are circumcised in the hospital and attend a big initiation ritual later. Still others are circumcised in the hospital and never experience initiation. All the Mandinga boys I met who were born in Portugal, in contrast, were circumcised in the hospital. Whereas I did meet a few parents who told me that they wanted to send their sons to a big initiation back in Guinea-Bissau, none of them have ever actually done it, at least to my knowledge. Indeed, big initiation rituals in Portugal seem to have been replaced by Muslim-style coming-out ceremonies like the one I describe in the opening vignette of this chapter.

Men's views on girls' initiation and female circumcision in Lisbon were more complex and contradictory than their views on male circumcision. Many men I spoke with told me that female circumcision and initiation are "women's business" and claimed they did not have much to say about them. In contrast, Mandinga men who had studied the Qur'an, had made the hajj, and stressed their inclusion in the *umma*, the global community of Muslims, opposed initiation and female circumcision and enthusiastically shared their views with me. For example, when I engaged these men on the link that Mandinga women make between female circumcision and Islam, they told me that women "don't know anything about Islam." They explained that because women do not study the Qur'an, they commonly misunderstand and misconstrue many of Islam's central teachings. These men contend that girls' initiation and female circumcision, like other Mandinga life-course rituals, are African customs, not Muslim ones. In their view, the link that women make between female circumcision, cleanliness, and prayer is actually a misunderstanding resulting from falsely conflating Mandinga ethnicity and Muslim identity, two things that should remain separate. While a Mandinga person acquires the former naturally through a father's name, a mother's breast milk, and customary life-course rituals, a person becomes a true Muslim only by observing the five pillars of faith. As such, many Mandinga men I worked with in Portugal were opposed to female circumcision, and some had even forbidden their wives from circumcising their daughters. At the same time, however, many of these men claimed they would not marry an uncircumcised woman, nor would they allow their sons to do so.

I suggest that men's changing, albeit contradictory, views on initiation and circumcision must be analyzed in terms of three major issues: global Islam, the media, and attitudes toward sexuality. Remaking Islam in Lisbon has afforded Mandinga men a relatively privileged position compared with that of Mandinga women. Men have more free time for religious activities, such as prayer and Qur'anic study, and as I explained in the introduction of this book, they attend Friday prayer at Lisbon's central mosque more frequently and with less harassment from "Arab" and "Indian" Muslims than do women. Men also travel and make the hajj more frequently than their female counterparts do. Considering this, men are more secure about their status as global Muslims and are wary of anything that might threaten this status.

Many Mandinga men I spoke with in Portugal, for example, are very aware of the fact that not all Muslims practice female circumcision. Wolof peoples in

Senegal and the Gambia, they explained, are good Muslims, but they do not circumcise women. Nor are Saudi Arabian women circumcised, and no one would ever accuse them of being bad Muslims. Consider the following portion of an interview I conducted with Al-Hajj, a Mandinga man in his late fifties who works as a Qur'anic teacher and Muslim healer-diviner in central Lisbon. Although he was born in a Mandinga village in southern Senegal, he spent most of his life in Guinea-Bissau before migrating to Portugal.

> MJ: Mandinga women claim that uncircumcised women are unclean and can't pray. Is this true?
>
> Al-Hajj: It's a lie! Women don't have to be circumcised to pray. The Qur'an doesn't say that. Saudi Arabian women are Muslims, they all pray, and they are not circumcised.
>
> MJ: Some Muslim healer-diviners in Guinea-Bissau and Portugal have told me that the Qur'anic passage about female circumcision is secret and can't be seen by young or unlearned people. Is this true?
>
> Al-Hajj: These men may claim to be Qur'anic scholars, but the truth is that they can't read Arabic. So how do they know what the Qur'an is? They say the passage is secret so they can hide that they can't read Arabic and that they know nothing about Islam.
>
> MJ: Do you think female circumcision should end?
>
> Al-Hajj: Female circumcision is something that women themselves should decide to do. If they want to do it, then let them. But if they don't want to do it, then they shouldn't be forced. It will be difficult to end the practice because it's custom; women have been doing it for generations.

Men's views are also profoundly shaped by the media, which lump all forms of female circumcision together under the term *female genital mutilation* and condemn it as a human rights violation. Countless newspaper articles, documentary programs, and news stories circulated during my fieldwork, many of which I watched and discussed with my Mandinga interlocutors in Lisbon. Men expressed concern over how Europeans and other Muslims might view them as a result of this media attention. Such concern was also widespread among non-Muslim African immigrants in Lisbon. Several non-Muslim men from Guinea-Bissau told me that they received more stares shortly after the airing of a French documentary program about female genital mutilation on Portuguese television. One man told me that Portuguese women will no longer date African men because they are afraid that these men will force them to be circumcised.

Despite these changing views, however, many men I spoke with in Lisbon remained conflicted about the future of girls' initiation and female circumcision. When I asked men who opposed the practice if they would allow their sons to marry an uncircumcised woman, many claimed they would not. I suggest that this conflict can be explained in part by the elusive link between female circumcision and sexuality. In contrast to attitudes about gender and sexuality in the West, women in the Muslim world are often thought to have a stronger sex drive than men. Female circumcision, many Mandinga told me, normalizes this drive, making it equal to men's sex drive. Uncircumcised women, according to the men I spoke with, want sex often. Their husbands, who are busy or may have other wives, might not be able to please them, so they take lovers. As one Muslim healer-diviner explained, "If you cut just a little bit of a woman down there [i.e., if you circumcise her], she will be calm and won't need sex so often." Men agreed that in normalizing women's sex drive, female circumcision makes women better wives and mothers. A few men who opposed the practice, however, claimed that a proper upbringing, not a ritual, makes women good wives and mothers.

The link between female circumcision and sexuality becomes even more complicated when one considers non-Muslim views on the practice and its alleged consequences for sexuality, which contradict men's views. All of the non-Muslim men from Guinea-Bissau I spoke with during my fieldwork claimed that female circumcision creates sex-crazed, promiscuous women. In their view, the practice reduces a woman's sex drive. Because circumcised women cannot be "reached" by men (i.e., because they are never satisfied sexually), they become obsessed with sex and seek out lovers, who they think can please them. Several men, even one practicing physician I met in Bissau and later spoke with several times in Lisbon, blamed Bissau's rising prostitution rate on the increase in female circumcision practices resulting from conversion to Islam. As a non-Muslim man in his midthirties told me in Lisbon, "Female circumcision is bad. Women have a slower sex drive than men. In the past, it was common for Muslim women to marry men who were twenty years older than them. If a young man can hardly reach a woman [please her sexually], then imagine an older man. It worsens the situation when you reduce a woman down there [circumcise her]. That's why circumcised women have so many lovers."

It is interesting that non-Muslim men attribute Muslim women's alleged obsession with sex and promiscuity to female circumcision, the very practice that Muslim men believe make women less obsessed with sex and more faithful. When I discussed non-Muslim views about female circumcision and sexuality with Mandinga men, they simply attributed them to the influence of the West and to the rise of anti-Islamic sentiment in Guinea-Bissau and especially in Portugal. My Mandinga interlocutors told me that Guinea-Bissau's revolutionary hero, Amilcar Cabral, once said, "Political power must never pass to those who wear the hats [i.e., the Muslims]." As more and more Muslims in Guinea-Bissau secure political positions (indeed, the country elected a Muslim president in 2009 and another one in 2019), non-Muslims grow more and more nervous. As my Muslim interlocutors put it, "Christians [i.e., non-Muslims] are telling lies about our customs to try to ruin us."

UNCERTAIN FUTURES: WOMEN'S VIEWS

One morning during my fieldwork, I met Gabriela at a café in central Lisbon. A mutual friend had introduced us several weeks previously at Morabeza, where I told Gabriela about my research over heaping plates of "food from the homeland." Gabriela claimed to know a lot about female circumcision in Guinea-Bissau and enthusiastically agreed to an interview. A Balanta woman in her midforties, she described herself as an educated woman from Bissau. She worked as a teacher for many years before coming to Portugal. Before the war, she traveled frequently between Bissau and Lisbon.

I told Gabriela that the Mandinga women I worked with claimed that female circumcision allowed women to pray, making them respectable Muslims and full Mandinga persons. "Those women told you that because they don't want traditional circumcisers, who are more than likely their relatives, to lose their power and status in their communities," she responded. "Do you know how much traditional circumcisers make?" Gabriela pretended to shovel rice into her mouth with her right hand, a Guinean gesture signaling a full belly and thus a good life, not necessarily the result of honest work. "That kind of life is hard to give up," she added. Gabriela identified sexuality, not ethnicity or Islam, as the real reason behind female circumcision: "Animists, like the Balanta, can sleep with whomever we want any time. But Muslim women are forced to marry men they hardly know. They're circumcised, so they don't feel anything during sex. So, they arrange lovers, which causes them problems. Female circumcision leaves women scarred, both physically and psychologically."

Gabriela claimed that female circumcision is changing, but the changes are difficult to see. She told me about several Muslim women she knows personally who at the time of their initiations paid the circumciser not to cut them. "The circumciser accepted the bribe and pretended to cut the women, leaving their genitals perfectly intact," she claimed. Gabriela believes, however, that female circumcision is an African custom that will not easily end. In her view, change must start with Muslim women themselves, and migration, which some scholars have described as a new coming-of-age ritual (e.g., Jónsson 2012; Kleinman 2016) will play a key role: "Muslim women living in Portugal will soon return to Guinea-Bissau and tell their sisters and friends the positive aspects of intact genitalia: a healthy body and pleasurable sex. Then their sisters and friends will open their eyes and refuse to have their own daughters circumcised."

The above vignette, full of confidence and clarity about the past, present, and future of initiation and female circumcision, conceals a multilayered set of concerns, one that is transnational in scope and fraught with uncertainty. Two crucial issues make the situation especially complicated for women, confronting them with more difficult choices than men concerning their ritual practices. The first is women's views on female circumcision, Mandinga ethnicity, and Islam. In contrast to Mandinga men, who are challenging the once-solid relationship between these concepts, Mandinga women remain overwhelmingly convinced that female circumcision is central to their identity as Mandinga persons and as Muslims. More specifically, they insist that in order to be fully Mandinga, they must be good Muslims. This requires that they pray, and they must be clean in order to pray. In their view, female circumcision makes them clean and allows them to pray.

I spent a lot of time in Lisbon with Muslim healer-diviners' wives, most of whom were extremely skeptical of their learned husbands' views that female circumcision is not required for prayer and has nothing to do with Islam. One of these women, Kadija, became a close friend. When I first met her in 1999, Kadija's husband had recently returned from making the hajj and had started his own Muslim healing-divining business in a Lisbon exurb. The couple had two daughters, one who was born in Guinea-Bissau and was circumcised there as a young girl and another who was born in Portugal and had not yet been circumcised. Kadija told me that her husband claimed that female circumcision was an African custom, not a Muslim one. As such, he refused to have their youngest daughter circumcised. Kadija was very confused by her husband's views and felt caught between being a good wife and respecting her husband's wishes and being a good mother and taking responsibility for her daughter's Muslim identity. She voiced this dilemma clearly to me in 2001: "If I obey my husband, I spoil my daughter's prayers." When I returned to Lisbon in 2003, Kadija was considering either sending her daughter to Guinea-Bissau to have her circumcised or taking her to a traditional circumciser in a nearby Lisbon exurb. Dilemmas like Kadija's are common in Lisbon, and although I know of a few that were resolved (one woman, for example, had her daughter circumcised in Guinea-Bissau against her husband's wishes), to my knowledge the majority have not been.

A second factor limiting women's choices is the lack of hospital circumcisions. Whereas remaking Islam for Mandinga men in Lisbon has meant replacing traditional, bush initiations with hospital circumcisions and Muslim-style coming-out ceremonies, this is not an option for Mandinga women. When I asked women about this inequity, they told me that although they are perfectly content to have their sons circumcised in the hospital, they would never want their daughters circumcised there. According to the women I spoke with in both Guinea-Bissau and Portugal, the cutting itself is important—if someone other than a traditional circumciser performed it in a hospital, it would not have the same meaning. As one woman put it, "If a girl were circumcised in the hospital, her prayers wouldn't count."

Unlike the men I spoke with, whose memories of their initiations were over-whelmingly negative, women reported very positive experiences of both initiation and circumcision. Fewer women than men reported abuse from elders or painful circumcisions, for example, and many women's eyes welled up with tears when they recalled their personal experiences of these rituals. Whereas most of my male interlocutors did not want their sons to endure what they had endured when they were initiated, most women felt that they did not want their daughters to miss what they had experienced in the bush.

More women than men also spoke about the magical elements of initiation rituals, such as the power of the circumcision knife, the girls' masquerade figures, and the extraordinary skills of traditional circumcisers. If someone sees the circumcision knife, many women told me, she will go blind or will hemorrhage during childbirth. To be a traditional circumciser, my female interlocutors explained, one must "have a head," or have the power to see and combat witches and evil spirits and to perform supernatural acts. As one woman explained, "A traditional circumciser can simply look at your genitals as she slices a lemon, and you'll be circumcised." The women I spoke with claimed that it is this aspect of traditional initiation rituals that is most difficult to maintain in the contemporary era, since fewer people today have a head. Indeed, I met many daughters of traditional circumcisers who themselves refused to "take up the knife" and become circumcisers like their mothers because they claimed they did not have the head for the work. Several of these women now sell clothing or work in restaurants, which they claim is easier work and earns them more money.

Positive memories of the big initiation aside, all of the women I spoke with agreed with the men that the small initiation, circumcision, was the most important part. As one elder woman explained, "If anyone tells you that initiation is more than circumcision, like drums, masquerade figures, and parties [coming-out ceremonies], they're lying. The important thing is that when you give birth to a girl you take her into the courtyard and circumcise her. You put leaves [traditional medicines] on her, she heals, and it's finished. You don't need a big party. That's just an opportunity to show everyone that your daughter was circumcised. It's about nothing more than spending a lot of money and making people happy."

Like their male counterparts, the Mandinga women I spoke with in Lisbon were aware of the global condemnation of female genital mutilation and were deeply affected by media portrayals of the practice. Many women spoke to me at length about the French documentary program I mentioned earlier in this chapter. A few claimed that shortly after the airing of the program, checkers in grocery stores refused to take money directly from their hands, insisting instead that they place the money on the counter. Others reported that white people refused to sit next to them on the bus or metro. As one woman put it, "It was as if they looked at us and all they saw were mutilated genitals."

A Maternal Kin Club member told me that because of the negative media attention, club women avoid discussing female circumcision at meetings. She told me that her own views on the subject, however, had changed significantly as a result of the French documentary program. She explained, "One day, I'm going to introduce it [the topic of female circumcision] at a meeting and say I'm against it. I was circumcised, and so was my oldest daughter. But my younger daughters, the ones who were born here [in Lisbon] will not be circumcised. It [female circumcision] is not good for women's health, and many young girls have even died from it. The elders say that the deaths are from witchcraft, but they are really from blood loss. Using the same knife on all of the initiates causes infection. I saw it on the program."

Shortly following the airing of the program, several women I worked with closely became more reluctant to talk openly with me about their views on female circumcision. Those who did share expressed considerably more insecurity about their knowledge and opinions, asking me if I was going to "put that in my book for everyone to read." I worked very closely with one woman in her midtwenties who was circumcised in Guinea-Bissau and moved to Portugal when she was four years old. When I spoke with her about the effects the media seemed to be having on Mandinga immigrant women, she explained, "Many white people go to Africa to study female circumcision, and they end up reporting everything on the news. They show pictures of women being circumcised and portray it as a terrible thing. They don't explain why we do it; they just say that it's a violent act. This makes us [Mandinga women] feel badly, and that's why we're afraid to talk to outsiders about it."

In both field sites, I waited several months before asking women about their experiences of initiation and circumcision. After gaining their trust,

I promised not to include anything they deemed secret in my writings, and I promised to use pseudonyms when necessary. But talking about initiation and female circumcision always seemed to make people feel vulnerable, even those I came to know best. Toward the end of my 1999 fieldwork in Lisbon, one of my closest friends, Awa, agreed to a taped interview about initiation and female circumcision. A Mandinga woman in her midfifties, Awa is the daughter of a traditional circumciser in Guinea-Bissau. She refused to follow in her mother's footsteps because she felt she didn't have the head for the work. During the interview, Awa sang some initiation songs for me and explained their deep meanings. She told me the story of her own initiation and circumcision and shared with me her views on the condemnation of female genital mutilation in the media. There were several things she asked me not to write about, and I promised her that I would honor her wishes as well as protect her identity in my publications (Awa is a pseudonym).

When I returned to Portugal in 2001, I visited Awa in her apartment in a suburb of Lisbon. She told me that some Portuguese journalists had recently visited her, asking her if they could interview her about female circumcision. Assuming that I had sent the journalists, Awa agreed to talk to them but was very upset by some of the questions they asked. I explained that I did not know the journalists and most certainly had not sent them, but I can never fully be sure that Awa believed me. This incident underscores the power inequality inherent in anthropological research and in the global debate surrounding female genital mutilation. After this experience, I decided to use pseudonyms when writing about female circumcision, even when this went against the wishes of those who asked me to "put their names in my book and make them famous in America."

Films and journalists are not, of course, Mandinga women's first experience of outsiders' attempts to alter their initiation rituals. During the war of liberation, PAIGC (the African Party for the Independence of Guinea-Bissau and Cape Verde) leaders sought to improve women's lives by banning several traditional practices they believed had negative consequences for women, including polygyny, forced marriage, and denial of divorce rights. They omitted female circumcision from their list, however, because local women themselves did not deem it oppressive. Furthermore, leaders worried that banning it might cause women to lose trust in the PAIGC and lead them to circumcise girls in secret (Urdang 1979, 186).[13]

Recent efforts by NGOs have been less sensitive to local women's views or even outright dismissive of them. One woman I worked with extensively in Guinea-Bissau and then later in Portugal, another daughter of a traditional circumciser, told me about a meeting that members of one NGO organized shortly before my arrival in 1996. The members invited several prominent elder Muslim women in Bissau with the intent of "educating" them about the harmful consequences of female genital mutilation. They suggested that the women end the practice altogether or, at the very least, replace clitoridectomy with incision (the slightest form of female circumcision) and use sterile materials.[14] This woman told me that the NGO members had shown them pictures of women's bleeding genitals, including women who were "all sewn up" (referring to infibulation, a form of female circumcision that is not practiced in Guinea-Bissau). She found the images both confusing and offensive and told me that local women responded simply by moving female circumcision from a public ritual to a private one.[15]

During my 2003 fieldwork in Bafata-Oio, the Mandinga village in Guinea-Bissau where I had conducted research in the 1990s, I had the opportunity to attend a seminar for rural Muslim women entitled "Reflections on Some Common Problems Affecting Women in Guinean Society" (my translation from the Portuguese). About fifty Muslim women from several villages in the Oio region attended the conference, which was, ironically, both organized and led by men and conducted in Kriolu, a language that most of the women I knew in the Oio region did not speak or even understand. At one point, one of the conference leaders held up a large poster entitled "Negative Aspects of Women's Lives." Underneath this heading was a list, including arranged marriage, having too many children, and "excision." After the conference, I asked several women I knew well if they agreed that excision was a negative aspect of their lives. They responded that they both disagreed with this statement and were deeply offended by the choice of language and by the fact that they had not been involved in the planning of the conference. They stressed the importance of excision (the women themselves did not use this term) for prayer and for being a good Muslim. In their view, these could only be positive aspects of women's lives.[16]

The global clamor surrounding female genital mutilation and the experience of remaking themselves and their religion in Lisbon have not provided easy answers for Mandinga immigrant women who, in deciding the fate of their own identity and ritual practices, are struggling to reconcile men's changing views, media images, and their desire for inclusion in (or exclusion from) global Islam. For the women I worked with, the stakes are high, and they abound with uncertainties and contradictions. This was especially evident to me in 2003 in Lisbon, when I witnessed a very rich and complicated dialogue about girls' initiation and female circumcision.

After a delicious meal of rice and peanut sauce, I spent the afternoon with three Mandinga women I had come to know very well during my fieldwork, Ousmana, Binta, and Sanya, in Damaia. We lounged on Sanya's bed, chatting and watching Brazilian telenovelas (soap operas). The big news in the Mandinga immigrant community that week was a coming-out ceremony to be held the following month in Chelas. Attempting to stir up some interesting conversation, I asked the women if they were planning to attend and if it was a boys' or girls' ceremony. "It's a boys' ceremony, for sure," Ousmana responded. "You have to be very careful about girls' initiation here, because Europeans don't like it." I told Ousmana that Europeans and even many Africans don't like circumcision because they believe circumcised women can't enjoy sex. Kadi responded, "That's a lie. I went to a Fula initiation when I was four years old. It took four women to hold me down, and they totally cleaned me [a reference to excision]. I didn't feel anything, but it hurt afterwards whenever I peed. It took me almost two months to heal. But I enjoy sex very much. I feel it. It's Christians [non-Muslims] who say that Muslim women, circumcised women, don't feel anything during sex. This is just about competition between Christians and Muslims. Christians try to ruin us by telling lies that make Muslims seem backwards."

Ousmana recalled her initiation: "I also went to a Fula ritual and was totally cleaned. I spent six months in the bush, and all I remember was suffering. If someone cooked palm oil and another cooked peanut sauce, the elders would mix them together and feed it to us. They made us eat the leftovers the next day, even if they were spoiled."

The women chatted about the traditional circumcisers living in Lisbon whom they knew of, as well as different circumcision styles. Ousmana told us that she wants to have her daughters circumcised, but it is difficult. One daughter lives with her in Lisbon, and the other lives with her husband's relatives in Bissau. She explained, "I want to take my daughter to a traditional circumciser in Lisbon, but my husband doesn't want me to. I don't know what to do. I don't want her to remain uncircumcised. What if she grows up and wants to marry a Muslim man? What will she do then? I don't want my daughter to marry a non-Muslim. My husband's [female] relatives want to have my [other] daughter circumcised in Bissau. I want her to be circumcised, but not in a big ceremony because that just means trouble."

The women agreed that having one's daughter circumcised back home involves considerable risk. They shared stories of people they knew who were circumcised with no problem but who died later in a big ceremony from witchcraft. "If your daughter is circumcised in Bissau," Binta asserted, "you won't know if she'll be cut the Mandinga way or the Fula way." She recalled her own initiation: "I went to a Beafada initiation. They barely cut me, and I didn't feel a thing. It was like someone took a razor blade and nicked me with it. Fula women are spoiling girls' initiation for everyone. Mandinga and Beafada just make a small cut so blood drops, but Fula take everything."

The women also agreed that initiation is spoiled now and that there are no more public rituals in Bissau. "People are afraid to admit they circumcised their daughters since the government is against it," explained Binta. "But they will never be able to end it. People just do it secretly now, just like they're doing it here in Lisbon." Ousmana told us about a government official in Bissau who came out publicly against female circumcision. "A few days later, he was dismissed from the government, and he is now mad. They spoiled his head!" When I asked the women to specify exactly who had spoiled the government official's head, the women argued whether it was the elders, the traditional circumcisers, or the other government officials, but the point of Ousmana's story is clear: despite the ambiguities and upheavals, the custom of girls' initiation will not end easily.

As Mandinga men remake Islam in African Portugal, the future of their rituals and the consequences for their identity—both ethnic and religious—are relatively clear: they can forgo the African custom of initiation, have their sons circumcised in the hospital, and celebrate their initiated status in a coming-out ceremony. For them, this change does not entail a sacrifice of their identity as Mandinga or as Muslims. For women, however, the path forward is less clear, and the consequences for identity more ambiguous. For them, the cutting itself remains tied to African custom in ways that the cutting for men does not: even if hospital circumcisions were legal (and they are not), women would deem them unacceptable. Furthermore, there is no place for circumcision, let alone initiation, in global Islam. While Mandinga immigrant women debate among themselves and with their male counterparts the future of their rituals, their children remain in limbo: uninitiated and uncircumcised, their identity as Mandinga and as Muslims remains incomplete, a fact that their mothers find deeply unsettling.

NOTES

1. I use the term *circumcision* to refer to genital cutting for Guinean Muslim men and women because they are familiar with this phrase and prefer it to both *genital cutting* and *genital mutilation*. The term *female circumcision* captures the fact that Mandinga women themselves liken the practice to male circumcision.

The terms *clitoridectomy* and *excision* are both too specific and thus do not account for the fact that Mandinga women may practice either. I discussed this extensively with my interlocutors in both sites before deciding on this term.

2. All boys in Guinea-Bissau are initiated and circumcised, though the rituals vary considerably according to ethnic group. The situation for girls is more complex. Whereas girls' initiation is pervasive, not all girls are initiated, and only three ethnic groups, the Fula, the Mandinga, and the Beafada, circumcise girls. Because these three groups are Muslims, female circumcision is considered a Muslim practice in Guinea-Bissau (Johnson 2000, 2007). This characterization is unique, however, since not all Muslims in West Africa circumcise women and many non-Muslims do (Gruenbaum 2001, 60).

3. These findings are consistent with published works addressing female circumcision in Guinea-Bissau in general and among Mandinga specifically. Urdang (1979, 185–86) defined partial clitoridectomy (removal of the tip of the clitoris) as the most common form of female circumcision practiced in the country. Carreira (1947, 82) documented that "genital mutilation" for Mandinga women consisted of "excision of the tip of the clitoris" (my translations from Portuguese).

4. Gruenbaum (2001, 2–3) identifies three forms of female genital cutting known to anthropologists. The first type, which she terms *Sunna* circumcision, involves the cutting, pricking, or partial removal of the clitoris. *Sunna* means "tradition" in Arabic, referring to what the Prophet Mohammed was described as doing in his life. The second type, excision or clitoridectomy, involves the removal of the clitoris and at times part of the labia minora. The third type, Pharaonic circumcision or infibulation, is the most rare and severe form of genital cutting. It involves the removal of the clitoris and the labia minora and majora. The two sides of the wound are sewn together, leaving a small hole for the drainage of urine and menstrual blood. It is practiced in and around the horn of Africa. See Shell-Duncan and Hernlund (2000, 3–7) for a slightly different description of the various practices.

5. Muslims and non-Muslims alike insisted that Muslim (i.e., Mandinga, Fula, and Beafada) initiations were the best because the circumcisers were well trained (quick and accurate in cutting) and the celebrations were the most elaborate and fun, complete with drumming, dancing, and Kankurang, the boys' masquerade figure. Muslim initiations were also thought to be the most effective in teaching young boys to "know the eye."

6. Mandinga marriage is processual, involving two phases that can take up to seven years to complete. In the first phase, the couple's families exchange kola nuts. The couple is then considered married, but they continue to live apart with their respective families. During this time, they can have sexual relations and may even have children, but their marriage is incomplete. In the final phase, the

entire village accompanies the husband as he brings his wife to his compound to live jointly.

7. The "Mande caste system" was codified during the colonial period and included three groups: nobles or freedmen, artisans and bards, and slaves (Conrad and Frank 1995, 7). Although still acknowledged today, these categories are considerably more fluid and occasionally challenged in practice.

8. Knowing the eye for Mandinga parallels the notion of social sense described by Richards (1982, 123) for Bemba in Zambia and Riesman (1998, 127–29) for Fulani in Burkina Faso. Social sense for Fulani is inherently tied to ethnic identity in that it defines *pulaaku*, or those qualities considered to be most appropriate for Fulani people, such as a sense of shame and a mastery of one's needs and emotions.

9. Scholars working on female circumcision in Africa have made similar arguments. Gosselin (2000, 54) writes that Malians term both male and female circumcision *seliji*, or "prayer water," which refers to the ritual ablutions that Muslims perform before prayer. In Mali, circumcision is thought to render both men and women fit for Muslim prayer. Muslim Jola in Senegal believe that female circumcision allows a woman's prayers to "take" (Dellenborg 2004, 82).

10. See Johnson (2000, 220–21) for a longer and slightly different version of this story. My Mandinga interlocutors, both men and women, often argued whether it was the Prophet Mohammed's or the Prophet Ibrahim's second wife who was first circumcised.

11. See Davidson (2016) for parallel stories about generational conflict over initiation and other religious practices among (non-Muslim) Jola in Guinea-Bissau. Ampa Badji, one of Davidson's key research participants, encouraged his own children to choose education over initiation as a way of escaping "a dead-end life in the village" (2016, 77).

12. A number of people I met during my fieldwork claimed to know, or even to be, a *kondoron*, a person circumcised by nonhuman agents. There are two types. First, a person may be born circumcised, as Mandinga believe that God circumcises some babies before birth. Second, a spirit may circumcise a person at night. *Kondoron* are thought to be auspicious and are highly respected in Mandinga society.

13. The PAIGC was successful in encouraging parents to have their sons circumcised in clinics rather than in the bush (Urdang 1979, 188).

14. See Hernlund (2000) for a successful example of "ritual without cutting" in the Gambia.

15. There was one dramatic exception during my fieldwork in Guinea-Bissau to the increasingly secret or private nature of girls' initiation and female circumcision. Women in the town of Mansoa held what local radio reports described as the largest public girls' initiation ritual in the history of the Oio region.

The women considered the ritual an act of protest directed toward the government and NGOs for launching anti–female genital mutilation campaigns without taking into account local women's views.

16. Prazak (2016, 1) makes a compelling case for the importance of context when working on female genital cutting in Africa, arguing that "only through a holistic approach do these practices make sense," both for anthropologists and for local practitioners. Prazak's book is a model, in that it is based on "more than two dozen years of experience within a particular Kenyan community" (Prazak 2016, 2).

FOUR

DISTANT DEPARTURES

Funerals, Postburial Sacrifices, and Rupturing Place and Identity

ONE LATE MORNING IN LISBON, I accompanied two of my closest research participants and friends, Alaaji and his wife, Aminata, to a funeral in the Lisbon suburb of Bobadela. When Alaaji parked the car on Amilcar Cabral Street and turned off the engine, we could hear women's wailing coming from an open window of an apartment building nearby. Aminata had called me early that morning with the news. Musukuto, a woman in her midfifties and a prominent member of the Maternal Kin Club, had just lost her twenty-year-old daughter to tuberculosis in Guinea-Bissau. "The hardest thing about it," Aminata said as we walked up the steep cement staircase to the apartment, "is that Musukuto hadn't seen her daughter in more than ten years."

When we arrived, Musukuto's small apartment was already packed wall to wall with mourners. Musukuto sat on the floor on a *spuma*, a foam mattress that people typically sleep on in Guinea-Bissau, covered with a white sheet. Her back was against the wall, her head was covered with a white scarf, and she held her mobile phone in her right hand. Aminata and I greeted her and sat beside her. "Everyone told me that you were coming," she said. Weeping, Musukuto recounted the story of how she had almost collapsed at work from the shock when a relative called her from Guinea-Bissau with the news. Although Musukuto hoped to travel to Guinea-Bissau later in the month to attend a postburial sacrifice, flights from Lisbon to Bissau had not yet resumed since the start of the war. In the few minutes that Aminata and I sat with Musukuto, she received seven calls on her mobile phone. Some people called to say they were on their way. Others who had gotten lost on the way called for directions. Those who could not attend relied on their mobile phones to transmit the wails and blessings that accompany a Guinean Muslim's journey from this world to the next.

Although Musukuto's story, like all stories, is unique and specific, it is hardly exceptional. Indeed, my field notes are filled with stories of "distant deaths," of Muslims in Guinea-Bissau holding funerals for relatives who died in Portugal, or Guinean Muslim immigrants in Portugal attending postburial sacrifices for people who died "back home" in Guinea-Bissau. The rupture between place and identity that characterizes contemporary life for Guinean Muslims, no matter where they may be, has in some ways reinforced and in other ways recast how they understand and ritually mark death. Indeed, as Guinean Muslim immigrants remake Islam in Portugal, funerals and postburial sacrifices, like other life-course rituals, are currently altering their understandings of themselves as Africans, as members of distinct ethnic groups (Mandinga and Fula), and as Muslims in a changing world.

DYING AT HOME AND ABROAD: FUNERARY RITUAL IN A TRANSNATIONAL ERA

In order to understand the complex and gendered discourses surrounding distant deaths, some ethnographic details are necessary. How do Guinean Muslims, at home and abroad, conceptualize death and mark it ritually? Here I focus specifically on Mandinga funerary ritual, since I know it best. In villages and towns in Guinea-Bissau, death is announced by the characteristic wailing of the deceased's female relatives. This is followed by the thumping sound of large wooden mortars and pestles as the women of the deceased person's household pound rice for *munkoo* (rice flour sweetened with sugar or honey), which mourners distribute to guests following the burial. The preparation of funerary munkoo acts as an official acknowledgment of the death, marking the end of the period of shock and the beginning of the period of work (i.e., ritual). After a death, the deceased's relatives cannot carry out their daily chores, engage in conversation, or even exchange greetings until they have made munkoo.[1]

The importance of munkoo was made clear to me on one particularly memorable occasion in Bissau in 1997, when I had planned to meet with Aisatu, an elderly Mandinga woman who was a traditional circumciser. Arafam, my Mandinga teacher and field assistant, had agreed to accompany me and assist with translation. We caught the *toka-toka* (public city transport) to Bairro Militar, a neighborhood with a sizeable Mandinga population. When we arrived in Aisatu's compound, we were struck by an eerie silence. No one greeted us or even acknowledged our presence. Furthermore, when I gave my *semola* (offering) of tobacco, sugar, and white candles to Aisatu, she did not give me the customary blessings. It was obvious that all was not well in the compound. A novice fieldworker at the time, I assumed that Aisatu did not want me there. Perhaps she had heard about the *Tubaaboo* (white person) who had come to discover the "deep secrets" of Mandinga initiation and return to America to publish a book about them? But before I had the opportunity to voice my concerns to Arafam, he told me that one of Aisatu's sisters had just died, and she had not yet made munkoo. Needless to say, our meeting was postponed for another day.

As the news of death spreads, people gather in the deceased person's compound for preparations for the burial. In accordance with Islam, men wash and dress the body of a deceased man whereas women wash and dress the body of a deceased woman (Denny 2016, 282). A deceased man's body is wrapped in a large white cloth that covers the head and is tied at the neck. A deceased woman's body is dressed in a white waistcloth, a long white shirt, and a white head tie and is then wrapped in a large white cloth.

Once the preparations for burial are complete, a Muslim holy man inquires about the deceased person's outstanding debts and transgressions, asking all present whether pardon is possible or compensation is necessary. This practice, which my interlocutors called the "rite of pardon," is said to render the heart of the deceased "light," a prerequisite for entering paradise. This lightness is not simply metaphorical. If the deceased's sins were not forgiven, people explained, no one would be able to lift the body. On several occasions over the years in both Guinea-Bissau and Portugal, I heard the story of Kumba Gloria, which underscores the importance of this rite:

> There once was a man who married a woman named Kumba Gloria. They were married for thirty-six years, and their marriage was sweet. Kumba Gloria's husband met all of his wife's needs as a good husband should, and Kumba Gloria did everything that her husband asked her to do. But while on the surface their marriage was sweet, there was something very wrong. Every time Kumba Gloria's husband wanted to sleep with her, she refused. Since he was a peaceful and respectful man, he never forced his wife, nor did he ever complain to her relatives that she continually refused him. During the thirty-six years that they were married, the couple never once had sex.
>
> One day Kumba Gloria got very sick and died. Everyone in the village gathered in the compound for the funeral. The woman washed and prepared Kumba Gloria's body for burial. But when two men tried to carry the body to the burial grounds, they were unable to lift it. Four men joined them, but the six men still could not lift the body. Finally, four more men joined the group, making ten men in total, but they still could not lift it.
>
> A holy man approached Kumba Gloria's husband and said to him, "Today you declared publicly that your marriage was sweet and that your wife never

wronged you. Did you speak truly?" Kumba Gloria's husband came forward and addressed the crowd. "What I told you today was a lie. During the thirty-six years that I was married to this woman, she never once slept with me. But now that I see my wife lying here dead, I forgive her." Then two men lifted Kumba Gloria's body with ease and carried it to the burial grounds. The holy man explained, "God punished the woman for her sinful act by giving her a heavy heart, a heaviness that could only be lightened by her husband's forgiveness."

In providing the opportunity to render a heavy heart light, the rite of pardon serves as a ritual safeguard for the deceased's soul. In completing the rite, the bereaved can rest assured that they have done their part in facilitating the entry of the deceased's soul into paradise. After completing the rite of pardon, holy men offer prayers and inter the body. A man is placed in the grave lying on his right side, his head pointing east (toward Mecca), while a woman is placed on her left side, her head also pointing east. Relatives and guests comfort the bereaved, especially the wailing women, telling them to "suffer" the death and assuring them that "it was God's will."

Mandinga hold several postburial sacrifices in honor of the deceased, the first of which takes place on the day of the burial. Subsequent sacrifices are usually held on the third, seventh, fortieth, and one hundredth days after the burial. Postburial sacrifices follow the same general structure. Guests gather in the morning at the deceased's compound, and a goat or sheep is slaughtered. Holy men recite the Qur'an and give blessings to the attendees, who raise their palms upward to receive the blessings, tapping their foreheads and saying *ami-ini* ("amen"). After the meal, people receive their allotted shares of munkoo, kola nuts, and meat, officially marking the end of the ritual.[2]

Funerals and postburial sacrifices in Portugal take place in much the same manner, with a few notable exceptions, the first being the setting. Whereas these rituals usually take place outdoors in Guinea-Bissau, they more commonly occur indoors in Portugal. Most Portuguese apartment complexes lack spacious compounds, and the colder weather is often not conducive to long periods spent outside. Logistics aside, my interlocutors told me they prefer to hold rituals inside, away from the gaze of their Portuguese hosts. Many were anxious about how their neighbors and passersby might react to seeing African rituals held in the streets of Lisbon. A second difference is that in Portugal the preparation of the body and the burial itself shift from the house to the mosque. Finally, since great distances often separate Mandinga immigrants in Lisbon, news of the death is transmitted by mobile phone.

Once the death is announced, however, the events that follow are similar to those in the village. Women begin to wail. An elder (usually male) takes the phone to inquire about the details surrounding the death and the plans for the funerary rituals, and then all present prepare to travel to the deceased person's home, where close relatives will stay, work schedules permitting, for up to three days. When a death occurs at night in Guinea-Bissau, Mandinga wait to spread the news until morning, since the shock is said to be too difficult to endure at night, an inauspicious and dangerous time, and ritual preparations cannot be performed anyway until the next morning. Mandinga immigrants in Portugal, however, often do not uphold the customary prohibition on announcing death at night. My interlocutors often told me they dread receiving phone calls late at night, since they anticipate that these calls might bring news of death.

Postburial sacrifices in Portugal are almost identical to those in Guinea-Bissau except for one difference. In Portugal, the mortars and pestles used by Mandinga immigrants to make munkoo are much smaller, because they must be shipped from West Africa and stored indoors. Because of the smaller size of the mortars and pestles, people can pound only a small amount of rice at any given time, which makes it difficult to produce the large quantities of munkoo needed for a funeral or postburial sacrifice. For this reason, in Portugal, munkoo is usually reserved for the writing-on-the-hand ritual, for which it holds special significance. At funerals and postburial sacrifices, munkoo is commonly replaced with Spanish Maria biscuits, purchased in economy-size boxes and placed in a calabash from Guinea-Bissau. Each person receives a package of biscuits before departing. In response to my surprise on seeing Maria biscuits replacing munkoo, people responded, "Flour is flour." No one seemed to mind that Maria biscuits are made from wheat rather than rice.

The above ethnographic description, which I pieced together from interviews with Mandinga in Guinea-Bissau and Portugal and from my own observation of dozens of funerals and postburial sacrifices over two decades of fieldwork in both locales, is an idealized one, since every funerary ritual I attended was unique. This observation is nothing new, of course. Anthropologists have long argued that lived experience and scholarly representations of it are rarely, if ever, mirror images of one another.[3] Ethnographic accounts are inventions rather than representations of social reality: they are "partial—committed and incomplete" (Clifford 1986, 7), and Mandinga funerary rituals are no exception. Whereas the ritual treatment of the corpse is front and center in the above ethnographic description, for example, more than half of the Mandinga funerals I attended during my fieldwork occurred in the absence of bodies. An even greater number of postburial sacrifices I attended were held in a different locale,

Figure 4.1. Preparing Maria biscuits for distribution at a postburial sacrifice, 1999. Photograph by the author.

Figure 4.2. Maria biscuits substituting for munkoo at a postburial sacrifice, 1999. Photograph by the author.

whether a village, town, or capital city, from the burial site. This disparity is evident in the opening vignette, when Musukuto, who was unable to return to Guinea-Bissau during the war, had no choice but to mourn her daughter's death in Lisbon, receiving condolences via mobile phone. Such separations and absences, although common, were very difficult for people in both sites. As Guinean Muslims remake themselves and their religion in Portugal, the struggles accompanying distant departures often escalate into community-wide conflicts, which spread rapidly by mobile phone through Lisbon's urban spaces. I turn now to explore the complex, gendered nature and meaning of these conflicts.

"A CALL IS WORTH MORE THAN A PILE OF MONEY": FUNERALS AND FORGETTING IN THE DIASPORA

During my fieldwork in Lisbon, I spent a lot of time with Odette, a Fula woman from Guinea-Bissau who lived in Quinta do Mocho, a neighborhood settled exclusively by immigrants from all of Portugal's former African colonies. On one occasion after a long day of visiting, Odette and her husband, Saliyu, accompanied me to the bus stop, where we met a large group of Guinean immigrants who were waiting for transportation back to central Lisbon. We exchanged greetings in Kriolu and joined them. Across the street, a hearse drove up to an apartment building. We all watched as two Portuguese men dressed in formal black business suits entered the building, carrying a silver coffin. A few minutes later, the men exited the building and placed the coffin in the car. Then they carefully draped a white cloth over the coffin, closed the door of the hearse, and drove away. Several of the Guineans we stood with at the bus stop made sounds and gestures of disapproval. "If that were an African's apartment," one woman said, "it would be full of people. Just look at it. It's completely empty." Agreeing with the woman, Odette said, "When you die in Europe, you die alone."

Brief moments like these were deep reminders to the Guinean immigrants I met in Portugal that they were far away from home, in a very different place. Such moments also brought sharply to the surface Mandinga immigrants' deepest concerns, even their fears, concerning their identity, the current and future states of their ritual practices, and their place in a changing world. Whenever they talked to me about death and funerary rituals, my interlocutors made a simple distinction between "the Mandinga way" and "the white people's [Portuguese] way." They imagined the Portuguese experience of death (and, indeed, other life passages, such as birth) as solitary, brief, and medicalized. This contrasted sharply with death in their own culture, which they described as a highly social event, involving many people and taking place over an extended period.

But the Mandinga I came to know best in Lisbon explained to me that as time goes on, more and more immigrants forget their own ways of doing things. In their minds, however, forgetting was rarely, if ever, unintentional. Rather, it was a conscious shift in priorities that inevitably involved some neglect of social obligations to members of the wider immigrant community in Portugal and even to relatives back home. Some common examples of forgetting were failing to attend a funeral or postburial sacrifice or neglecting to call the bereaved if one could not attend in person. In some instances when people were accused of forgetting, they sent large sums of money as compensation, which many people interpreted as further evidence of forgetting. Indeed, during my fieldwork in Lisbon, I attended several funerals and many more postburial sacrifices during which arguments over such attempts to make up for forgetting often escalated into conflicts that people throughout the immigrant community talked about for months, even years.[4]

Two incidents, both of which occurred in 1999, were particularly noteworthy. The first involved an elder Mandinga man in his midsixties, Al-Hajj, whose brother died in the town of Farim in northern Guinea-Bissau. Al-Hajj's niece, whom I knew very well and visited often in her apartment in Cacém, called me on my mobile phone with the news. I immediately made preparations to go to Al-Hajj's rented room in the Lisbon neighborhood of Santos to give him "funerary greetings" (*mantenya di tchur*, in Kriolu). When I arrived, the guests were already spilling out into the hallway and onto the balcony adjacent to the small room. I greeted Al-Hajj, who immediately showed me a framed picture of his brother and him, dressed in their finest "big clothing," sitting on prayer rugs outside the Farim mosque in Guinea-Bissau. "This one is finished" (*Nying, a banta le*"), Al-Hajj said in Mandinga, pointing to his now deceased brother in the photo.

A large, elderly woman who commanded a presence arrived and greeted Al-Hajj. Using what my interlocutors called "deep Mandinga," a metaphorical speech style used by elders when they want to be discreet, the two began lamenting that once young people discover the "sweetness" of Portugal, they forget who they are and their obligations to their relatives. I averted my eyes and pretended not to be listening, a sign of respect I performed automatically after many years of fieldwork with Mandinga. But Al-Hajj, who knew me well and always showed genuine concern for my research, ignored my polite gesture and drew me straight into the conversation. "I learned of my own brother's death, Fatumata, only when people started arriving at my door, giving me funerary greetings," he told me. "I have never been so ashamed." Al-Hajj was particularly upset by the fact that his nephew, his deceased brother's son, did not even bother to call him. Just then, four more people arrived at the door. The eldest man in the group informed Al-Hajj that they had come to make a formal apology on behalf of Al-Hajj's nephew for failing to deliver the news of the death. He then placed a pile of money on Al-Hajj's prayer rug and covered it with a bag of kola nuts, a gesture of respect believed to neutralize the danger and ambiguity of cash. "Money has no place in this affair," Al-Hajj told the men calmly but sternly. He reached for his mobile phone, held it in his right hand, and said, "When my brother dies, his sons become my sons. A call is worth more than a pile of money."

The second incident occurred at the first postburial sacrifice held for Musukuto's daughter, the woman who died from tuberculosis in Guinea-Bissau. Aminata told me that Musukuto's deceased daughter's husband, who at the time had been living in Portugal for ten years, never sent money home to his wife and three children. "Even when he found out his wife was ill, he still didn't send money," Aminata stated. "That's how Guinean immigrants in Lisbon are. They only care about cars, gold jewelry, and mobile phones. They see these sweet things and forget their people back home." I caught a ride back to Lisbon with Aminata, her husband, and a group of female clothing merchants, who had taken advantage of the community gathering to sell the latest clothing styles out of Dakar, Lagos, and Mecca. The merchants complained that the holy men had criticized them for shamelessly using a postburial sacrifice to further their business interests and had chased them out the door. The conversation soon returned to the deceased woman's husband, who had finally arrived minutes before the end of the ritual. One of the merchants explained, "He placed forty thousand escudos in the middle of the room where the holy men were sitting. They were so angry they didn't even greet him."

These two accounts highlight the difficulty of "living together in a foreign land," as my Guinean Muslim interlocutors put it, and the continued importance of ritual and its accompanying social obligations in the contemporary diaspora. As evident in the above vignettes, community members, especially elders and holy men, are critical of immigrants who forget their obligations to their relatives, especially young immigrants who, in their struggle to make a living in Lisbon, put money before people. At the same time, however, my interlocutors in Lisbon were well aware of the challenges and constraints that immigrant life poses. Lisbon's urban sprawl is vast, and community members often live far away from one other. Contrary to common depictions of transnationals as highly mobile subjects (e.g., Appadurai 1996), the majority of the people I met in Lisbon did not travel frequently and easily between Lisbon and Bissau. They complained that airline tickets were expensive and travel difficult. Movement between the two countries was rendered even more difficult when flights from Lisbon to Bissau were canceled for nine months after the start of the war. Indeed, my interlocutors' experiences of transnationalism seemed more akin to those of Sierra Leonean immigrants living in Washington, DC, as described by JoAnn D'Alisera (2004), for whom the idea of homeland is bound up with nostalgia and a sense of permanent displacement.

Beyond transnationalism, I was even more surprised by how infrequently some migrants moved within Lisbon's urban spaces. Several elder women I worked with who lived in apartments in the suburbs claimed they had not been to central Lisbon since they arrived at the airport from Guinea-Bissau a decade previously. I met two sisters, one who lived in Damaia and the other in Outerela (about an hour to an hour-and-a-half trip by bus), who had never been to each other's houses and who saw one another only at Maternal Kin Club events or Muslim holiday celebrations at the central mosque. When I asked one of them why she did not go to Damaia to visit her sister, she told me that the place was too far and she feared she might get lost. Many women described public transportation as confusing and costly (the men complained only about the cost), and work and school schedules made it difficult for many people to attend community gatherings held during the week or late at night. In the case of funerals and postburial sacrifices, phone calls provided a way for immigrants to fulfill their social obligation to greet the bereaved when they were unable to be there in person.

Many migrants complained, however, that people often neglected even to call, as evident in the above vignettes. Although they might have had valid excuses—perhaps the money on their mobile phone was "eaten up," or, at least in the early days of my fieldwork, they did not own a mobile phone and could not find anyone willing to lend them one—those who failed to call were often accused of forgetting. In an attempt to make up for this, some people presented cash gifts to their relatives after the fact. But community members, especially elders and holy men, rarely, if ever, viewed money as appropriate compensation for forgetting.

Indeed, migrants held highly ambivalent views about money. Nearly all of my interlocutors at some point mentioned money as a common source of suffering in the diaspora. On the one hand, they were aware of how essential it is to life in Lisbon, much more than in Guinea-Bissau, where even without money one could always at least eat. In Lisbon, money is difficult to obtain and even harder to hold on to. Having it means that others, especially relatives back home, expect their share. This reality put a significant amount of pressure on the immigrants I knew in Lisbon. Many people contrasted the dream (or rather, the expectation) of making it in Europe with the reality that despite one's daily struggle to earn an honest living, one rarely, if ever, had enough money. A few people in Lisbon I came to know well confessed that the real reason they had never returned home, even to attend a funeral, was that they would not be able to bring gifts and money back to everyone who expected them. They avoided having to admit to everyone back home that life in Europe was not what they had imagined and that they had failed to make it in Portugal. One woman, whose family had "jumped into" an unfinished high-rise building with no finished door or windows and no indoor plumbing, told me, "If I explained my living conditions to my relatives back home they would not believe I was in Europe." Many immigrants considered it better to never return home than to face such humiliation.[5]

On the other hand, my Guinean Muslim interlocutors in Lisbon mistrusted those who desired money too much, those who had a lot of it, and especially those who seemed to acquire it effortlessly. James Ferguson (2006, 72) writes that in Africa, the production of wealth is inseparable from the production of social relations and can be considered prosocial and morally valuable or antisocial and destructive of community. Specifically, people in southern and central Africa made this distinction by contrasting "sweat" with "eating the sweat of others." The young immigrant men I met in Lisbon made a similar distinction between working in construction, which they viewed as difficult but "clean" work, and "going to Spain" (a euphemism for the drug trade), which, despite its monetary rewards, was "dirty" work, inappropriate for good Muslims. Elders and holy men in Lisbon were critical of the accumulation of money by any means as an attempt to build one's name in the immigrant community, especially since this process, as they saw it, inevitably entailed some degree of forgetting one's obligations to the wider immigrant community, one's relatives back home, and one's Muslim identity. As one healer-diviner put it, "A person is not respected in Lisbon unless he [or she] owns an expensive car, a gold watch, and a mobile phone. That's why immigrant bellies get bigger and bigger while people back home in Guinea-Bissau suffer. God doesn't want that."[6]

The elders and holy men I worked with in Lisbon commonly linked forgetting to religion. While one could expect such behavior from non-Muslims, true Muslims put people above everything, especially above money. This explains why the holy men in the above vignette, for example, accused the female clothing merchants of being more concerned with getting rich than with praying for the deceased's soul. For their part, however, the merchants

Figure 4.3. "Dirty hands, clean work" in Lisbon, 1999. Photograph by the author.

did not see it this way. When I asked them about this, they just asked, "How can struggling to earn a living in a foreign land be un-Islamic?"

As Mandinga immigrants remake themselves and their religion in Portugal, the place of money in social and ritual obligations is only one of several issues creating tensions and divisions between men and women, elders and youth, and those who aspire to global Islam and those who remain more comfortably rooted in African custom. I turn now to discuss two other issues, the ritual of the left-handed handshake and ritual wailing at funerals.

THE LEFT-HANDED HANDSHAKE:
A RITUAL OF SEPARATION

In Africa, as in many parts of the world, most daily activities, especially shaking hands, eating, and receiving gifts, are performed with the right hand, while the left hand is reserved for more nefarious activities, such as sexual play, cursing someone through witchcraft, and wiping one's backside after defecating. In his classic article on the subject, Robert Hertz (1973) argued against the temptation to understand the universality of the preeminence of the right hand in exclusively biological terms. In his view, it was more accurately a matter of culture, which must be interpreted within the overarching symbolic dualism defining "primitive religion" (Durkheim 1965), the sacred and the profane. Hertz wrote (1973, 6), "The fact is that right-handedness is not simply accepted, submitted to, like a natural tendency: it is an ideal to which everybody must conform and which society forces us to respect by positive sanctions."[7]

I learned early on in my fieldwork in Guinea-Bissau that Mandinga are no exception to this rule. Indeed, to use the left hand rather than the right hand when shaking hands or giving or receiving something is akin to an insult or even a curse. Considering this, I was surprised by a Mandinga practice I learned about for the first time in 1997 as I prepared to travel to Dakar, Senegal, for an academic conference. I stopped at each compound on my way out of the village of Bafata-Oio, where I was living at the time, to bid my hosts farewell and to receive blessings for a safe journey. But as I extended my right hand to the first person I encountered, he demanded my left hand instead. "Before traveling, you must shake with the left hand," he asserted. As I shook the left hands of a hundred people or more along the three-kilometer dirt path to the paved road where I would catch a *kandonga* (bush taxi) to Bissau, I pondered this seemingly subversive practice. Durkheim (1965) and Hertz (1973) wrote about the tendency for people to inscribe onto their bodies their most cherished conceptions of social order. In their view, adopted later by Mary Douglas (1966), social norms are really reflections of religious ideas. What possible religious significance might shaking with the left hand hold for Mandinga, both at home and in the contemporary diaspora?

In his work on separation and reunion in China, Charles Stafford (2000) argues that in order for people to effectively deal with the ambiguities and dilemmas that separation entails, the act of separation is universally ritualized. "Rituals of separation," in his view, "make manifest the collective, i.e., *social*, need to transcend the dilemmas imposed by . . . separation" (2000, 21; emphasis in original). For Mandinga, shaking with the left hand engages several dilemmas. First, there is the obvious question of whether or not the people about to be separated will eventually be reunited. Like Muslims in other parts of the world, Guinean Muslims believe that death is an immutable part of an individual's life trajectory as determined by God, who decides the time and place of a person's death at the time of his or her birth. Palestinian Muslims as described by Hilma Granqvist (1975, 36–37), for example, believe that at the time of a child's conception God places a handful of dust in the woman's womb from the physical place where the child will eventually die. That dust, in turn, is thought to call that person back to the place where he or she is destined to die. My Mandinga interlocutors reported similar beliefs. As one Mandinga woman in her late thirties in Lisbon explained, "People always know their place of birth, but only God knows where they will die. God has chosen a place for each person to die. A man can be young and strong and living a healthy and successful life in Europe. But one day he decides to go home [to Guinea-Bissau] or to take a trip to somewhere else, and he dies there. God chose that specific place for him to die. God called him to that place, and he answered."[8]

Travel inevitably involves risk and thus reminds people of the possibility that separation might be final rather than temporary. Shaking with the left hand, as my Mandinga interlocutors explained, expresses a wish for this not to be the case by bestowing a blessing on the traveler for a safe journey and a safe return home. It expresses the wish that "As sure as one's left hand will return to one's backside, may you also return home." This act, however, is a reciprocal one: although only one person is departing, two people are being separated, and thus both people feel the ambiguity brought on by that separation. Will the departure be temporary or final? The basic message of shaking with the left hand might be, then, "May the one who departs not die on the journey and may the one who stays not die in the waiting." Symbolically, the ritual of the left-handed handshake can be interpreted as a wrongful act that provides the people involved with a future opportunity to correct it. That is, if and when both people meet again alive and well, they can shake with the right hand, ritually resolving the ambiguity of the separation (i.e., whether it will be temporary or final).

Shaking with the left hand also underscores a basic paradox of Mandinga belief: although people affirm that the time and place of one's death are predetermined by God, this tenet is profoundly difficult to accept, especially in an era in which long-distance separation has become more commonplace, and more people are dying and being buried abroad. I do not want to suggest, however, that the dilemmas and paradoxes associated with separation, the symbolic links between place, death, and predestination, are themselves recent products of transnationalism or globalization. Rather, these long-held associations have simply become intensified in the transnational era.

Mandinga uphold a connection between death, place, and identity. Although this connection is recalled in the ritual of the left-handed handshake, it can be found in other more mundane situations—for example, in the Mandinga practice of interring hair, toenail and fingernail clippings, and other bodily substances (e.g., placentas and foreskins) in the earth. People told me that death is "a return to the earth," and burying bodily substances in the ground in which one's own body will likely be buried is thought to facilitate the journey of the soul from this world to the next, rendering it quick and painless. Like other peoples in West Africa, such as Maka and Ewondo in Cameroon (see Geschiere 2005) and Igbo in Nigeria (see D. Smith 2004), Mandinga, no matter where they may spend their lives, want to be buried in their home village, "where their umbilical cord is buried." People explained that interring bodily substances in one's home village serves as a wish to be buried there, that after death one's body will be reunited with rather than separated from the substances it shed during life. In his work on burials and belonging among Igbo-speaking peoples in Nigeria, Daniel Smith (2004, 569) argues that "the intense desire and expectation on the part of rural-urban migrants in numerous African societies to be buried 'at home' in their rural villages is one of the most powerful symbolic indicators of the continuing (and perhaps, growing) strength of ties to place of origin."[9]

Considering the historical importance and prevalence of travel to Mandinga and the continued emphasis on migration and diaspora for their contemporary identity, being buried "at home" is more often an ideal than a reality even in Guinea-Bissau. Bodies must, in accordance with Islam, be interred within twenty-four hours of death. Because of the country's poor road conditions and the fact that rivers and swampland make up about a quarter of the landscape (Forrest 1992, 3), travel is often slow and difficult, and those who die away from their homes are often buried among strangers. The challenge of efficient travel is intensified for Guinean Muslims who have immigrated abroad. Considering the limited number of flights per week connecting Lisbon and Bissau, and the expense of airline tickets, sending bodies back to one's home village in Guinea-Bissau is not always possible.

Mandinga beliefs about the mobility (or immobility) of bodies can be contrasted with those held by non-Muslim ethnic groups, for whom it is common to wait some time before burying the dead.[10] The waiting period leaves ample time to transport the body and allows relatives living in neighboring countries or even as far away as Europe to attend the funerary rituals. Non-Muslims also hold very different beliefs about the commemoration of the dead and the influence of the dead on the living. Eric Gable (2006) documents that when Manjaco die in Dakar, Paris, or Lisbon, relatives in their home villages replace absent bodies with head-shaped bundles of funeral cloth draped over vaguely corporal forms. To remember the dead, villagers also carve wooden images of the deceased and install them in ancestral shrines. According to Gable (2006, 390), "Long-distance death continues to be treated as if it were local and tactile." Furthermore, death becomes a form of repatriation through which Manjaco at once celebrate and mitigate what they refer to as the "brokenness" of the land, the disjunction between place, death, and identity.[11]

Unlike members of non-Muslim ethnic groups, Mandinga do not carve images of the deceased or erect ancestor shrines, since doing so would be contrary to Islam. Gravesites in Mandinga villages are unmarked and invisible to the untrained observer. The ritual of the left-handed handshake thus underscores the longstanding reality, intensified in the transnational era, that when Mandinga die and are interred abroad, continuity between death, place, and identity is forever ruptured. Indeed, as travel and migration intensify and transnational communities expand, continuity between body, place, and identity, symbolically affirmed in the ritual of the left-handed handshake and other practices, such as interring bodily substances in the ground of one's home village, is more of an ideal than a reality. When Mandinga die in Portugal, their bodies are only sometimes sent home (and this is very costly), and Mandinga immigrants often have no other option than to mourn their relatives' deaths back home on another continent, transmitting wails and blessings via mobile phone.[12]

When I engaged women about the connections between death, place, and identity, they shared with me some alternative views. They claimed that beyond bestowing wishes to die at home and for a quick and painless journey of the soul to the afterlife, the practice of burying bodily substances is a way of preventing witches and malevolent spirits from "working" with them (i.e., using them to harm others). Furthermore, fewer women than men I spoke with seemed satisfied with the wish for continuity between death, place, and identity bestowed by the ritual of the left-handed handshake. Although women generally traveled less frequently than men did, they were more inclined to consult a Muslim healer-diviner to "read the road" for them before they traveled and more likely to alter their travel plans based on the outcome of the visit. Women in both field sites also took more seriously the prohibition of traveling on Mondays and Fridays, since they were more inclined than men to believe that "big spirits" prowl the roadways on these days. These spirits are said to put their hands over drivers' eyes, preventing them from seeing the road and thus causing accidents. Women told me countless stories of people who had ignored a Muslim healer-diviner's advice concerning a trip and had died. The only men who seemed to share these beliefs were healer-diviners themselves (whom I explore in the next chapter), who did not consider their craft to be contradictory to Islam, even when it involved the use of tarot cards to determine whether a death was caused by witchcraft.

My interlocutors described witches (*buwaa*) as human beings with extraordinary powers. They shapeshift into different forms (e.g., owls or airplanes) and attack their victims internally, "eating" their organs until they become thin and weak and eventually die. People claimed that witches prey on the vulnerable (e.g., initiates or infants) and those with extraordinary luck, talent, or wealth. Indeed, witches are said to be motivated by jealousy and greed. Whereas some anthropologists (e.g., Beidelman 1993; Jackson 1989) have imagined witchcraft as a quintessential traditional African belief or practice, others (e.g., Auslander 1993; Geschiere 1997) have highlighted the modernity of witchcraft, seeing the elaboration and increase of occult activities as responses to changing economic and social conditions in postcolonial African societies. Peter Geschiere (1997, 8), for example, underscores the "ease with which witchcraft discourses in Africa incorporate the money economy, new power relations, and consumer goods associated with modernity." The question of whether witchcraft is traditional or modern for Guinean Muslims is only relevant, I contend, as they remake Islam in Lisbon. Ironically, what is most modern about witchcraft beliefs and practices is their recent relegation to the domain of custom, at least by some in Lisbon. Whereas most, if not all, Guinean Muslims generally accept the power and influence of nonhuman spirits (*iran*) as beings that God created out of fire, some are more skeptical of witches, or human beings who harm others out of unbridled jealousy and desire for power and wealth. These skeptics claim that "there is no room in Islam for witchcraft." Many Guinean Muslims, however, continue to believe in both spirits and witches at the same time as they assert that "it is God who does everything." I continue to explore this conflict below and in the chapters that follow.[13]

"WHAT KIND OF A FACE WILL I HAVE?": GENDERED PERSPECTIVES ON RITUAL WAILING

One evening in 1999 in Lisbon, I was sitting with Jiba, her daughter, Adama, and Adama's husband in their apartment in Amadora, a twenty-minute train ride by commuter train from central Lisbon. Jiba, who was my neighbor and close friend in Bissau, had recently joined her relatives in Portugal shortly after the start of the war. We were conversing and watching the evening news when the phone rang, startling Jiba. Still traumatized by the recent experience of shelling in Bissau, Jiba jumped at the slightest noise. "Who could it be at this hour?" Adama remarked to her mother in Mandinga before answering the phone in Portuguese. The rest of us shifted our attention from the television to Adama, who let out a short cry, "*Weh!*" followed by a long, drawn-out wail, "*Wayoooo!*"

a typical female response to news of death, especially the death of a close rela-tive. Adama fell on the floor suddenly, crying over and over again in Kriolu, "*Ña tiu murri!*" ("My uncle is dead!") As she stumbled into the hallway, crying, no one rushed to calm her. Between Adama's regular, almost rhythmic wails, Jiba and Adama's husband commented on Adama's "foolish" behavior: "Every little thing and she falls apart." Switching back to Mandinga, Jiba informed us that the old man, who was blind, had been ill for a long time. She had not received news recently and thus suspected his condition had worsened. Considering this, she was not shocked by the news. Adama, now calm, announced firmly, "I'm going to Chelas." Adama's husband, who was fully engrossed in a tele-vised soccer match, reminded Adama of the train strike, which would surely complicate the already long trip to the Lisbon suburb. "Besides," he added, "it's already too late to go." Adama protested, "I have no choice. If I wait until tomor-row morning, what kind of a face will I have?" Reluctantly, Jiba and Adama's husband complied with her wishes and prepared to make the hour-and-a-half journey to Chelas by commuter train and bus, despite the strike.

The above vignette provides a short glimpse of the conflicting views sur-rounding emotional reactions to the news of death. More specifically, it engages gendered perspectives on ritual wailing as Guinean immigrants remake Islam in Portugal. Although Islam does not forbid weeping for the dead as an expression of grief, it does discourage loud lamentation, such as ritual wailing. Muslims view strong emotional displays of shock, grief, sadness, or anger as expressions of the unjust nature of a particular death: an impossibility in a religion that sees every death as part of God's divine plan. Jane Smith and Yvonne Haddad (1981, 59–60) note that some hadiths take this prohibition one step further, suggest-ing that weeping may actually intensify the suffering of the dead.[14]

My Guinean Muslim interlocutors in Guinea-Bissau and Portugal con-trasted stoic Muslim responses to death with emotional non-Muslim ones. They told me that, as Muslims, they believe that human beings remain igno-rant of their own prescribed life trajectories set by God and can do very little, if anything, to alter them. Death can strike at any moment and without warn-ing, and the appropriate thing to do is to "suffer" the death, to endure it, as God's will. Men often viewed emotional outbursts of anger or sadness as dis-respectful of, even a challenge to, God. Boubakar, a Mandinga man from the Gambia who worked as a clothing merchant in Bissau, told me confidently one afternoon in his compound as we were having tea that there were no real Muslims in Guinea-Bissau. He supported his claim with stories of emotional responses to death, which he viewed as contradictory to Islam. He explained, "When someone dies, all of Bissau knows because the women start wailing. If these people were true Muslims, they would quietly suffer the death, remembering that God can take a life as quickly as he can begin one."

My interlocutors were even more critical of the fact that emotional outbursts by animists often take the form of dramatic protests directed at God. Baba, a Mandinga man who owned a small shop in Bissau, told me about his Mankanya (a non-Muslim ethnic group) neighbor, who, on receiving the news of his brother's untimely death, had aimed a shotgun at the sky and yelled at God for taking his brother from this world. Another man told me that he had observed his animist neighbor enter his spirit house after a funeral and yell and curse at several carved images of his ancestors for not having warned the living of the death. My Guinean Muslim interlocutors, men and women alike, found these stories fascinating, albeit horrifying, because they underscore a relationship between the human and the divine profoundly different from their own.

When I engaged people specifically on the practice of ritual wailing, however, their views on the subject varied sharply according to gender. Whereas men, especially those who had studied the Qur'an or had made the hajj, most often upheld the official Muslim view, women's views were more variable and contradictory. On the one hand, women often gave me the line offered by men: proper Muslims should suffer every death quietly as God's will, so ritual wailing is contrary to Islam. On the other hand, many of these same women admitted that they regularly wailed at funerals and described it as a Mandinga custom. When I pushed further, many women specified that ritual wailing was actually something they *had* to perform when they first heard the news of the death and right before the body was interred. Ritual wailing takes on a rather dramatic quality. On entering the house of the bereaved, mourners fall to the ground, one by one, before the closest relative of the deceased and cry, "Waay, my mother!" or "God help me!" repeatedly until someone says, "That's enough," at which point the mourner stops wailing immediately and takes her place among the gathered guests.

Women commonly expressed concern about the nature and timing of such performances. On several occasions during my fieldwork in Guinea-Bissau and Portugal, I heard a woman ask, "Should we wail now or later?" or "What kind of face do I have?" (i.e., "Do I appear upset enough?") When I inquired about the apparent concern about the performance of ritual wailing, women explained that the deceased's relatives might openly criticize unimpressive wailers for being ambivalent about their loss. Worse yet, they might accuse them of having had a hand in the death, an allusion to witchcraft. This was precisely what Adama in the above vignette was concerned about when she asked her husband what kind of face she would have if they waited until the next morning to greet the bereaved at her deceased uncle's house. In the morning, the shock of death and the strong emotions that accompanied it may have lessened, and Adama might have found it more difficult to wail on greeting her bereaved family members.

Adama's mother, however, did not share her daughter's concern and was even critical of Adama's dramatic expression of grief. A postmenopausal woman who had made the hajj, Jiba's religiosity was intensified and her beliefs were more in line with men who have studied the Qur'an, have made the hajj, and aspire to global Islam. She prayed faithfully five times a day, attended Friday prayer at Lisbon's central mosque (whenever she could arrange a ride), and joined the male elders in Qur'anic recitation at life-course rituals. She wore a head scarf over her *tikoo* (head tie) and openly expressed her desire to align her religious practices more closely with Islam as practiced by Arabs. She confided in me her fear that her daughters, on moving to Portugal and being surrounded by non-Muslims, might "fall from Islam." That is, they might stop praying and start eating pork and drinking alcohol. Jiba's concern was not unfounded. During my 2003 visit to Lisbon, Adama and her husband, who described himself as a "son of Muslims," showed me the video of their mixed wedding combining Muslim and Portuguese elements. During my 2017 visit, I learned that their marriage had ended.[15]

As Mandinga men, especially those who have studied the Qur'an and made the hajj, remake Islam in Portugal, they emphasize their inclusion in the *umma*, the global community of Muslims, over Mandinga custom. Many men I spoke with deemed the practice of ritual wailing un-Islamic and discouraged women from engaging in it. They blamed women's inappropriate responses to death on their alleged inability to read Arabic and thus on their ignorance of true Islam. For their part, women blamed men for abandoning cherished Mandinga traditions for a new religion and found it difficult, if not impossible, to believe that men could so easily suspend their belief in witchcraft. These statements underscore Mandinga immigrant women's insecurities about their inclusion (or lack of it) in global Islam. Many women complained that they did not have the opportunity to study Arabic, and when their husbands were praying or attending mosque, they were cooking and taking care of their children. As one woman in Portugal put it, "Mandinga women don't have time to be good Muslims."

Beyond ritual wailing, women take their skepticism of the Muslim belief that all deaths are God's will one step further when they consult healer-diviners to investigate the possibility that a death might have been caused by witchcraft. A vignette from my 1997 fieldwork in Guinea-Bissau illustrates this point. On one occasion, one of my neighbors in Bissau, whom I called Kamaraba (literally,

"Big Kamara," Kamara being the woman's clan name), received the shocking news that her only son had died in Portugal. He was in his late twenties or early thirties at the time and had been living in Lisbon for many years, where he worked at a luxury hotel. When I inquired about the details, all Kamaraba told me was that her son woke up one morning and, feeling quite sick, decided to stay home from work. He developed a high fever in the evening and was taken to the hospital, where he inexplicably died later that night.

When I arrived at Kamaraba's compound for the first funerary sacrifice, her house was packed with people who had come to show their support and to mourn her son's death. Kamaraba's long periods of rhythmic waling were interspersed with loud cries, "My mother!" Her male relatives attempted to quiet her, urging her to suffer her son's death as God's will. They discussed whether they should attempt to have the body sent home or whether Kamaraba's son should be buried in Lisbon. Others asserted that at the very least Kamaraba should travel to Lisbon to see her son's face one last time.

In the end, Kamaraba's son was buried in Portugal, and she never made it to Lisbon. Although she went to the Portuguese embassy in Bissau several times to inquire about the possibility, she was simply told that she lacked the proper documents and was sent away. Although male relatives and Muslim holy men continued to assure Kamaraba that her son's death was God's will, she was unconvinced. "People were jealous of my son's success and the money he sent to me," she explained. She confessed to me in private that she planned to consult a healer-diviner to explore the possibility that her son's death might have been caused by witchcraft.

Gendered discourses surrounding distant departures, already common in Guinea-Bissau, intensify as Guinean Muslims remake themselves and their religion in Portugal, as they engage various groups of others (e.g., increasingly secular Roman Catholics and "Arab" and "Indian" Muslims), and as they come to terms with their own inclusion and exclusion vis-à-vis these others. In deeming ritual wailing un-Islamic, Mandinga men in Portugal assert their identity as pious Muslims and the superiority of true Islam based on the five pillars of faith over their own version, which has long mixed freely with African custom. In defending ritual wailing as an obligatory custom and consulting healer-diviners about the causes of particular deaths, women express skepticism about the Muslim belief that all deaths are God's will and resist male constructs of piety. But these gendered discourses are often ambiguous and contradictory. "Good Muslims" who assert that all deaths are God's will, for example, undermine this certainty when they engage in the ritual of the left-handed handshake, a wish for continuity between death, place, and identity in an era where migration and the uncertainty associated with it have intensified. Furthermore, Muslim healer-diviners who have been to Mecca and pride themselves in their ability to read and write Arabic and understand the deep meanings of the Qur'an make their living by "reading the road" for those who, despite their longing to be global Muslims, are reluctant to abandon their belief in the power of witches.

NOTES

1. Anthropologists have argued that drumming and transition are symbolically linked (e.g., Goody 1962; P. Metcalf and Huntington 1991; Needham 1967). Although Mandinga drum at initiations and weddings, most consider it un-Islamic to drum at name-giving rituals and funerals. The rhythmic pounding of mortals and pestles as the women prepare munkoo, however, might be interpreted as playing a similar role as drumming, marking important transitions that are thought to occur at death.

2. Carreira (1947, 116) documented that postburial sacrifices took place after the burial and on the third and seventh days after the death. He described the third sacrifice as the most important, as it marked the time at which Mandinga believed the soul left the body for the afterlife. No one I spoke with, in contrast, was able to tell me when the soul leaves the body.

3. See, for example, Abu-Lughod (1991), Bruner (1986), Jackson (1989), and Stoller (1989).

4. This parallels Weiss's discussion of forgetting among Haya in Tanzania. He argues, "Forgetting . . . is not merely an ineffective attempt to retain information, or an unintended consequence of the production of new forms of knowledge. Rather, forgetting can in some instances be seen as an intentional and purposive attempt to create absences that can be crucial to the reconstruction and reevaluation of social meanings and relations" (1997, 164). Weiss treats forgetting as a form of memory.

5. Geschiere (2005, 55) explains that funerals in Cameroon engage similar anxieties and conflicts concerning money between urbanites, who are obligated to return to their home villages to attend funerals, and their relatives back home. Urbanites often dread returning home for funerals and fear aggression from their relatives, who might accuse them of not sharing their wealth.

6. For ethnographic discussions on the ambiguity of money in Africa, see Hutchinson (1996, 2000), Weiss (1996, 2009), and Comaroff and Comaroff (1993). For a different take on the relationship between money, morality, and Islam, see Stoller (2002).

7. See also Wieschhoff (1973) and Needham (1973) for analyses of right/left symbolism in Africa.

8. J. Smith and Haddad (1981, 35–36) and Jackson (1989, 81) report similar beliefs about the link between death, soil from a particular place, and predestiny for Muslims in general and for Kuranko in Sierra Leone, respectively.

9. Mebenga (1991, 234) explains that for Ewondo peoples in Cameroon, burying the placenta reminds a child that "he should never forget to return to the place where his placenta is buried. This act ties any Ewondo to his village, like a child is tied to his mother by the umbilical cord. Indeed, this conception demands that every Ewondo be buried in his village of origin so as to reaffirm this union forged by his birth" (cited in Geschiere 2005, 53; Geschiere's translation from the French). Geschiere (2005) argues that in the 1990s in Cameroon, conflicts over returning home for funerals engaged ideas about belonging.

10. See Davidson (2004), Einarsdóttir (2004), and Gable (2006) for examples among Jola, Papel, and Manjaco peoples in Guinea-Bissau.

11. In a similar fashion, Toba Batak people in Indonesia erect monumental village gravesites for their deceased relatives who spent their lives seeking their fortunes in the city. Bruner (2005, 471) writes, "The bones of the deceased are literally fixed in concrete, immobilized, yet the graves themselves are symbols of mobility, dispersal, of movement."

12. In his study of death and migration among Cambodian and Filipino immigrants in the United States, Becker (2002) found that the most common factor determining whether or not remains are sent home is where the majority of the deceased relatives live, either back home or in the United States.

13. See Daswani (2015, 113–19) for a similar discussion of witchcraft beliefs and practices as both traditional and modern, as well as similar debates about the place of witchcraft in Christianity among Ghanaian Pentecostals.

14. Anthropologists working with Muslims in Africa and Asia have documented this belief extensively. Jackson (2011, 19) writes that Kuranko in Sierra Leone believe that "excessive weeping and lamentation at a funeral will make it difficult for the spirit of the deceased to pass into the place of the dead." See Geertz (1960, 72) for a similar example from Java.

15. In the wedding video, Adama wore a white dress and hat, her husband wore a suit and tie, and guests wore European clothing. The food included a whole roasted pig (complete with an apple in its mouth), and beer and wine bottles lined the table. Before the ceremony, two praise-singers dressed in African clothing sang Muslim chants to the wedding couple, which Adama described as "the Muslim part."

PART II

REMAKING ISLAM THROUGH RITUALS BEYOND THE LIFE COURSE

FIVE

—ᴥ—

REVERSALS OF FORTUNE

From Healing-Divining to Astrology

WHILE I WAS CONDUCTING FIELDWORK in Lisbon, I spent most of my days with immigrants from Guinea-Bissau, in the neighborhoods where they lived and in the public spaces they routinely frequented. I did, however, make a few Portuguese friends, who taught me "proper Portuguese" and gave me a different perspective on African immigrants in Lisbon. Maria was one of them. When I met her in 1999, she was a strong but gentle woman in her midfifties who worked as a cleaning lady in the building where I usually stayed during my visits to Lisbon. She loved to tell me stories about her life: how she gave birth to her son in the back of a taxicab, how Portugal suffered during the Salazar years, and how the country changed after entering the European Union.

One morning in May, I greeted Maria as she was beginning her daily routine of cleaning the guest rooms. She seemed agitated and upset. She told me that her twenty-eight-year-old son was struggling with drug addiction. In the hope that a recent treatment program would cure him, Maria was making daily offerings to Santa Rita de Cacilhas, the patron saint of impossible situations. Each night before bedtime, she lit three candles. But when they burned out, the melted wax formed the image of an animal, usually a dog or a pigeon. Maria was convinced that this was a bad omen, and sure enough, her son had relapsed during the night. The treatment program had failed.

I attempted to console Maria, asking her if there was anything I could do. She asked me to refer her to one of the healer-diviners I had been telling her about. Perhaps some "African magic," as she put it, could cure her son. One week later, I accompanied Maria to her consultation with Alaaji S., who operated his own healing-divining practice in his home in a Lisbon exurb, a forty-five-minute bus ride from central Lisbon. We greeted him, removed our shoes, and sat down on the prayer carpets that lined the marble floor of his small room. Maria explained her problem to Alaaji S. He assured her that he had successfully treated many clients, African and Portuguese alike, for drug addiction. He threw his cowry shells and informed Maria that the spirit behind her son was making him sick. He instructed Maria to make a sacrifice shortly after dusk: three bags of corn for the pigeons at Rossio square and three eggs in the Tejo River. He assured her that her son's condition would improve within three weeks.

Like many of his healer-diviner colleagues from Guinea-Bissau, Alaaji S. was remaking himself and his craft as he worked to earn a living in Lisbon by meeting the changing demands of a cosmopolitan clientele; struggled for inclusion in the *umma*, the global community of Muslims; and attempted to make a place for himself in a multicultural Europe. Healer-diviners in Lisbon encounter and must sort out the conflict between custom and innovation, in both their own identities and their healing-divining practices. Both gender and generation play roles in this process, as tensions emerge between old and young healer-diviners in Lisbon and as female healer-diviners (I met only one during my fieldwork in both Guinea-Bissau and Portugal) enter the field.

The relationship between healer-diviners, the Portuguese, and global Islam, as exemplified in the encounter between Maria and Alaaji S., speaks both to a colonial past and to a postcolonial present. It entails a reversal of fortune, one whose power relies on what Arjun Appadurai (1996, 3) calls the "work of the imagination" or what Richard Werbner (2002, 20) terms "flights of imagination by which people transcend what outsiders might call their marginality." As Muslim healer-diviners in Portugal remake themselves and their religion, marketing their powers for daily consumption by various groups of others in Lisbon, they must reconcile their identities as marginal immigrants and successful entrepreneurs, as African "astrologers" and cosmopolitan Muslims. And at the same time that the Portuguese deem healer-diviners primitive and doubt their authenticity, they attempt to tap into their powers by seeking consultations with them. In so doing, they renegotiate their relationship to their former colonial subjects, this time within their own borders, and struggle to make sense of the changing face of Lisbon during a time of increasing anti-immigration and anti-Islamic sentiment throughout Europe.

THE CUSTOM OF HEALING-DIVINING
FROM AFRICA TO EUROPE

Although there are a variety of healing traditions in Guinea-Bissau, healers are often lumped into two overarching groups: Muslim healer-diviners (*mooroo* in Mandinga) and "animist" (whom I prefer to call "indigenous") healer-diviners (*jambakus* in Kriolu). The latter typically belong to ethnic groups that practice African indigenous religions, and they specialize in both healing with medicinal plants and divination. Muslim healer-diviners are from Muslim ethnic groups in Guinea-Bissau (Mandinga, Fula, and Beafada), and, like indigenous healer-diviners, they also work with medicinal plants and divination techniques.

Despite a similarity in approaches and skills, Muslim healer-diviners define themselves in sharp opposition to indigenous healer-diviners, and this perceived difference is an important feature of their identity. The Muslim healer-diviners I worked with told me that *jambakus* "work with trees"— that is, they rely on expert, often secret knowledge of plants and animal parts (e.g., hair and horns) for their treatments. When I pointed out that Muslim healer-diviners also use these in their own work, they explained that the difference lies in the source of their power: whereas an indigenous healer-diviner's power comes from the bush, a Muslim healer-diviner's power comes from God.

If Muslim healer-diviners readily employ indigenous methods in their own work, the reverse is also true for indigenous healer-diviners, who borrow freely from Muslims. On one occasion during my fieldwork in Guinea-Bissau, a Pepel (a non-Muslim ethnic group) woman from Bissau told me about her visit to a renowned *jambakus* in Keije, a non-Muslim neighborhood in Bissau. She explained that the medicine the *jambakus* had given her contained "very powerful Arabic writing." Commenting on this inherent overlap between the power of God and the power of the bush, Lamin Sanneh (1997, 8) writes, "Dreams, dream interpretation, healing, and amulets belong as much to the Muslim religious tradition as they do to indigenous therapeutic culture, and they thus defy any rigid attempt at separation." Although in practice people may routinely undermine the distinction between these two groups of healer-diviners, it remains key in the realm of identity. Consider this conversation I had with a Muslim healer-diviner in Lisbon:

MJ: What is the difference between a Muslim healer-diviner and an indigenous one?

Healer-diviner: A Muslim healer-diviner is one thing and an indigenous healer-diviner is another. Muslim healer-diviners work with the Qur'an. Indigenous healer-diviners treat people without knowledge of the Qur'an. They don't know how to write and they work with spirits.

MJ: Are there any Muslims who work as indigenous healer-diviners?

Healer-diviner: There are people in Africa, Muslims and non-Muslims, who work with things from the bush. If someone is sick, they know which

plants will cure that person. They use those plants to make medicine. They
know trees, but they don't know the Qur'an.

MJ: But don't Muslim healer-diviners also work with plants?

Healer-diviner: Yes, there are those healers we could call double healer-
diviners, who work with the Qur'an and who also work with plants.
But that has nothing to do with whether a person is a Muslim or not.
Everything cures. Most double healer-diviners give their clients medicines
made from plants and medicines they write from the Qur'an. They also
give them *duwaa* [blessings], since it is God who does everything [cures
people].

This conversation underscores the inherent ambiguity between these two
categories of healer-diviners. Although the distinction between Muslim and
indigenous healer-diviners remains important for religious identity, it often dis-
solves in practice. At the same time that the healer-diviner above claimed that
"everything cures" and that the distinction between Muslim and indigenous
healer-diviners has "nothing to do with whether a person is a Muslim or not,"
in the end, he embraced the predominantly Muslim perspective of "it is God
who does everything." Since this chapter concerns Muslim healer-diviners, I
use the term *healer-diviners* for the sake of simplicity, using *Muslim* or *indigenous*
only for emphasis.[1]

Scholars have used a variety of terms to describe Muslim healer-diviners,
the most common one being *marabout*. This term is a French gloss of the Arabic
word *murabit*, whose root means to "tie," "bind," or "fasten" (Denny 1988, 89).
Dale Eickelman (1977, 6) defines *marabouts* as "persons, living or dead, who
have a special relationship with God" and who "serve as intermediaries with
the supernatural" and "communicate God's grace (*baraka*)." My interlocutors
also described healer-diviners as being close to God, as people who mediate
between human beings, God, and nonhuman agents such as spirits and angels.
They consider healing-divining one of the noblest of professions, equal to that
of farmers, warriors, and traders.[2]

A person may become a healer-diviner in three ways. First, he may inherit
the knowledge and skills of the trade from a relative or a namesake. Second,
and most commonly, he may apprentice with a renowned healer, developing his
craft slowly over many years. Third, in a "sacrifice of identity" (Gottlieb 1989,
246), he may offer a child (or part of a child) or his wife's fertility to a spirit in
exchange for the knowledge and power necessary to become a healer-diviner.
Although the healer-diviners I worked with deplored this strategy, they told me
that, sadly, some shameless people occasionally resorted to it.

Healer-diviners perform two primary roles. As teacher-scholars, they operate Qur'anic schools where they instruct students in Arabic literacy, Islamic doctrine, and ritual practices. As diviners, they train the next generation of healer-diviners in the deep secrets of the Qur'an and see clients for a variety of problems or pursuits, including barrenness, success in business, a cheating spouse, drug or alcohol addiction, or securing a visa to "try one's luck" in Europe. Much like Tswapong wisdom divination as described by Richard Werbner (2015, 10), the craft of healing-divining for Guinean Muslims involves "the pragmatic search for the understanding of suffering, the grasp of clients' moral dilemmas in the face of uncertainties." Healer-diviners blend a variety of techniques in their treatments, including the magical manipulation of God's names and of Qur'anic verses, numerology and astrology, and medical knowledge of plants and animals. To determine the source of a client's misfortune and the most effective treatment, healer-diviners use a variety of divining techniques, including cowry shells (*kuuringo*), sand (*kenyoo*), the Qur'an (*Alikuraanoo*), kola nuts (*kuruwo*), and prayer beads (*tasabayoo*). Their most elaborate divination technique, however, is *lasitakaaroo*, or "dream-divination." As one healer-diviner explained, "When I dream-divine for a client, I perform ablution and pray. I ask God to show me the person's problem. I recite the *alifaatiyoo* [the opening sura of the Qur'an], and then I go to sleep. God shows me whatever the problem is through my dreams. I might see that the person should make an offering, such as distribute kola nuts or meat at the mosque."

Healer-diviners provide clients with three types of "medicines" (*booroo*). The first, called *safewo*, from the Mandinga verb meaning "to write," are leather-cased amulets into which Qur'anic verses are sewn. Amulets may provide generalized protection from misfortune, or they may achieve a seemingly endless array of more specific purposes. For example, when my husband, Ned, and I settled in the village of Bafata-Oio in Guinea-Bissau, the village's most renowned healer-diviner gave us "language medicine" in the form of amulets we wore around our necks. The amulets contained a mixture of Qur'anic verses, medicinal plants, and honey, which would "open our heads" and allow us to learn the Mandinga language quickly. People wear amulets on their bodies, around the neck, arm, waist, wrist, or ankle. They also put them on their livestock or suitcases to protect them from theft or on the steering wheels of cars or bush taxis for safety in travel. In making amulets, healer-diviners rely on the help of leatherworkers, who sew the bundle into leather cases and add strings. In Lisbon, leatherworkers sit at Rossio square to await business from healer-diviners and their clients.[3]

Figure 5.1. A leatherworker sewing medicine into an amulet at Rossio, 2001. Photograph by the author.

The second type is *boorijiyo*, or liquid medicine, which consists of water into which Qur'anic verses are dissolved or washed from wooden slates used by Qur'anic students. People either drink this medicine or wash their bodies with it. The last type involves the transmission of blessings (duwaa) through a healer-diviner's breath or spittle, which people rub into their faces, heads, and chests. The healer-diviners I worked with stressed the importance of duwaa, asserting, "It's the only medicine one needs." To help me understand the importance of duwaa, a healer-diviner in Lisbon once asked me how long it took me to travel from the United States to Portugal. "Seven hours by plane," I told him. He responded, "Duwaa is more powerful than airplanes; it can travel from here to anywhere in the world in less than a second!"[4]

Healing-divining is more than teaching the Qur'an and making medicines; it is, my interlocutors insisted, a total way of life. Ideally, healer-diviners live simply and refuse many of the material comforts of contemporary life. People told me that the most powerful healer-diviners, even today, still come from the bush, or small villages in Guinea-Bissau's interior. The most powerful of all are considered *woliyo* (holy man or saint), a step above a healer-diviner, whom people from all ethnic groups (Muslim and non-Muslim alike) travel long distances to visit for specific reasons or simply to receive blessings. During the time of my early fieldwork, a few of the villages in which famous holy men lived were regional pilgrimage sites to which people journeyed from all over the Senegambia and sometimes as far as Mali. Whereas healer-diviners are said to develop their craft slowly over many years and eventually gain a reputation based on a large following and their clients' success stories, a holy man's power is said to come straight from God. Holy men do not typically employ medicines in their work but rather rely exclusively on the God-given power (*baraka*) contained in their bodies, which they transmit to others through duwaa. Holy men also are commonly thought to receive messages from God in the form of predictions. Guineans credit several holy men in Guinea-Bissau with predicting the length and outcome of both the country's liberation war and the 1998–99 civil war, the War of June 7.

Much to my interlocutors' delight in both field sites, I visited several renowned holy men in Guinea-Bissau. Before Ned and I set out, our friends and neighbors, Muslim and non-Muslim alike, warned us that getting there would not be easy. God is said to determine if and when a person will meet a particular holy man face-to-face. Pilgrims cannot arrive at a sacred pilgrimage site, people explained, unless their hearts and heads are clean. Holy men are said to see pilgrims before they set out on their journey. God tells the holy men whether or not they should allow the pilgrims to come, and they are said to "spoil the road" for those who are not yet ready for the experience. On our first attempt to visit Konchupa Faati, Ned's only pair of sandals was stolen, preventing us from going. When, after two more attempts, we finally made it to the holy man's village, our friends and neighbors told us, "It was your time to go."

Because a healer-diviner's power and authenticity are linked to rural spaces, people tend to doubt healer-diviners the farther away they move from Guinea-Bissau's interior. People were always suspicious of healer-diviners in Bissau, even those who claimed village ancestry. Furthermore, they seemed convinced that healer-diviners who were born and raised in the capital city were fake. My interlocutors described these urban healer-diviners as self-centered individuals who took advantage of their clients in pursuit of money, fame, and power.

In an attempt to build their reputation against potential critics, healer-diviners perform authenticity in various ways. For example, they maintain an uneasy attitude toward money. Indeed, people assume that healer-diviners are more authentic and powerful the less inclined they are to accept cash as payment for their services. Holy men and famous healers prefer gifts in kind, such

Figure 5.2. Kola nuts from Guinea-Bissau purchased in Damaia, 2017. Photograph by the author.

as white cloth, candles, kola nuts, and bags of sugar or rice, in increments of three or seven, numbers Muslims deem auspicious. If clients insist on giving cash, healer-diviners often inquire about its source, whether it is "clean" (earned through agricultural or wage labor, a result of the "sweat from one's brow") or "dirty" (acquired through theft, witchcraft, prostitution, or the sale of drugs). Clients may avoid potentially uncomfortable questioning about the source of money by tying it to kola nuts, a sign of its purity.

People outright ridicule urban healer-diviners who demand cash payment, especially those who charge large sums of money for consultations. On one occasion in Bissau when I was suffering from a bout of dysentery, my research assistant, Arafam, brought a Muslim healer-diviner to see me. Using cowry shells, the healer-diviner diagnosed my problem as "wind," an illness I had contracted from a witch, who had "caught" me as I passed by unknowingly, without protective medicines. He informed us that the treatment, a body wash, would cost three million Guinean pesos (approximately US$30 at the time). Horrified, Arafam told the healer-diviner that we did not want his medicine, and the healer-diviner left abruptly. Arafam explained to me that the healer-diviner was obviously a fake, exemplified by his shameless desire for money.[5]

Figure 5.3. A healer-diviner studying the Qur'an, 2001. Photograph by the author.

Muslim healer-diviners also perform authenticity through their dress. They wear simple, Saudi-style robes and Muslim hats, and most do not wear shoes. Whereas even the poorest Guineans I met would run into their house to slip on a pair of Chinese-made plastic flip-flops before allowing me to take their photograph, healer-diviners routinely told me to wait until they had kicked off their leather sandals. Some holy men and very powerful healer-diviners refused to be photographed altogether. Others allowed me to take their picture but insisted that they were too powerful for my camera to capture their image. On several occasions, I asked healer-diviners if I could take their picture anyway. When I developed the photographs, their hands, feet, and faces either did not appear or were blurry, while the rest of the photograph was clear. In another case, a healer-diviner appeared in the photograph as a double image.

Healer-diviners also had mixed views about formal interviews. One told me that I could record our interview, but his words were "too powerful" for my machine [tape recorder] to capture. I recorded the interview anyway, but when I went home to transcribe it, there was nothing on the tape, even though it appeared that the interview had recorded normally. When I mentioned these phenomena, people described them as proof of healer-diviners' powers and laughed at my amazement: "Fatumata, healers are *very* powerful!" Other healer-diviners were pleased that I wanted to interview them, and some even asked me to photograph them after they had donned their finest Saudi-style robes. One even posed for a photograph with the Qur'an in one hand and my tape recorder and microphone in the other, saying, "Show my photograph in America and build my name, Fatumata!"

Aside from a constant concern with authenticity, my interlocutors explained that a healer-diviner's life, like that of a traditional circumciser, entails a considerable amount of suffering (*sabaroo*). Healer-diviners ideally spend every hour of the day in the service of God, their students, and their clients, and they dedicate what little free time they have to meditation and prayer. At night, when everyone sleeps, healer-diviners make medicines, and even when they sleep, they perform dream-divination. Because their livelihood depends on being available to receive clients at all hours, they often forgo travel and other leisure activities. As one of the healer-diviners I worked with in Lisbon told me, "Healer-diviners must stay in one place; we can't go anywhere."

TRANSNATIONAL MUSLIM HEALING-DIVINING

Despite their alleged rootedness, healer-diviners are agents of transnationalism. As such, they should be understood, as Clara Carvalho (2012, 317) puts it, "in the context of the transnational flows that characterize the modern age . . . as one of the best examples of cultural globalization." In Guinea-Bissau, they are an important link between those who migrate and those who stay behind. I heard countless stories of Guineans who consulted healer-diviners to help them get to Portugal. Some healer-diviners, my interlocutors explained, could give clients a bracelet that would make them invisible for twenty-four hours, just enough time to pack a bag and board a plane to Lisbon, no ticket, passport, or visa required. I met a healer-diviner from the neighborhood of Pilon, in Bissau, whom people described as a rich man. People claimed that he had made his fortune from the money and gifts he received from satisfied clients in Europe who "never forgot him."

Healer-diviners in Portugal play a similar role, facilitating transnational communication between immigrants in Europe and their relatives back home in Guinea-Bissau. When the War of June 7 was raging in Bissau, political refugees consulted healer-diviners regularly about their nightmares, their daily struggles with life in Europe, and their plans for returning home. Grieving immigrants consulted healer-diviners to uncover the cause of a relative's sudden or mysterious death back home. Soon after my arrival in Lisbon in 1999,

I was reunited with Aja, an elder Mandinga woman mentioned in the introduction of this book, with whom I had worked closely in Bissau and who had come to Lisbon, fleeing the war. When I heard that she might be in Lisbon, I found her by taking an eight-by-ten framed photograph of her to Rossio square and asking the merchants there if they knew where she was living. When we met, I asked Aja what she thought of life in Lisbon. She told me that it was hard. Her body ached from the cold, and people lived so far away from one other. She felt isolated and alone and suffered from nightmares about the war. She was tired of spending her days watching Brazilian soap operas in a language she did not understand while her daughter worked long hours cleaning apartments and office buildings. In short, she wanted to go home.

Aja's one solace was her weekly trip to central Lisbon to Bairro Santos (the Saints Neighborhood) to visit Master S. The two had grown up together in the town of Farim in Guinea-Bissau. For a small fee, Master S. would read the road, determining whether a client should or should not pursue a particular course of action at a particular time. During my first fieldwork in Lisbon, Master S. was helping Aja plan her return to Guinea-Bissau. She explained, "He dreams for me and tells me the result. If he says the road is sweet, I'll go. If he says it's spoiled, I'll wait." Aja introduced me to Master S., who eventually made me medicine for luck and success in my fieldwork. I also consulted him about how and when to send money and photos to my friends back in the village of Bafata-Oio in Guinea-Bissau. When Ned and I planned to return to Guinea-Bissau in 2003, Master S. read the road for us the day before we boarded our plane to Bissau. Before returning to the United States, we sought fertility medicine (our daughter was born in 2004).[6]

Master S. introduced me to the world of healing-divining in Lisbon. Soon I was spending many of my days visiting healer-diviners, all of whom operated Qur'anic schools, healing practices, or both out of their homes in Lisbon and its exurbs. When healer-diviners leave their homeland to try their luck in Portugal, and as they remake themselves and their religion in Lisbon, they struggle to balance an allegiance to their traditional craft with the need to earn a living in a cosmopolitan environment. Many told me that surviving in Portugal inevitably involves abandoning some techniques and adopting others to meet the demands of two disparate groups: nostalgic African clients, like Aja, who seek authentic healer-diviners who can reproduce treatments from home for reasonable prices, and potentially high-paying Portuguese clients, who have a different set of expectations about the power and capacity of "seers" (*videntes* in Portuguese) and who seek to tap into the "primitive" powers of their former colonial subjects, this time from within their own national borders.

Figure 5.4. Receiving blessings from a Muslim holy man en route to Bissau from Lisbon, 2003. Photograph by an unknown passenger.

Responding to this challenge, many healer-diviners in Lisbon call themselves "astrologers," "masters," or "scientists" and take out ads in local newspapers and magazines. Below is an example of one of these ads, which I translated from Portuguese, from a Lisbon newspaper in 1999:

Great Master
Astrologer Alaaji

African, great scientist, spiritualist, with powerful black and white super magic. Treatment and assistance in problem solving, whatever the case may be, however large, serious, or difficult. Rapid solution. Example: love, health, business, to seize or divert, drive away or attract loved ones, exams, sport, alcohol or drug addiction, spiritual problems, sexual impotence, luck. Future prediction through malevolent spirits and powerful talismans. Long-distance consults possible. Considered to be one of the best professionals in Portugal. Expect a result within two weeks. Payment plan options available. Appointments in person, by letter, or by phone. Monday through Saturdays; except Fridays for religious reasons.[7]

Aside from appearing in newspapers, ads such as these took the form of flyers that were distributed around Lisbon in African restaurants, in squares, in metro tunnels, and outside the mosque. During my 2011 fieldwork on a brief visit to the Algarve, I saw ads that had been placed on the windows of parked cars on the streets of Faro, the region's largest city. An interesting feature of these ads was that they were nearly identical in their format and wording. They included many terms that were not used in the local languages that healers spoke (Fula or Mandinga), such as *talisman* and *super-magic*. Before my fieldwork in Portugal, I had never heard of phone consultations with healer-diviners or payment plans.

When I asked him about the ads, Master B., who had arrived in Lisbon in the late 1980s and ran a healing-divining business out of his apartment near Lisbon's central mosque, responded, "Getting Portuguese clients isn't easy, Fatumata." He proudly showed me a stack of photographs of his "white" (non-African) clients, which must have numbered over a hundred. For Master B., these photographs were proof of his power and fame in Europe and beyond. As he showed me the tools of his trade—ink, pens, prayer beads, cowry shells, sand and water from Mecca, and a stack of tarot cards—Master B. explained that the key to attracting Portuguese clients is flexibility: "White people believe that African healer-diviners are witches or magicians," he told me. "That's why we advertise ourselves as 'great scientists,' 'masters,' 'seers,' or 'astrologers' when we come to Lisbon. Europeans respect those titles." When I asked another healer-diviner, whom I call Master X., about these new titles, he explained, "When Africans have powers that enable them to do great things, Europeans call them witches, who perform magic. But when Europeans have those same powers, they are called scientists and professors, and they become rich and famous." According to Master X., promoting themselves as astrologers or scientists in Portugal is one way in which healer-diviners attempt to earn respect in the eyes of Europeans, respect that was denied to them in the colonial period. But it is more complicated than this. In giving themselves these titles, healer-diviners openly confront persistent colonial attitudes in the postcolonial period, recasting them to their advantage in Lisbon. They also challenge the racism, inequalities, and anti-Muslim sentiment they encounter in their daily lives in Europe, experiences most did not have back at home in West Africa where they were members of a racial majority, where ethnicity rather than race was key in defining one's identity, and where they were surrounded by other Muslims.

Although united in their quest for respect, healer-diviners in Lisbon are in direct competition with each other for clients, and each must constantly defend his authenticity, power, and reputation against rival healer-diviners and disillusioned clients. Furthermore, as they remake themselves and their religion in Portugal, many healers have become increasingly concerned with their identity as true Muslims, whether or not their colleagues, their clients, and other Muslims in Lisbon perceive them as acting in accordance with Islam. The new titles that healer-diviners adopt for themselves in Lisbon and the new approaches they use in their treatments provide new challenges to this identity, as well as to ideas about what constitutes proper practice. For example, Master B. explained that African clients usually approach a healer-diviner with a specific problem or request, allowing the healer-diviner to seek a solution. In contrast, Portuguese clients feel that healer-diviners, as seers, should already know the reason for their clients' visits and should not have to be told. Master B. claimed that he did not mind this new technique and readily adopted it when he came to Lisbon. He explained, "When Portuguese clients come to see me, I ask them how I should divine the reason for their visit: cowry shells, prayer beads, or tarot cards. I don't need them to tell me their problems, because I know the stars. They tell me why my clients have come to me. When I tell my clients, they just look at me and say, 'That's right, Master B.; that's exactly why I've come.'"

But other healer-diviners in Lisbon, especially older ones who practiced most of their lives in West Africa before coming to Portugal, were critical of this new approach, and some even deemed it un-Islamic. One of these skeptics, Master D., trains healers and operates a Qur'anic school in his apartment in the Saints Neighborhood, in the same building as Master S. He told me that he does not claim to know his clients' problems before they relay them to him. "I'm just a healer-diviner," he told me. "I'm not God. How am I supposed to know a person's problem before they tell it to me?" Master D. lamented, however, that his loyalty to more traditional healing-divining approaches has cost him. "I don't have many Portuguese clients," he claimed. "I treat mostly Africans, which is why I'm not a rich man today." Furthermore, Master D. accused those healers who adopt techniques of the "infidels," such as divination with tea leaves and tarot cards, of spoiling the reputation of those healer-diviners who remain loyal to the custom of their craft.

Master D. also accused many of his healer-diviner colleagues in Lisbon of hypocrisy. The same young healer-diviners who abandon custom for more cosmopolitan practices, he explained, are the first to resurrect it for their own monetary gain. He told me that Master B., for example, once asked a friend to dress up as *Kankurang*, the Mandinga boys' initiation masquerade figure, to scare a disillusioned Portuguese client into paying him. However deplorable to Master D., this use (or abuse) of custom was indeed lucrative for Master B., who toward the end of my 1999 fieldwork moved his family from their small apartment near the mosque to a larger, more modern one in Queluz. When I returned to Lisbon for my 2003 fieldwork, Master B. informed me that he had made the hajj two more times.

Figure 5.5. A healer-diviner using his prayer beads in Lisbon, 2003. Photograph by the author.

Figure 5.6. A healer-diviner posing with his new sunglasses, 2001. Photograph by the author.

As healer-diviners remake themselves and their faith in Portugal, they are critical of each other's knowledge and practice of Islam. Young healer-diviners, especially those who attend Friday prayer at the mosque and have made the hajj, are especially concerned with whether or not the traditional methods their colleagues employ constitute proper Islam. Although young healer-diviners respect their elder colleagues' knowledge of the Qur'an's secrets and of their power to manipulate these verses in order to serve their clients, they claimed that these healer-diviners lack an understanding of these verses' meanings. Furthermore, they told me that despite older healer-diviners' ability to recite the Qur'an from memory, few, if any, of them could read or write Arabic.

Master B., who attended Friday prayer at the mosque, had studied Arabic, and had traveled extensively in the Middle East and North Africa, was particularly concerned when he learned that one of his older colleagues in Lisbon had obtained his knowledge of the Qur'an by drinking medicine his father had given him. He explained, "This gives African Muslims a bad name and makes Arabs think we know nothing about Islam." Master B. also told me that in order to compete with young healer-diviners, who are known for their Arabic literacy and mastery of the Qur'an, older healer-diviners purchase photocopies of medicines from their more Arabic-literate colleagues. Whereas some healer-diviners I spoke with considered photocopies an acceptable form of knowledge sharing and cooperation among members of the Muslim healer-diviner community, others, like Master B., were horrified that healer-diviners would give photocopied rather than authentic medicines to paying clients, especially to Portuguese ones, who did not know any better.

My healer-diviner interlocutors in Lisbon were also divided on how to handle occasional requests to use their knowledge and power in more nefarious ways. For example, most claimed to have received at least one request from a Portuguese client to kill someone, usually a boss, spouse, or in-law. Some healer-diviners felt strongly that using their power to destroy human life is contrary to Islam, since Muslims believe that only God should take a life. Others, however, especially those who took out ads in local newspapers and employed not-so-traditional methods, emphasized the need to serve their clients, however amoral or un-Islamic their requests may be. In their view, all Muslim healer-diviners have the God-given power to "build" (*dadaa*) and to "destroy" (*tinyaa*). "If these powers are both explained in the Qur'an," one healer-diviner told me, "how could they be un-Islamic?"

Nevertheless, several healer-diviners feared criticism from their colleagues and members of the wider Muslim community on this point and asked me to conceal their identities if I ever wrote about this issue. One healer-diviner,

Master Y., explained, "It's not difficult to kill someone. All I have to do is write the name of a person, a being God created out of earth, next to an angel or a spirit, beings God created out of fire, and tangle the two together. Within three days, the person will die." I asked Master Y. what God would think of healer-diviners killing people. He explained, "When a healer-diviner ends a person's life, he doesn't share his client's evil feelings toward that person. The healer simply channels the power, power that comes straight from God and the Qur'an. In the eyes of God, it's the one who asks the healer to kill a person who commits a sin, not the healer-diviner himself."

Unlike Master Y., Master D. was critical of healer-diviners who agree to kill people in exchange for money. Although he did not necessarily deny a healer-diviner's power to both build and destroy, he told me that using one's powers to end human life, especially the life of a European, only perpetuates racist stereotypes of African Muslims: "People call us witches and think that we work with the devil. These lies give African Muslims a bad name and make Arabs think that we know nothing about Islam. I'm not a witch. I only work by the power of God. I tell my clients that if they want me to help them, then they must first have faith in God."

Despite healer-diviners' claims that they possess the power to end human life, most confessed to never having used it. As Master X. put it, "I prefer to build, not to destroy. I only use my powers to destroy if it leads to something good." Several healer-diviners told me that they adopt strategies to discourage Portuguese clients from hiring them to kill people without making these clients lose faith in their powers. For example, Master X. told me that he sets the price for killing a person so high that no one would be able to pay it. "A Portuguese client may want someone killed, but most don't have the kind of money to actually hire a healer-diviner to do it," he explained.

To temper their critique of young healer-diviners in Lisbon, the older healer-diviners I worked with brought up the issue of economics. They explained that abuses of power are common and understandable for those who recently arrived in Portugal with nothing. Many young healer-diviners, they told me, joined their family members and friends in the *barracas* (slums) and found work in construction. "They became healer-diviners," one healer-diviner told me, "not because the work was in their head and heart, but because it was less physically exhausting and more profitable than mixing cement and carrying bricks." To set themselves apart from this new, emerging group of healer-diviners, older healer-diviners boasted, "We know no other job than healing-divining."

For their part, young healer-diviners disagreed with their older colleagues' traditional emphasis on simplicity. "Healing-divining is difficult work that requires discipline," one healer-diviner asserted. "We have a right to charge prices that will earn us a decent living." Master B. compared himself to other professionals in Lisbon: "Doctors and engineers have less training than I have, but they have much more to show for it; they are respected people." Young healer-diviners also had different ideas about suffering and its alleged positive effects on identity: "We've spent our entire lives suffering," one healer-diviner told me. "Now it's our turn to rest."

HEALING-DIVINING AND GENDER:
A FEMALE ASTROLOGER IN LISBON

Not only has the encounter between healer-diviners and global Islam in Lisbon created divisions based on generation, it also has done so in the realm of gender. When I asked people in Guinea-Bissau and Portugal about healing-divining and gender, everyone I spoke with insisted that both men and women can be healers. Despite this, I never met a female Muslim healer-diviner in Guinea-Bissau, although I knew of several indigenous ones. When I engaged people on this point, they assured me that female Muslim healer-diviners do exist, especially in Senegal, Guinea-Conakry, and the Gambia, neighboring countries with Muslim majorities and where women study the Qur'an as rigorously as men do. They explained that few women in Guinea-Bissau have the desire or opportunity to pursue Qur'anic study, and some men claimed that women lack the faith and discipline necessary to be healer-diviners. For their part, women agreed that men are better suited than women to be healer-diviners. "That's our custom," they told me. It is not that women believe they are incapable of learning the skills of the craft; they simply feel that their limited time and energy, at least for the majority of their lives, are better spent in the fields, at the market, or with their children.[8]

I did, however, meet one female Muslim healer-diviner in Lisbon, Master C. At the time, she was a large, relatively successful woman in her early sixties. She lived in an apartment complex in a Lisbon exurb with a sizeable Guinean immigrant population, a short bus or metro ride from Rossio square. Master C. was an active member of the Association of Guinean Immigrants in Portugal. She attended monthly meetings and worked closely with the group's president to plan events that brought all Guinean immigrants together, despite ethnic and religious differences.[9] She told me that she avoided the Muslim associations and culture clubs because she "didn't like their politics," though I often saw her at Maternal Kin Club events throughout the years.

After living in Lisbon for over thirty years, Master C. wore only Muslim clothing, ate only Guinean food, and did not speak Portuguese. She told me that other than traveling occasionally to London to visit her daughters and going to central Lisbon to buy things from the homeland, she did not leave the neighborhood. Indeed, whenever I visited, I found her at home, ironing or watching the news or reruns of *Buffy the Vampire Slayer.* "And people say that there are no witches in the land of the white people," she remarked one day as we watched together.

Although I spent a lot of time with Master C. during my 1999 fieldwork in Lisbon, she did not tell me she was a healer-diviner until several years later. One day, when I was telling her about the work I was doing with Muslim healer-diviners, she told me that she was one and offered to show me her *iran* (spirit), which she had acquired from a Manjaco village in Guinea-Bissau. She led me to her bedroom, reached under the bed, and pulled out a small, round vessel made of clay. Grayish in color and covered with dust and cobwebs, it contained two animal horns. When I asked Master C. to tell me about her healing-divining practice, she explained, "When clients come to me for a consultation, they buy some alcohol and bring some money. They tell me why they have come and ask the spirit for what they want. They don't pay anything more until they see a result."

Master C. told me that unlike other healer-diviners in Lisbon, she does not "eat" (spend) any of the money she earns through her practice. Instead, she saves it and eventually returns the money (*torna boka*, literally, "return the mouth") to the Manjaco people who still "own" the spirit. She told me that she had recently asked the spirit to help her daughters overcome their drug addiction in London. Eventually, Master C. wants to retire the Manjaco spirit altogether and shift the focus of her healing-divining practice to cowry shell divination. "That way, I can keep the money," she told me.

I asked Master C. if she considered her practice a Muslim one. She thought for a moment, and just when I thought she might not have understood the question, she responded, "It's not Muslim, but I'm a Muslim, so it doesn't matter. My people, the Beafada, are Muslims, and they work with spirits. All Muslims go to the spirits of the Kristons [non-Muslims], even if they don't admit it, and Muslim healer-diviners are lying if they claim they don't work with spirits. All they do is eat people's money."

Like the older, more established healer-diviners I worked with in Lisbon, Master C. remained rooted in her Muslim identity, which was shaped as much by African custom as by the five pillars of faith, including prayer and fasting during Ramadan. For Master C., as for many women in Guinea-Bissau and Portugal, working with spirits and working with the Qur'an were essentially one in the same. In this view, religion does not exist apart from the practices of daily life (in this case, healing-divining) in which it finds expression. Master C. did not attend Friday prayer at the mosque and did not feel the need to emulate other Muslims in Lisbon; the Beafada have, after all, been good Muslims for centuries. Like young healer-diviners in Lisbon, however, Master C. was not opposed to marketing her skills to potentially high-paying clients in order to improve her life in Lisbon. "Whether people like it or not, we [Africans] are here to stay, and we have a right to use what we know to make a decent living."[10]

When I returned to Lisbon for my 2003 fieldwork, I visited Maria at her apartment in central Lisbon. I asked about her son, and she told me that he was doing well. Her own health, however, had taken a turn for the worse. Every night before going to bed, she felt light-headed and short of breath. She slept fitfully and had frequent nightmares. When the results of countless medical tests were inconclusive, the doctor diagnosed her mysterious condition as "nerves." One night, Maria explained to me, she dreamed she was on her balcony, hanging laundry, when she tripped over a flowerpot. An African man dressed in a long white robe appeared suddenly and grabbed her arm, preventing her from falling eight stories to her death.

To Maria, the significance of her dream was clear: perhaps Alaaji S., whom she had not seen for over a year, could cure her illness. After a consultation, he asked her to sacrifice an egg at every crossroads from her apartment to her workplace and to wash her body with liquid medicine each day at sunrise and sunset. She gave him a large sum of money shortly after her condition improved. The next time she visited Alaaji S., she noticed that he had a new TV. "There's my money," Maria told me she had thought. She stopped seeing Alaaji S. but sent him several referrals. Soon, he started sending her a portion of the money he earned from consultations with these new clients. "Before long," Maria told me, "I had earned back all of my money and I bought myself a brand-new TV, just like Alaaji S.'s."

During my 2017 fieldwork, I met Maria for breakfast in central Lisbon. She had retired from her cleaning job and was taking advantage of Lisbon's now robust tourist economy by renting out her apartment while she lived with relatives. She asked how my research was going and then handed me a piece of paper filled with Arabic writing and geometrical shapes. She explained that an African man had given it to her on the streets of Lisbon after she had told him she wasn't sleeping well. She asked me if I could decipher any of the writing and if I knew whether it would help or hurt her. While I could not read the writing, I assured her that it was not a "curse" (her term) but was rather meant to help. I asked her if she had been back to see Alaaji S., and she told me she had not. She worried that her fascination with African healer-diviners and their magic might become a vice, and she was working hard to avoid vices in her life, which was hard to do, she claimed, as she struggled with new health challenges and making ends meet in what she described as a "changed Lisbon."

NOTES

1. A rigid separation between the powers of God and the bush rarely holds in West Africa. Kpelle healers in Liberia as described by Bellman (1975) claim that their medicines help people only when Xala (God) agrees to it. See Mommersteeg (2012, 24) for a discussion about the challenge of separating "doctrinal Islam" from "maraboutage" in Mali.

2. Healer-diviners are part of the group of nobles or freedmen in the Mande caste system (Conrad and Frank 1995, 7). See Eickelman (1977), Schaffer and Cooper (1987), Lambek (1993), McIntyre (1996), Sanneh (1997), Mommersteeg (2012), and Carvalho (2012) for accounts of Muslim healer-diviners in Africa or, in the case of Carvalho, among Africans in Europe.

3. Amulets figure prominently in Scottish explorer Mungo Park's eighteenth-century and nineteenth-century descriptions of life in the Senegambia. He described them as "Koranic verses encased in small leather pouches" worn "by animists and Muslims alike to guard against a variety of evils" (cited in Quinn 1972, 54).

4. The Mandinga term *duwaa* comes from the Arabic *du'a*, translated as "'[c]alling' upon God in supplication or petition. Spontaneous and individual prayer, as distinguished from the formal prayer service of salat" (Denny 2016, 403).

5. Einarsdóttir (2004, 115) makes a similar point about non-Muslim healers in Guinea-Bissau. Healers who demand initial payment rather than waiting until their clients' situations improve are described locally as "more scoundrels or money-makers than respectable professionals."

6. Other scholars highlight healer-diviners as agents of transnationalism. Senegalese desiring to migrate to Europe often call on marabouts to "ease the migratory path" (Riccio and degli Uberti 2013, 216). Many of the consultations that Graw (2012, 29) witnessed during his fieldwork in the Senegambia focused on what diviners and their clients called "the path of travel," or migration.

7. Healer-diviners in Madagascar call themselves "astrologers," even though they do not use astrological data in their work. They divine "the right course of action to be undertaken according to a variety of systems, some of which are of Arabic origin" (Bloch 1968, 292).

8. See Gemmeke (2009) for a study of two female marabouts in Dakar. Gemmeke (2009, 129) describes healing-divining, what she terms *Islamic esoteric knowledge*, as "a male-dominated field" in Senegal. Despite local claims that women could be marabouts, she met only three during her fieldwork, although

she heard of others. Mommersteeg (2012, 56) describes his visit to Maimouna Niafo, a female marabout in Djenné, after people assured him that "female marabouts don't exist."

9. Despite the organization's stated goal of inclusivity, it still attracted mostly non-Muslims, and Muslims described it as a non-Muslim group.

10. See Rasmussen (2006, chap. 8) for a discussion of the complex relationship between female herbalists and male marabouts among Tuareg in Niger. While some imagine this relationship as complementary—"like husbands and wives"—tensions are common.

"WELCOME BACK FROM MECCA!"

Reimagining the Hajj

DURING MY FIRST PERIOD OF fieldwork in Lisbon, Seku, whom I called Baba, or "father" in Mandinga, fulfilled his lifelong dream of making the hajj. Seku was one of a few Guinean immigrants whom I had actually known in Guinea-Bissau before I began working in Lisbon, and our shared experiences in the homeland provided a special depth to our relationship in the diaspora. In Lisbon, Seku worked as a Muslim healer-diviner, and over the years, he had built up an impressive clientele, which allowed him to save enough money to both build a house in his hometown of Farim in northern Guinea-Bissau to which he hoped to return one day (I learned during my 2011 fieldwork that he had done just this) and to go to Mecca to make the hajj.

When I heard that Seku had returned from Mecca, Ned and I went to visit him in his small rented room in Bairro Santos. Before catching the tram, we stopped at Rossio square to buy some tobacco from Guinea-Bissau. At that time, the police were cracking down on the merchants, who were selling without permits. Making sure that no police were watching, I discreetly handed a Fula merchant some money, and he pulled out three long tobacco leaves, which he rolled carefully into a small plastic bag. As I slipped the tobacco into my handbag, I told him we were on our way to see Seku, and the merchant told us to give Seku his greetings.

At Seku's rented room, we announced our arrival, saying "Asalamalekum" outside his door. He responded, "Malekumsalam," a clear signal that he was not with a client and that we could enter. Seku was sitting on a colorful prayer rug in his usual spot on the floor. Ned and I both extended our right hands in turn as we greeted him with his new title, Al-Hajj, reserved for men who have made the Mecca pilgrimage. He was dressed in a long, white robe with a Saudi-style head covering, a sure sign of his now "cosmopolitan" Muslim identity (see Schulz 2012). I handed Al-Hajj the local tobacco, and he showered us with Mandinga blessings. He then prepared his VCR to show us the tape he had brought back from Mecca, while we looked through photographs of him at all the sacred sites. A few of the photos featured other Guinean Mandinga immigrants from Lisbon, several of whom Ned and I enthusiastically identified. Al-Hajj informed us that a total of sixteen people from the Mandinga immigrant community in Lisbon had made the pilgrimage that year, an impressive number. As we watched the video, Al-Hajj narrated the major events: how he had "stoned Satan" at Mina and how he had finally managed with all his strength to push through the crowd to touch the Kaaba's famous Black Stone. Lighting his pipe, he told us about the scorching heat, about the hunger he had barely endured, and how he had gotten lost for twenty-four hours, nearly missing the bus to Arafat.

When we had finished watching the video, Al-Hajj reached into the closet and pulled out his suitcase, which was full of souvenirs from Mecca: prayer beads, head scarves, and costume jewelry. He pulled out a golden canteen filled with water from the sacred spring of Zamzam and poured Ned and me each a small cup. He instructed us to think of something we desired, whether health, luck, success, or fertility, and to drink the water, leaving a small amount. When we finished drinking, Al-Hajj poured the remaining water from our cups into our hands and told us to wash our heads, faces, and chests with it, in order to complete our requests to God. Next, he opened a plastic bag and gave us each four dates to eat. Finally, he reached into his suitcase and handed Ned a shiny golden ring, which he instructed him to place on my finger. We thanked Al-Hajj and gave him Mandinga blessings as he tapped his forehead with his right hand, saying, "Amini" (amen).

Al-Hajj explained to us that over the next few weeks he expected to receive many guests—relatives, friends, and clients—all of whom would want to welcome him back from Mecca. He would have to share something from Mecca with each person who came. I asked Al-Hajj how he felt now that he had made the pilgrimage. He responded, "I feel very different, more relaxed and at peace with myself and with God. When you go to Mecca, you leave war, problems, and all bad things behind. There are none of these things in Mecca, only peace." Al-Hajj explained that after making the pilgrimage to Mecca, he was more confident about the prospect of dying: "If death were to suddenly find me, I have now fulfilled one of Islam's most important obligations," he told us. Suddenly, Al-Hajj's new alarm clock—a miniature replica of Mecca, perched on top of his television set—illuminated and sounded, informing him that it was time for afternoon prayers. This was the first time that I had ever seen him excuse himself to pray in the presence of clients or guests. Soon after Al-Hajj completed his prayers, two clients arrived, and he escorted us out of his room for their consultations. After seeing his clients, Al-Hajj invited Ned and me back in and told us that he expected to receive many more clients now that he had made the hajj. Indeed, from the perspective of a healer-diviner like Seku, the pilgrimage to Mecca is both a transformative spiritual experience and a boon to one's business.

When I initially went to Guinea-Bissau in the late 1990s, I was a graduate student who was interested in learning about a topic that at the time epitomized the local: life-course rituals, especially girls' initiation. But in engaging my interlocutors on the subject of traditional Mandinga rituals, I was surprised by how often conversations with people, whether old or young, drifted away from Guinea-Bissau and toward Saudi Arabia. My field notes are full of stories of people who dreamed of one day either sending a parent to Mecca or making the pilgrimage themselves. In both Guinea-Bissau and Portugal, people shared with me their concerns about obtaining the necessary funds, ascertaining the most appropriate time to go, and how what one would see in Mecca might forever change one's life.

About five months into my fieldwork in Guinea-Bissau, I was overjoyed when Jiba (mentioned in chap. 4), a respected elder woman in Bissau whose mother had been a traditional circumciser, agreed to let me interview her about Mandinga girls' initiation rituals and the practice of female circumcision, my first recorded interview on my official research topic. When I arrived at Jiba's compound with butterflies in my stomach on the morning of our scheduled interview, I found her sitting on the veranda dressed in her finest Muslim outfit. After we exchanged greetings, she informed me that while I would soon learn much about Mandinga initiation, she first wanted to tell me about the hajj. Jiba had made the pilgrimage to Mecca the year before my arrival in Bissau, and it was still very much on her mind. As she shared with me the details of her encounter with Islam's most sacred places, I began to realize the importance of the pilgrimage for Mandinga. Indeed, the hajj is perhaps one of the most dramatic and meaningful experiences of their religious lives; it is also, I soon learned, an experience fraught with ambivalence. On the one hand, it is the time at which Mandinga feel most intensely their belonging in the *umma*, the global Muslim community. On the other hand, however, the hajj often provokes deep feelings of estrangement from this same community.

It is this sense of ambivalence that I hope to capture in this chapter as I recount Mandinga experiences of the hajj. I show how the sacred pilgrimage engages both local and global identities and shapes (and remakes) the religious imagination. Although the allure and experience of the hajj are profoundly global, I reveal the local cosmology that frames people's experiences of it. This emphasis on locality stems in part from the frustrations Mandinga feel when their own engagement with global Islam does not match their expectations for full inclusion in the umma—when they feel different, marginalized, and excluded—and how they respond to these feelings and experiences.

As anthropologists continue to shift their focus away from village contexts to the experiences of displacement, tourism, and diaspora communities, it is an especially appropriate time to reexamine the place of pilgrimage in people's religious lives (Lamb 2000; Dubisch and Winkelman 2005). The hajj has long been—and continues to be—perhaps the most dramatic symbol of the unity and diversity of Islam. As such, it plays a particularly important role as Guinean Muslims remake themselves and their religion and as they look increasingly beyond Africa for a "truer," more "authentic" model of Islam to which to aspire than the one they have always known.

In this chapter, I explore how Guinean Muslims in Lisbon reimagine the hajj, themselves, and Islam. Specifically, I highlight Mandinga experiences of the pilgrimage to Mecca, their personal encounters with Islam's most sacred sites, and the inner transformation that these encounters engender. I also examine the varied social consequences that the journey holds as Mandinga immigrants attempt to differentiate African custom from global Islam and as they struggle for full participation in the umma. I highlight how and why my Mandinga interlocutors in Lisbon decided to make the hajj, how the journey changed them personally, and how it affected their relationships with the communities, both local and global, of which they are a part. The hajj, an event of global importance to Muslims, shapes how Mandinga imagine themselves as Africans, as Mandinga, and as Muslims. I demonstrate that local ideas about gender and the life course, however, remain prevalent even when Mandinga emigrate to Portugal, and these continue to shape immigrants' perceptions and experiences of the hajj. I draw here on classic and contemporary works in the anthropology of pilgrimage (e.g., Coleman and Eade 2004; Delaney 1990; Turner and Turner 1978; Thayer 1992; Eickelman and Piscatori 1990; Morinis 1992). In exploring *buunyaa*, or "welcome back from Mecca," ceremonies and a case of "untimely pilgrimage," I argue that the hajj, like other Mandinga life-course rituals I have explored thus far, is a powerful site of tension in Lisbon as Guinean Muslims remake Islam in Europe. I begin with a brief description of the hajj.[1]

THE HAJJ

The pilgrimage to Mecca is the fifth pillar of Islam, in addition to the declaration of faith, prayer, almsgiving, and fasting during the holy month of Ramadan, and is arguably one of Islam's most dramatic ritual practices. It occurs annually during the last month of the lunar year and is required once in a Muslim person's lifetime if he or she is physically and financially able. Making the hajj involves extensive preparation and planning, which has become big business for travel agencies and tour groups (see Schulz 2012), which aid in this process. Only a certain number of people are allowed to make the pilgrimage each year, and there are quotas from each of the Muslim countries. Individuals must thus apply to make the hajj and are not necessarily guaranteed a slot. These logistical details provide a degree of challenge, even mystification, for Muslims in under-represented countries, those who live on "the edge of Islam" (McIntosh 2009).

On arriving in Mecca, men perform ablutions and don the ihram, the pre-scribed dress for all male pilgrims. This garment consists of two seamless white pieces of cloth, one that wraps around the waist and reaches to the knees and the other that drapes over the left shoulder and attaches around the torso. Male pilgrims must leave their heads uncovered and wear only sandals. In contrast to the men, women wear traditional clothing from their respective countries. As such, their dress is considerably more varied than that of their male counter-parts. Women's clothing must be modest, however, covering all parts of the body except the hands and face. Pilgrims' gendered clothing styles underscore the unity and diversity of the Muslim world: while the ihram represents unity, women's varied dress reflects the "diverse and creative character of Islam as a global community of faith" (Denny 2016, 123).

The term *ihram* refers not only to pilgrims' special attire during the hajj but also to the state of purity required of them. All pilgrims, male and female alike, must abstain from sexual activity, contact with the opposite sex, wearing perfume or jewelry, trimming their nails, quarreling, or harming any living thing. Men must either remove or at least trim their facial hair. Once ready, the pilgrims first enter the sacred mosque, stepping with their right foot through the Gate of Peace to visit the Kaaba, a large rectangular black stone structure. The Kaaba is draped with the kiswa, a black cloth with gold-embroidered Qur'anic verses, which is replaced every year. The pilgrims circle the Kaaba seven times counterclockwise, each time either touching the Black Stone or, if that is not possible due to the crowds, simply extending their arms toward it. The Kaaba has a centering power for Muslims everywhere. It is the focal

Figure 6.1. The wall hanging of the Kaaba given to me by Maternal Kin Club members, hanging in my office, 2019. Photograph by the author.

point toward which they orient their prayers and the place where prayers are considered to be the most powerful and effective. It also determines the direction in which the deceased are placed in their graves, as I discussed in chapter 4. The orienting nature of this structure for Muslims was especially evident in Lisbon, because nearly every Mandinga household I knew of had a wall hanging of the Kaaba in their apartment, which they had usually purchased outside Lisbon's central mosque. In several cases, this was the only decorative item in a person's apartment, and it was usually the first thing that a Guinean Muslim immigrant acquired after arriving in Lisbon and finding a place to live. After I completed my first year of fieldwork in Lisbon, Maternal Kin Club members presented me with one to take back to the United States to remember Lisbon and Mecca.[2]

After circling the Kaaba and offering prayers in the sacred mosque, the pilgrims collect water from the sacred spring of Zamzam. Muslims believe that the angel Gabriel uncovered this spring with his wing when Hagar and her son were lost in the desert and were desperately searching for water. Muslims everywhere consider water from Zamzam to be the purest, most sacred water in the world, and pilgrims often bring several bottles of it home with them to share with those who have not yet made the hajj. After visiting the Well of Zamzam, pilgrims perform the *sa'y*, which involves walking or jogging back and forth seven times between the two hills of al-Safa and al-Marwa. This point completes the "lesser hajj." At this point, pilgrims must either get a haircut or have a small piece of hair removed in symbolic fashion before embarking on the "greater pilgrimage," the rites that take place at Arafat, Muzdalifah, and Mina.

The pilgrims travel next to Arafat, a vast, arid plain where thousands of tents are erected to accommodate them. Here the pilgrims reflect on the Prophet Ibrahim's decision to sacrifice his only son, Ishmael. Some perform the "standing ceremony," in which they stand in meditation and praise of God from before noon until just before sunset. Others may climb the Mount of Mercy. The standing ceremony is considered to be the heart of the hajj, and if pilgrims fail to observe it, "the whole pilgrimage will be null and void" (Denny 2016, 125). After evening prayers, the pilgrims travel to Muzdalifah, an open plain lying between Arafat and the town of Mina. Here the pilgrims collect either forty-nine or seventy small stones to take to Mina.

After midnight, the pilgrims begin the journey to Mina, where they will stay for two nights. Over the next three days, the pilgrims perform the "stoning of the devil" ceremony, in which they throw the stones they collected at Muzdalifah at three whitewashed stone pillars representing Satan. They perform this in honor of Ibrahim's and Ishmael's courage. As Ibrahim was preparing to sacrifice his son, Satan is said to have appeared to Ishmael, urging him not to follow through with God's command. Ishmael picked up some stones and threw them at the devil. The stoning ceremony is thought to symbolize the pilgrims' own struggles with temptation and the rejection of evil.

Before returning to Mecca, each pilgrim must sacrifice a goat or sheep in commemoration of God's replacement of Ishmael by a ram. This is followed by the Festival of Sacrifice, which Muslims in West Africa commonly term Tabaski. On this day, Muslims everywhere sacrifice an animal in symbolic communion with the Mecca pilgrims. As such, the Feast of Sacrifice connects Muslims in the periphery with those at the center, in Mecca. After completing the specific obligations of the hajj, many pilgrims end their journeys by traveling to the city of Medina, about three hundred miles north of Mecca, where they visit the sacred sites of the Prophet Mohammed's mosque and tomb. Although this visit is not officially part of the hajj and is not required, pilgrims consider it a way of showing respect to the Prophet and of gaining his favor. As a hadith states, "Whoever visits my tomb, my intercession will be granted to him" (Denny 2016, 128).

Figure 6.2. Alaaji Djana in Mecca on the hajj, early 2000s. Photographer unknown.

Figure 6.3. Al-Hajj Sané in Mecca on the hajj, late 1999. Photographer unknown.

TRAVEL AND TRANSFORMATION: THE
CULTURAL VALUE OF PILGRIMAGE

In order to understand the importance of the hajj for Guinean Muslims in Lisbon, it is first necessary to address the cultural centrality of travel for them more generally. While I focus specifically on Mandinga culture, which I know best, much of what I describe here is also true for members of other Muslim ethnic groups in Guinea-Bissau, such as Fula and Beafada peoples. Mandinga value travel of all kinds, whether to a village to seek blessings from a renowned holy man, to the Middle East or North Africa to study Arabic or the Qur'an, or to Europe to "try one's luck." Travel is not new to Mandinga, who have a long history of movement and migration for the purposes of conquest, trade, and religious proselytizing (Schaffer and Cooper 1987, 5) and are very proud of that history. When I first explained my research project to people in the village of Bafata-Oio in Guinea-Bissau, they were less impressed with my desire to study their culture than with the fact that I had traveled all the way from America to do it.

When about halfway through my stay, Ned and I had the opportunity to take a road trip to Mali, the place from where Guinean Mandinga originally came, our hosts were delighted and encouraged us to go, and our firsthand experience of the Mande heartland deepened our relationships with the villagers when we returned. "You have seen the birthplace of the Mandinga people," they would suddenly say to us, even months after the trip. Indeed, the value of journeying great distances to seek knowledge, to deepen one's relationship with God, or to improve one's life conditions is captured by the Mandinga proverb *Ni I mang taamoo, I buka je* ("If you don't walk [travel], you won't see"), which I heard often during my fieldwork in both Guinea-Bissau and Portugal.[3]

Travel has social consequences as well as personal benefits, because it creates boundaries and distinctions (see Eickelman and Piscatori 1990). This was evident in my experience with my interlocutors in both field sites. The Muslim healer-diviners I described in chapter 5, for example, had earned their reputations in part by traveling to other Senegambian countries, such as Senegal or the Gambia, to apprentice with a renowned healer-diviner, or to the Middle East or North Africa to study Arabic or the Qur'an. Similarly, those who make the hajj earn the respect of everyone in their home communities and in the global Muslim community, which is demonstrated in part by the official titles that pilgrims adopt when they return: Alaaji (or Al-Hajj) for men and Aja for women. This respect can also be observed in the clothing styles that those who make the pilgrimage choose to don on their return.

People were very articulate about the transformative power of travel, especially to Mecca. Many explained that "a person is not the same" when he or she returns from making the pilgrimage. To help me understand this transformation, Yaya told me the story of "Cat's Trip to Mecca" one night as we drank tea in Bafata-Oio. I heard similar versions of the story in Lisbon.

Cat's Trip to Mecca

One day, Cat called all the mice in his compound and announced to them that he was going to make the pilgrimage to Mecca. The mice were impressed but also surprised, and even a little bit dubious. "Could it be true?" they asked. "Would Cat really go all the way to Mecca to make the pilgrimage? Perhaps he's just fooling us again." But soon after Cat told this to the mice, he informed them of the day he planned to return, and he left. The mice discussed the issue and devised a plan. They decided to meet Cat at the airport when he returned from Mecca. That way, they could see for themselves if he was telling the truth. "If Cat really makes the pilgrimage to Mecca, then he'll return a changed Cat; he'll be uninterested in chasing us," the mice agreed.

But the mice knew from experience to be cautious when dealing with Cat. As soon as Cat left, they started to dig an underground tunnel all the way to the airport. The mice worked and worked, and they finished the tunnel on the day that Cat was scheduled to return. They built a door to the tunnel right near the main entrance to the airport, and they waited for Cat. When Cat arrived, he saw the mice and immediately started to chase them. Startled but prepared, the mice ran into their underground tunnel and slammed the door. They didn't stop running until they were safely home. The mice knew from Cat's behavior that he had lied to them: he had not made the pilgrimage to Mecca. Cat was furious that the mice had discovered the truth. After that day, the mice never trusted Cat again.

In explaining the story's meaning, people told me that when a person makes the hajj, he or she "leaves all bad things behind" and returns with a "clean heart" and a "clean head." A person who has made the pilgrimage to Mecca is incapable of harming another person, they claimed, or any living creature. Had Cat truly made the hajj, he would not have been able to chase even mice, his most natural of enemies. Indeed, Mandinga described the hajj as so transformative that making it would give a cat, or any other animal or living being, the ability to overcome the most instinctual of desires. When I asked people to identify the source of this transformative power, they explained that it was "seeing" (in the sense of experiencing firsthand) the sacred sites of Mecca and Medina, especially the Kaaba. My interlocutors who had made the pilgrimage described seeing the Kaaba with their own eyes and touching the Black Stone as the most important and meaningful experiences of their lives. The transformative power of the hajj and its sacred sites is captured in the following excerpt from an interview I conducted with Alaaji B. in Lisbon:

MJ: How did you feel when you went to Mecca?

Alaaji B.: When you go to Mecca, I don't mean the city itself, but the Kaaba, that thing we circle around, hey! The first time I saw the Kaaba, I cried because I never thought I'd make it there. If you're a true Muslim and you reach the Kaaba, all of your ideas about the world no longer matter. The only things that matter are God and the next world.

MJ: Did you feel different after you made the hajj? Does a Muslim change once he or she makes the hajj?

Alaaji B.: Yes, a person does truly change. Ever since I went to Mecca, God put something inside me; I can hardly believe it myself. Before I went to Mecca, I often went to *discotecas*. But ever since I returned from Mecca, I don't even like the thought of going dancing. Now only my house, my wife, and my children matter to me. I stay at home and read the Qur'an instead of going out. I just think of God and the next world. I used to fear many things, but I'm a stronger person since I went to Mecca. When you go to Mecca, you see things that you can't see anywhere else in the world; you only find them in Mecca. Where else can you see millions of people who have the same one thing on their mind and in their hearts? Nowhere but Mecca! After the pilgrimage, you only think of good things; it's very difficult for you to forget God.

Not only do Mecca returnees feel different after making the hajj, they act differently as well, and others treat them differently. Aside from carrying themselves with a new air of confidence and piety, Mecca returnees are expected to set an example for others to follow. They must now pray five times a day without fail and fast during the holy month of Ramadan. Returnees are reminded of these new expectations by the title that will henceforth become a part of their name (and may even replace it) and, by extension, their identity. I suggest that their status as changed people, however, is captured most dramatically and given a distinctly local flavor in the buunyaa ceremony, which Mandinga in Lisbon hold to officially welcome back the pilgrims from Mecca.

PILGRIMAGE AND PURITY:
WELCOME-BACK-FROM-MECCA CEREMONIES

Buunyaa ceremonies are held for forty days after the return of the pilgrims from Mecca. Although I was told that buunyaa ceremonies are also held in

Guinea-Bissau, no one I knew made the pilgrimage during my fieldwork, so I was unable to actually experience one. I suggest, however, that the buunyaa takes on new meaning and importance for Mandinga immigrants in Lisbon as they become part of a large and diverse group of Muslim immigrants from outside of Africa and as they remake Islam (and religion more generally) in Europe. During my fieldwork in Lisbon, buunyaa ceremonies took place every weekend during the forty-day period after the hajj season and were especially joyous occasions for members of the Mandinga immigrant community. On several occasions, these ceremonies took on a transnational, cosmopolitan flair, as Mandinga immigrants from Senegal or the Gambia who were living in France, Spain, England, or Germany traveled to Lisbon to attend them. This was seldom, if ever, the case with other life-course rituals I attended in Lisbon and have described in previous chapters, which were local events attended exclusively by Mandinga, and on occasion, Fula immigrants, in Lisbon. Despite their cosmopolitan feel, however, buunyaa were quintessentially Mandinga events that engaged local beliefs about Islam, pilgrimage, and the life course.

My interlocutors explained, for example, that people who return from making the hajj remain in a state of purity for forty days. This state of purity is the basis for an important reciprocal relationship that ensues between the Mecca returnees in a given year and members of the wider immigrant community. Community members are obligated to hold a buunyaa for their relatives or friends who have returned from Mecca during the forty-day period in order to welcome them back, to mark and celebrate publicly their newly acquired status, and to share the benefits of their state of purity with others. As Alaaji B. explained, "We believe that Mecca is the house of God and the Prophet Mohammed. We must welcome back every person who goes to this house and returns because now they are respected people. They have seen the house of God and the Prophet. We must hold a buunyaa for them because before they made the hajj they were people, but now they are different people, people who are respected in God's eyes. That's why we hold these ceremonies."

During the forty-day period of purity, Mecca returnees have an obligation to the community at large, especially to their fellow Muslims who have not yet had the opportunity to make the hajj. It is up to the returnees' relatives and friends to provide the space in which the returned pilgrims may carry out their ritual obligations. Mandinga believe that God will grant any request that a Mecca returnee makes during the forty-day period. Community members with specific problems or special requests—for example, a barren woman who desires a child, an undocumented immigrant who wants desperately to secure a residence permit to stay legally in Portugal, or a student who needs to perform well on an upcoming exam—will attend as many buunyaas as possible in order to optimize blessings from the Mecca returnees during the forty-day period.

Those who host buunyaa ceremonies also receive special benefits. Indeed, holding a buunyaa in one's home is thought to be an effective way of ensuring good fortune, because the blessings conferred at the ceremony are said to literally settle in the place where they are given. This was certainly on Aminata's mind as she planned her husband's buunyaa on his return from Mecca. Aminata and Alaaji B. had been renting a small apartment in central Lisbon since their arrival in Portugal, and they eventually hoped to save enough money to buy a larger apartment in the exurbs. Aminata explained that when she shared her plans to hold her husband's buunyaa with other community members, they told her that their apartment was too small and encouraged her to rent a larger space so that the guests could feel at ease. But Aminata felt strongly that holding the buunyaa outside of her own place would be a waste of the blessings. In the end, she decided to hold the buunyaa in her small apartment, and the ceremony was very well attended. When I returned to Lisbon two years later, I visited the couple in their newly purchased, spacious apartment located twenty minutes outside of Lisbon by train. I admired the place and recalled Aminata's dilemma regarding Alaaji B.'s buunyaa. She recounted, "I refused to hold Alaaji's buunyaa anywhere but in our apartment. If we had held it elsewhere, where would the blessings have gone? When the guests left, the blessings would have just stayed there for nothing. I didn't listen to those people who told me that our place was too small. We held the ceremony at our place, and the blessings stayed with us. Look at us now; God has given us our own spacious house."

I attended many buunyaa ceremonies during my fieldwork in Lisbon, and although there are some variations, they share a common structure. The women in charge of cooking the afternoon meal meet early in the morning and sometimes even the night before to make preparations and begin cooking. Guests arrive around noon, well before the sacred hour of two o'clock in the afternoon, the time when the elders and holy men give the blessings. The guest of honor dresses in his or her finest outfit, usually Saudi-style clothing purchased in Mecca, and sits on prayer rugs that have been laid out on the floor in the central room. Men who have previously made the hajj join the guest of honor, whether male or female, in the central room, while women who have previously made the hajj gather in a separate room. Elder men, healer-diviners, Qur'anic scholars, and postmenopausal women also gather in the central room to read aloud from the Qur'an.

As the guests arrive, they greet the elders and holy men, as well as the guest of honor, in the central room. Those who wish give them small offerings of money or kola nuts, and the elders announce their names at the sacred hour, adding a personal touch to the general blessings conferred. Young women and children gather in a separate room where they visit, waiting for the blessings and the afternoon meal. Unmarried men sit in another room. If the apartment becomes too crowded with guests, members of this group move outside. At two o'clock, the scholars and elders recite the Al-Fatiha and give dozens of blessings: "May God give you a long life," "May God bless you with health and happiness," and, most important in the case of a buunyaa, "May God show you the road to Mecca." All present at the ceremony extend their hands, palms up, as the Al-Fatiha is read; then they respond to each blessing by tapping their right hand (or sometimes both hands) to their foreheads, responding, "Amini." After the final blessing is said, they rub their hands over their heads, faces, and chests, literally bathing their bodies with the blessings and ensuring that the blessings stay with them. Then the women serve the afternoon meal.

Food at a buunyaa typically consists of rice or couscous with a sauce containing halal meat (goat or lamb) purchased near the mosque. Each group described above, based on age, gender, and marital status, also eats separately, with each designated room receiving one large bowl that everyone shares. I have described elsewhere the social and spiritual benefits of eating from a common bowl for Mandinga (Johnson 2016) in both ritual and nonritual contexts. I suggest, however, that sharing food takes on an even greater importance at a buunyaa. In her book on childhood in Sri Lanka, Bambi Chapin (2014, 65) describes the common belief in South Asian cultures that "sharing food creates and affirms sameness" and, beyond this, has the power to change who one is. This same idea sheds light on why my Mandinga interlocutors who had not yet been to Mecca told me that they would never miss the opportunity to eat a meal at a buunyaa. In sharing food with people who have been to Mecca, Mandinga ingest the sacred, enhancing their own spirituality and bolstering their chances of eventually going to Mecca.

While Mandinga in Guinea-Bissau and Portugal often eat with spoons, food served at ritual events, such as life-course rituals and buunyaas, is deemed sacred and eaten only with the right hand. An exception is often made, however, for foreigners or special guests, who receive their food separately and are usually given a spoon. At the first few buunyaas Ned and I attended in Lisbon, an elder pulled us away from our respective groups and gave us our own bowl to share, as well as two spoons. We initially accepted the arrangement, as we were familiar with this common expression of Mandinga hospitality. Our hosts were delighted, however, when at subsequent buunyaas we refused this special treatment. Eventually, people treated us like everyone else and left us

Figure 6.4. Women fan the Mecca returnees at a buunyaa ceremony in Lisbon, 1999. Photograph by the author.

to eat with our respective groups based on our age, gender, and marital status. This marked a new phase of my research and signaled our deeper belonging in the Mandinga immigrant community.

After the meal, the elders divide among the guests the kola nuts presented to the Qur'anic scholars at the beginning of the ceremony. At this point, the guests may depart if they wish. If the guest of honor is female, however, women often gather to sing praises to her, fanning her with their colorful head scarves. After about an hour of singing, the women may linger for some friendly conversation before returning home.

After receiving buunyaa blessings, guests avoid shaking hands with another person for the remainder of the day in order to prevent the blessings from leaving their own bodies and benefiting someone other than the person for whom the blessings were intended. This highlights a very different understanding of personhood, one in which boundaries between bodies are fluid and in which substances—such as blessings and even personality traits (see Riesman 1992)— readily flow from one person to another. Since Mandinga consider it impolite for a person to refuse to shake another person's hand, however, people who have received blessings at a buunyaa will extend their forearm instead, as blessings are thought to leave one's body only through the right hand.

TIMELY PILGRIMAGE: LIFE COURSE,
PERSONAL DESTINY, AND THE HAJJ

One day during my first stay in the village of Bafata-Oio in Guinea-Bissau, Ned and I sat drinking tea with a large group of young men and women who had gathered in our compound. The women lounged on woven mats, plaiting one another's hair, protected from the scorching afternoon sun by the pleasant shade of a mango tree. The young men chatted, waiting for Idrissa to finish brewing the first round of tea. Al-Hajj Daabo, a respected elder who had made the pilgrimage to Mecca the previous year, joined us for a visit. A young boy quickly brought him a chair as we all exchanged greetings. Al-Hajj handed me a small Viewmaster along with several rounds of slide cards of all of the major sacred sites of Mecca and Medina. As he sipped the first round of tea, I loaded one of the slide cards into the Viewmaster and flipped through the images of the kiswa-cloaked Kaaba, the Gate of Peace, the Sacred Mosque, the plain of Arafat, and thousands of pilgrims stoning Satan in Mina.

I passed the Viewmaster to Lamini, a boy in his early twenties, and asked him if he wanted to go to Mecca. "Yes, of course," he responded. "But I'm not ready yet; I'm still a young man." My research assistant and one of our closest friends, Numoo, who was about the same age as Lamini, shared with us his life aspirations to complete school, go to America, and send his mother to Mecca. "When I do all of these things, then I'll be ready to make the hajj myself."

Anthropologists who have studied pilgrimage often contrast this experience with life-course rituals such as initiation (e.g., Martin 1987; Turner 1974). They contend that whereas those who go on a pilgrimage choose to do so, and they may go at any time in their lives, initiation and other life-course rituals take place at more prescribed periods of the life course. But the timelessness of pilgrimage is often assumed and may be overstated, at least among some Muslims. Indeed, when one considers how people in local contexts view the issue of timing, pilgrimage appears to be similarly connected to the life course and might itself take on the qualities of a life-course ritual. For example, Sarah Lamb (2000) explains that while Bengali women in India can always go on a pilgrimage, there are more appropriate and easier times in a person's life to go. This is especially true in the case of women, who during their childbearing years are often too constrained by their children and domestic routines to go on a pilgrimage. There is also a spiritual dimension at work here, both for Bengali women and for my Mandinga interlocutors. Bodily processes such as menstruation and childbirth affect young women's purity, a point that I made in chapter 3. As women age and their children become occupied with their own children, they have more freedom to travel, and postmenopausal women no longer have to be concerned with compromised purity associated with bodily processes. Furthermore, going on a pilgrimage for Bengali women is a good way to "cut maya," (Lamb 2000, 157) or the ties that bind human beings to one another, to possessions, and to the material world, preparing them for death.[4]

This powerful life-course dimension is also relevant for the Mandinga I met in Guinea-Bissau and Portugal. As I conducted my fieldwork and spoke to Mandinga about the hajj, I was surprised by how many people told me that they were not ready or too young to make the pilgrimage to Mecca, even when they had long since attained puberty and had the money, health, and desire to go. I soon learned that for Mandinga, any time is not necessarily a good time to make the hajj. Part of this, of course, might be explained by the fact that for many West Africans, even those who have migrated to Europe, making the pilgrimage to Mecca is still more of a dream than a reality. Timing is therefore of the utmost importance: when one goes on the hajj, one should make it count. To understand this, it is necessary to explain Mandinga views on religious identity, gender, and purity as these relate to the life course.

One major point that has pervaded this book is that although all Mandinga define themselves as Muslims, individuals vary in the extent to which they conflate Islam with custom, associating it with ethnicity (belonging to a Muslim ethnic group) and ritual practices, or rather see Islam as something beyond this, a codified religion based on the five pillars of faith that unite Muslims everywhere. But wherever they fall along the spectrum, people I spoke with agree that making the hajj requires that they fully devote themselves to Islam on their return. Considering this, a person should wait to make the hajj until he or she is able to do so. This depends on both age and gender. Mandinga believe that most young people lack the discipline and education to commit to practicing Islam to the fullest after making the hajj. If young people make the hajj too early in life, they will inevitably act in ways that will, as my interlocutors put it, "spoil" (tinyaa) their pilgrimage. This is especially important when one considers that, unlike Saudi Arabians, who, people told me, can make the pilgrimage whenever they want, most Mandinga will go once in their lifetimes, if they go at all. It is for this reason that Mandinga identify later life as the appropriate period for making the hajj. As an elder man in his late sixties explained,

> When a person makes the hajj, all of his [or her] sins are immediately absolved. The pilgrim is pure and innocent again, just like a child. This is why people should wait to go to Mecca until their sinning period is over, because human beings are sinners; that is something that simply cannot be avoided,

especially for young people whose hearts are not cool [who cannot control their emotions and are quick to anger]. If someone says something that you don't like and you say, "You're worthless," then you have sinned. When you're older, you're wiser, more patient, and less likely to talk a lot [to say things that you will regret later].

For Mandinga, aging is conceptualized as a process of cooling, one that brings about emotional as well as physical changes in the body: one is calmer, more able to control one's emotions, and less likely to have strong emotional responses to situations. Attaining this state is a process and does not happen at the same time for every person. But when I asked people to identify a specific age or point in the life course at which it begins to happen, many specified the age of forty. Others told me that it begins when one's own children have children. In determining the appropriate age to go to Mecca, however, one must consider both age and gender, and the effects of both on the development of religious identity through the life course. In Guinea-Bissau, boys attend Qur'anic school more frequently and spend more time reading the Qur'an and praying than do girls. This gender disparity continues through the life course, as men's daily routines leave more time for religious practice than do women's routines. Although Mandinga boys and girls both attend Qur'anic school in Lisbon, men still pray and attend mosque more frequently than do women, a point that I have made in previous chapters. Considering this, the acceptable age for making the hajj is younger for men than for women.[5]

My interlocutors explained that once a woman is past her childbearing years, when she has stopped menstruating and has "white hair" and her body is "dry," she is considered an elder. At this point, Mandinga women enter a new phase of their religious lives. They often adopt a more Arab style of dress, consisting of long Muslim robes with colorful head scarves. They may pray more regularly and attend Friday prayer at Lisbon's central mosque, and they are free to mix with elder men at life-course events and Muslim holiday celebrations hosted by the various culture clubs. It is at this time of their lives, women told me, that they prefer to make the hajj, if they are able to at all. Mecca was very much on the minds of the Mandinga immigrant women I met in Lisbon. During my 2001 fieldwork, I learned that the members of the Maternal Kin Club had created a fund to sponsor one member a year to make the hajj.

Aside from ensuring that one's hajj will count, however, respecting Mandinga beliefs about pilgrimage and the life course is also, many people claimed, a matter of personal safety. There are some things in life that are too "strong"— that is, too powerful—for young people to see. Objects such as circumcision knives, certain types of medicines (amulets) worn on the body, and specific Qur'anic passages are some common examples. The forty-day postpartum confinement period, which Mandinga in Portugal continue to uphold, is designed in part to protect mothers and their babies from medicines worn on the body that are deemed too strong for their vulnerable bodies (see Johnson, n.d.). A person's ability to handle the power of these things, however, is believed to increase as one progresses through the life course. Healer-diviners who have reached the age of forty are able to work with Qur'anic passages that are deemed too strong for younger healer-diviners. Such passages are powerful enough to "ruin one's head," leading to temporary disorientation or even insanity. The Mandinga I came to know in both Guinea-Bissau and Lisbon extended these beliefs to the hajj, arguing that the sacred sites in Mecca and Medina are too strong for people under the age of forty; indeed, seeing them prematurely could lead to blindness or insanity.

Although the majority of my Mandinga interlocutors in Lisbon acknowledged and accepted these beliefs, I did meet a few "native skeptics" (Gable 1995) who claimed that they were simply a means for elders to maintain the traditional structure of power and authority. More specifically, they blamed elders for inventing beliefs about "strong" sites and their perilous effects on the body in order to prevent young people from going to Mecca before them and to thus limit the knowledge, status, and influence of youth in the religious sphere. This is especially relevant in Lisbon, they claimed, where Muslim healer-diviners are in direct competition with each other, as we saw in chapter 5, and where there is considerable tension between older, more traditional healer-diviners and younger ones who read Arabic and claim allegiance to a truer version of Islam. Several younger healer-diviners told me confidently, for example, that Islamic law does not stipulate an appropriate time for people to go to Mecca as long as they are adults, meaning that they have attained puberty. When I shared this perspective with some elder healer-diviners, however, they were horrified by the accusation that traditional beliefs about the life course and the hajj were invented, and they became defensive: "If young people want to waste their money and spoil their heads by doing things before they are ready, then let them. They'll just come running to us [older healer-diviners] later for cures; then they'll see that we're right."

Aside from the appropriate age at which one should make the hajj, discourse in the Mandinga community highlighted beliefs concerning the pilgrimage to Mecca and death. People explained that anyone who dies while making the hajj is guaranteed salvation. They agreed that while it would be auspicious to die while making the pilgrimage, it would be sinful to go to Mecca in poor health in an attempt to actually die there. This would be, in their minds, a violation of God's will. As we saw in chapter 4, Mandinga believe that God sets the time and place of a person's death at his or her birth, and attempting to alter one's destiny is thought to be disrespectful of God. Destiny aside, my interlocutors agreed that making the pilgrimage is so physically and emotionally exhausting that one must be in good form—old enough but not too old—to go. Seku described the conditions on the pilgrimage as extremely difficult: the heat is intense, pilgrims have to walk a lot, there are so many people, and preparing food is difficult. "I lost five kilos," he claimed. When I asked Jiba if she wanted to make the hajj again, she laughed: "I'm only strong enough to do that once, Fatumata. Once is enough!" She also complained about the heat, how she was unable to touch the Black Stone due to the crowds, and how she almost gave up trying to stone Satan at Mina, since she had such bad aim.

Personal destiny, which people identified as the most important factor in one's ability to make the hajj, challenges both the (Islamic) obligatory nature of the pilgrimage and (Mandinga) beliefs about when one should make it. Indeed, I was told that people can wait until they are forty years old, save up all their money, carefully plan their trip, and purchase airline tickets, but if it is not their destiny to make the hajj, then they will not make it. I engaged my interlocutors on this issue: if every able-bodied, financially capable Muslim must make the hajj at least once in his or her life, then why wouldn't God simply make this a part of everyone's personal destiny? I always got the same answer: God does, but one's death (set by God on the day of one's birth) might simply precede one's time to go to Mecca. That is, one's death might precede one's pilgrimage on the divine timeline. As Alaaji B. explained,

> When I arrived in Mecca, I cried. I thought of my mother and father. I thought of them because they never made it to Mecca. But that wasn't their fault: God ended their lives before they had a chance to go. I was planning to take my mother to Mecca. When I had finally made all of the preparations, just as I had saved all of the money I needed to take her, she died. So she never went to Mecca. But I went there; I went to Mecca. I didn't do a thing for God that would make him want to take me there. It was just my personal destiny. That's why I cried.

Like Alaaji B., Seku also spoke of the role of personal destiny in his making the hajj:

> A few years ago, I started seeing Mecca in my dreams. I would dream that God was showing me the road to Mecca, and I was looking at it. But I didn't think the dream meant that I would go to Mecca just yet; I thought it meant

something different. But then the dreams became more frequent. I started seeing the Prophet Mohammed pointing the way to Mecca; he showed me the road to Mecca just like God had done for me earlier. That's when I knew it was time for me to go. I didn't tell anyone about my dream. I just started making preparations, collecting the necessary documents and saving money. Then I told people, "This year, God willing, I will make the hajj." When I arrived in Mecca, I just thanked God. I told him, "My father was a king, but he never went to Mecca. My mother was a king's wife, but she never went to Mecca. But you have brought me here, and I say, thanks be to God."

We have seen that the hajj, although an obligatory rite of Islam, is infused with Mandinga customary beliefs about the life course and personal destiny. These beliefs highlight age, gender, and purity and establish when it is appropriate to make the hajj and why. They also clearly distinguish desire and agency from personal destiny, as determined by God. But such beliefs are destabilized as Mandinga immigrants remake Islam in Lisbon—as they come into increased contact with Muslims from outside of Africa and as they become more aware of their inclusion in (or exclusion from) the umma, the global Muslim community. As is the case with other ritual practices described in previous chapters, this process has sparked tension and debate between men and women, elders and youth, and those who remain comfortably rooted in African custom and those who seek a truer model of Islam, one based on the five pillars of faith that unite Muslims everywhere.

UNTIMELY PILGRIMAGE: AJA FATIMA'S STORY

Nowhere was the conflict between African custom and global Islam more salient than in the case of one young girl's untimely pilgrimage, which sparked community-wide controversy. I met Aja Fatima at a buunyaa ceremony in the neighborhood of Bairro Santos in central Lisbon during my 1999 fieldwork. At the time, she was a charming and very bright nineteen-year-old who had recently made the hajj with her father, who worked as a healer-diviner in a Lisbon exurb. Fatima was working as a checkout clerk at the popular French supermarket chain Carrefour when her father invited her to make the hajj with him. Her boss would not give her the time off from work, so she quit. When she returned from Mecca, she resumed school and hoped to attend college and eventually go to medical school or travel to the Middle East or North Africa to pursue Islamic studies. Aja Fatima was well aware that she was the youngest person in the Mandinga immigrant community ever to have made the hajj. What she did not know, however, was that her untimely pilgrimage would soon be the subject of a community-wide debate in Lisbon.

Several weeks after my first encounter with Aja Fatima, Ned and I were invited to her buunyaa. When we arrived at her apartment, we greeted the elder men who were seated on colorful prayer rugs in the central room. They had not yet started reading from the Qur'an, and they amused themselves by watching a Portuguese film and chatting. I left Ned in the front room with the men and went to the other rooms to greet the women. Aja Fatima sat in the back room on a bed with the rest of the women in the Mandinga community in Lisbon who had made the hajj that year. She was dressed in a beautiful maroon Saudi-style gown and matching head scarf that she had purchased in Saudi Arabia. Delighted at the opportunity to chat more extensively with Aja Fatima, I asked her how she felt now that she was called "Aja," one who has made the pilgrimage to Mecca. She responded, "I'm very happy." She then began recounting her experience in Mecca and how the factors of gender and age had directly shaped that experience.

Aja Fatima told me that going to Mecca had "opened her eyes." It made her more aware of her identity both as an African (and her racial identity as a black person) and as a woman. "It was strange to be an African woman in Mecca," she said. "There were so many people there—Arabs, Indians, and even Chinese—but I could count the number of black people on my fingers. There were not many of us, and even fewer of us were women." Aja Fatima told me that it was difficult for her to relate to the lives of Saudi Arabian women, especially how they dressed in purdah and what she described as their lack of independence from men. Fatima was disillusioned: was this the model that she and other Mandinga in Lisbon were supposed to look toward and were trying so desperately to follow? As a young, single woman accompanied only by her father, who spent most of his time with his fellow male pilgrims, Aja Fatima was unprepared for the logistical difficulties she faced in Mecca. Mandinga pilgrims commonly have Polaroids taken of them at the sacred sites of Mecca and Medina, like the two included earlier in this chapter. On their return, they prominently display these photographs for their relatives and friends to see at their buunyaa. I received many such photos as gifts during my fieldwork in Lisbon. People also often have them professionally enlarged and framed, in which case they become the most treasured centerpieces of their homes. Aja Fatima regretted that, unlike most Mandinga Mecca returnees, she had no pictures to show me of herself in Mecca: "When I asked to have my picture taken, the man just looked at me and asked where my husband was. I told him I wasn't married, and he told me that if I wanted my picture taken, I would have to have permission from a male relative, and he would have to appear with me in the photograph. My father wasn't there at the time, so I couldn't have my picture taken."

When it was time for lunch at Aja Fatima's buunyaa, I left her company and joined a group of married women in another room. One middle-aged woman said she felt it was wrong for Aja Fatima's father to have taken her to Mecca. "She is far too young to have made the hajj," she asserted. Another woman agreed: "Her mother hasn't even been to Mecca; it's not right." One woman defended Aja Fatima's father, explaining that he would have taken his wife to Mecca, but she had been sick for some time and was not yet well enough to go. But the middle-aged woman had another theory. She believed that Aja Fatima's father took his daughter to Mecca so that she would agree to an arranged marriage with a Muslim Guinean man, who was studying in Egypt. She told us that Aja Fatima was actually in love with another man, but that her parents did not approve of him because he was a Balanta, a non-Muslim (the very word *Balanta* means "I refuse [Islam]" in Mandinga). Although this man had allegedly converted to Islam, he was born a non-Muslim, and for Mandinga, as I have argued in this book and elsewhere (Johnson 2000, 2006), being Muslim is as much an ethnicity as it is a religious identity. A woman in her late twenties chimed in: "If they [Aja Fatima's parents] think that taking their daughter to Mecca will make her accept an arranged marriage, they're wrong: she has spent most of her life in Europe and will do what she pleases." But the middle-aged woman disagreed: "No, she won't. The girl has been to Mecca; she can't refuse her elders' wishes. If they say that she must marry the man, then she has no choice but to marry him." Another young woman interjected, "If that's what going to Mecca is about, then I don't want any part of it." Several of her friends nodded in agreement. The middle-aged woman had the last word: "They have ruined the girl."

Several weeks after Aja Fatima's buunyaa, people in the Mandinga immigrant community were still talking about her untimely pilgrimage to Mecca. Most people blamed Aja Fatima's father's poor judgment in taking his daughter to Mecca. "Take a child to Mecca, what for?" they asked. Others blamed Aja Fatima's parents for conflating the sacred pilgrimage with Mandinga custom—for treating it like an initiation ritual. Just as traditional African initiation rituals commonly subjugate youth to the elders' power and authority, Aja Fatima's parents had used the hajj to make their daughter act in accordance with their wishes—to make her marry the husband they had chosen for her. But since Aja Fatima had grown up in Lisbon, her wishes would most likely contradict those of her parents, and her pilgrimage would thus "amount to nothing," as they put it. Community members agreed that using the Mecca pilgrimage as a means of tightening control of one's daughter in Europe is wrong. Mandinga, like all Muslims, believe that people should make the hajj with only one thing "in their head"—only one intention, to fulfill their promise to God.

Indeed, Alaaji B. explained to me that the problem of taking young people to Mecca is compounded by the problems involved in raising Mandinga children in Europe. He explained,

> The reason we say young children shouldn't go to Mecca is because we go to Mecca to ask for God's forgiveness. In Europe our children hear all about their friends, who go to *discotecas*. Here our children don't practice their religion as much as [people do] back home. If you take a child to Mecca, they see God's and the Prophet's house and other sacred things. But then what if they come back and break the law? Then they'll truly shame their mother and father and spoil their parents' names. People will say, "Look at what that child has done, even after going to Mecca." That's why we believe it's not good to take a child to Mecca. But if you raise your child correctly, you won't have that problem. Children are like plants. The way you plant them and care for them, that's how they become. If you plant them, leave them alone, and never water them, they'll be ruined. So many Guineans in Europe do just this: they ruin their children. They raise them here and never tell them to pray. They grow up unable to speak their own language. How can children be Muslims if they can't even speak their [indigenous] language? To make up for this, parents just say, "Well, I have a lot of money, so I'll just take my child to Mecca." You can take them, for sure, but that doesn't mean they'll start acting like Muslims. It's not like this in Africa. There children study the Qur'an. If you take them to Mecca, they'll continue to study and practice their religion because that's all they know. They see what their father and mother do, and they do the same thing. It's good to take those children to Mecca. But here in Europe, why waste your money on taking your children to Mecca? Use your money instead to hire a Qur'anic teacher for your children, and don't stop paying him until your children can read the entire Qur'an.

Alaaji B., who was not yet forty during my early fieldwork in Lisbon, had already made the pilgrimage to Mecca several times. A successful healer-diviner, he took pride in his ability not only to read the Qur'an but also to understand its deep meanings. And unlike other healer-diviners, who, Alaaji B. claimed, only memorized Arabic words, he could read, write, and speak Arabic. He accused members of the Mandinga community of conflating African custom and Islam. In his mind, the real problem with taking children to Mecca is not that they are too young—that they are under the age of forty—but that Mandinga parents are failing to bring up their children as good Muslims in Portugal.

If Alaaji B. was critical of children going to Mecca, he was also critical of women who make the hajj. He explained that many Mandinga immigrant women who make the Mecca pilgrimage are less interested in fulfilling their obligation

Figure 6.5. Mandinga women at the mosque. The woman dressed in Saudi-style clothing had recently returned from Mecca and was inviting everyone to her buunyaa the following day, 2017. Photograph by the author.

to God than they are in using the hajj to start a business by purchasing clothes and other high-status items from Saudi Arabia that they can later sell in Lisbon. Although pursuing business interests with other pilgrims while on the hajj is considered lawful, especially if it can help defray the costs associated with the sacred journey (Martin 1987, 340), many Mandinga men told me that purchasing merchandise to improve one's lot in life during the month of the hajj spoils one's pilgrimage, rendering it worthless in God's eyes. That many women consider the hajj a mere business opportunity was an attitude shared by many men and even some women I came to know in Lisbon. Many women openly admitted to me that the best part of buunyaa ceremonies was the opportunity they provided to purchase big Muslim clothes such as Arab-style dresses and head scarves, as well as body lotions, prayer beads, and perfumes from Saudi Arabia. As one woman remarked after purchasing an outfit on credit at a buunyaa ceremony we both attended, "I might not be an Aja yet, but at least I can dress like one."

In the introduction to their book on pilgrimage and healing, Jill Dubisch and Michael Winkelman (2005, xxii) write, "The voluntary character and the sense of empowerment and of personal connection with spiritual power that pilgrimage can provide make it an appealing ritual for the socially disadvantaged and marginalized." Whereas Mandinga in Guinea-Bissau are mildly aware of their marginalization in the wider Muslim world and strive for greater inclusion in the umma, this awareness and desire intensify as they confront Lisbon's transnational Muslim community face-to-face. They soon learn that belonging is difficult to attain. Mandinga immigrants in Lisbon are doubly marginalized as African Muslims (from the perspective of "Arab" and "Indian" Muslims) and blacks (from the perspective of their former Portuguese colonizers). In the contemporary diaspora, they feel they are often objects of racism and anti-Muslim sentiment. My interlocutors told me that people stare at them when they wear their big clothing on the streets of Lisbon while others avoid sitting next to them on the metro or commuter trains and even occasionally tell them to go back where they came from. The pilgrimage to Mecca offers both hope and healing from such experiences.

But the hajj also engages the tension between African custom and global Islam as Mandinga remake themselves and their religion in Lisbon. As we have seen, this tension finds expression in gender and generation as men and women, elders and youth, attempt to draw (and redraw) the lines between these two categories and define (and redefine) appropriate Islamic belief and practice. This debate, as I have shown throughout this book, takes place most dramatically through ritual practices, of and beyond the life course. On one occasion at a buunyaa ceremony, the Mecca returnees demanded that the Mandinga praise-singers who had come to entertain the guests sing only Muslim chants to God and the Prophet Mohammed. They also forbade the praise-singers from playing the drums, which they deemed un-Islamic, at the ceremony. At first, the praise-singers were angry and argued with the Mecca returnees, explaining that they did not know many Muslim chants and that their job, as traditional Mandinga praise-singers, was to sing praises to the various clans and recall their historical importance to Mandinga, no matter where they lived. Unwilling to miss an opportunity to make a living, however, the praise-singers acceded to the wishes of the Mecca returnees and chanted the same two Muslim chants—the only ones they knew—all afternoon.

NOTES

1. I rely on Denny (2016), Amin (1978), and Martin (1987) in piecing together this general description of the hajj.

2. See D'Alisera (2004, 42–45) for a discussion of the image of Freetown's Cotton Tree, which she states "represents both 'home' and the longing for 'home'

that comes from living abroad" (2004, 44) among Sierra Leonean Muslims in Washington, DC. Like the Cotton Tree for Sierra Leonean immigrants in America, wall hangings of the Kaaba engage Guinean Muslim immigrants' complex emotions of belonging to (and exclusion from) multiple communities.

3. For Mouride traders as described by Ebin (1996, 98), travel is a sacred activity that is thought to lead to knowledge and to a better understanding of the world. She writes, "The number of countries one has 'done' . . . and the languages one speaks are frequent subjects of conversation at Mouride gatherings."

4. See Rasmussen (1997) for a similar discussion of personal destiny and the life course among Tuareg in Niger.

5. In her work on female marabouts in Dakar, Gemmeke (2009, 140) writes that the number forty has particular significance because it is the age at which people in Senegal believe the Prophet Mohammed began preaching.

—◆—

EPILOGUE

Faith, Food, and Fashion—Religion in Diaspora

I HAVE ARGUED IN THIS book that as Guinean Muslims leave their homeland and make their way in Lisbon, they encounter new versions of Islam and
different ways of thinking about religion more generally. Guinean Muslims
have long conflated ethnicity and religious identity, such that to be Mandinga
or Fula is to naturally be Muslim. Life-course rituals—naming, hand-writing,
initiation and circumcision, and funerals—as well as ritual practices beyond
the life course, such as healing-divining and pilgrimage, celebrate the fusion of
ethnicity and Islam and inscribe it onto bodies, living and dead.

I have also highlighted the changing role of diasporas in this complicated
process of identity-making. Fula and Mandinga have always defined themselves as diasporic peoples, whose histories, identities, and daily lives extend
beyond the borders of their "home" country, Guinea-Bissau. As such, they have
aligned themselves more closely with other Muslim peoples in Senegal and the
Gambia than with members of non-Muslim ethnic groups in Guinea-Bissau.
But their diasporic identity shifts and intensifies when Guinean Muslims
immigrate to Lisbon and join two new and dynamic diasporas: immigrants
from Portugal's other former African colonies and a diverse group of Muslims
from North Africa, the Middle East, and South Asia. I have demonstrated
in this book that members of this latter group have been most central in the
process of remaking Islam for Guinean Muslims in Lisbon. As they engage
more intensively with "Arab" and "Indian" Muslims, who hold different ideas
of what it means to be Muslim, they are beginning to question and revise
their understanding of proper Muslim belief and practice and to separate
African custom—exemplified by embodied ritual practices—from a more

cosmopolitan, global Islam, emphasizing Arabic literacy and the five pillars of faith that unite Muslims throughout the world. Beyond inspiring debates about ritual practices, their encounters with Muslims from beyond West Africa are leading some Guinean Muslims to alter their understanding of religion as a concept. Religion is not something that one receives from a father's name, a mother's breast milk, and passage through customary life-course rituals. It is different from and bigger than this, something one chooses, even achieves, to follow, comprising beliefs and practices that Muslims everywhere embrace. Religion looks not to an imagined traditional past anchored in the homeland but rather to a more global, emerging present and imagined future, full of possibilities and aspirations.

I have also argued that while Guinean Muslims in Lisbon themselves imagine and talk about African custom and global Islam in binary terms, in practice these often converge and overlap. These two orientations—which I have represented here by the cultural spaces of mosques and culture clubs—are best imagined as points on a continuum, along which people move back and forth at different times, even during fleeting moments, throughout their lives. The various points themselves and the ideas about one's actual or imagined location in relation to them at any given time are inspiring lively debates as Guinean Muslims remake themselves and their religion in and beyond Lisbon.

These debates, as I have demonstrated in this book, highlight gender and generational differences among Guinean Muslims in Lisbon. Men who can read and write Arabic, have traveled to the Middle East for study or pilgrimage, and regularly attend Friday prayer at Lisbon's central mosque aspire to be cosmopolitan Muslims. For them, belonging to a Muslim community whose borders extend beyond Guinea-Bissau, or even West Africa, involves, among other things, a commitment to replace African custom with global Islam. Guinean Muslim women, most of whom have not studied the Qur'an formally, do not read or write Arabic, and have not visited any Muslim country beyond West Africa, feel that global Islam is beyond their reach. Choosing to remain rooted in African custom, they have created culture clubs, alternative Muslim spaces in Lisbon where they can hold life-course rituals and Muslims holidays according to their own terms, those of the homeland. Culture club events, as I have shown, celebrate the fusion of ethnicity and Islam in embodied, meaningful ways. Although the heightened awareness surrounding what it means to simultaneously belong to an African ethnic group and practice the world religion of Islam and the debates that this awareness inspires have been unfolding in Guinea-Bissau for a long time, I have argued that these have intensified in Lisbon, where their contours are different and the stakes higher.

The ethnographic vignettes featured in this book highlight the continued importance of religion among African migrants in Europe. Indeed, while scholars have focused extensively on transnational migrants' political and economic activities, far fewer have highlighted the role of religion (Levitt and Glick Schiller 2004, 1026). Drawing inspiration from Sophie Bava (2011, 494), who writes that "religious processes are at the core of migratory practices and that migration is at the heart of religious issues," I have focused exclusively on Guinean Muslim immigrants' religious lives in the context of a changing and expanding diaspora as they sort out what being African and being Muslim mean in Europe. Through stories of named individuals who have shared their lives with me over two decades, I have also underscored the complicated nature of Guinean Muslim men's and women's choices as they live their daily lives in Lisbon and struggle to raise their Muslim children in a very different place than where their own parents raised them. These challenges are compounded by immigrants' experiences of racism and anti-Islamic sentiment as they become members—most for the first time in their lives—of racial and religious minority groups in Lisbon. Indeed, for the majority of my interlocutors in Lisbon, ethnicity—their identity as either Mandinga, Fula, or even Muslim peoples—has been the central defining feature of their identity in West Africa. Being forced to rethink themselves as Guineans, as Africans, and especially as black people is a new experience for most, one that brings novel questions and challenges, especially considering the changing political climate in Europe, in which secularism and anti-immigrant sentiment are on the rise.

During my 2017 fieldwork in Lisbon, my goal was to explore the continuities and ruptures in the Guinean Muslim immigrant community since my 2011 fieldwork. I spent my mornings at Rossio in central Lisbon with a group of female merchants I came to know well, who sold kola nuts, fruits, vegetables, and clothing items, such as Muslim head scarves, from Guinea-Bissau or Senegal. In the afternoons, I traveled to households in Lisbon's exurbs for extended visits with community members I became closest to, many of whom I have known since 1999 and others whom I had met during more recent fieldwork periods.

The first Friday during my 2017 fieldwork began as any other day. After having breakfast at a café near my rented room in central Lisbon, I walked to Rossio to help the merchants get ready for the day. Kadi was the first to arrive, and after exchanging greetings in Mandinga, we gleaned the nicest plastic buckets, crates, and flattened cardboard boxes we could find from a nearby construction site trash heap, which she expertly fashioned into tables and chairs, on which we carefully arranged her wares: roasted peanuts (both Portuguese and Guinean varieties), cashew nuts, baobab fruit, and vegetables from Guinea-Bissau. Three more merchants soon joined us and set up their wares, and we chatted and waited for the first customers to arrive. Curious, I asked the women about their plans for Friday prayer—if they planned to go to Lisbon's central mosque or the Rossio mosque, which was located just a few steps from where we were sitting, or if they would skip Friday prayer altogether. They told me they had planned to go to the central mosque. I recalled a recent conversation I had had with some men who owned or worked in the shops at Rossio, which sold dry goods and other products from West Africa. They had given me a tour of the Rossio mosque and had emphasized that while it provided a convenient place for the merchants at Rossio to pray, it was not meant to substitute for Friday prayer at the central mosque.

Around midday, I helped the merchants pack their wares into their large, colorful bags. Nyamo announced that she would stay behind, since she had arrived late. Assuming I would accompany the rest of the group to the mosque, Kadi said, "Let's go, Fatumata," and we carried the bags to the nearest taxi stand and piled into the first available cab. As our driver navigated the heavy traffic around Rossio, the women discussed the weather and their plans to attend the infant name-giving ritual that would be held the next day. Aja complained, "I couldn't sleep at all last night; my body hurts all over from work." She asked me if I had brought "strong medicine from America" and smiled when I handed her my water bottle and two acetaminophen tablets.

As we approached the mosque, I felt conflicted. On the one hand, I knew that going, especially on Friday, was important for my fieldwork, and I was thankful for the opportunity to accompany my merchant friends. On the other, I recalled how complicated many of my previous visits to the mosque had been, both for my Guinean Muslim interlocutors and for me as an anthropologist. As I have shown in this book, many women I knew well in Lisbon did not frequent the central mosque, claiming that Arab and Indian Muslims at the door frequently questioned their Muslim identity or even refused to let them in. During previous fieldwork periods, I struggled to find a balance between staying behind with the women and helping them prepare the afternoon meal, and going to the mosque with their husbands, who always encouraged me (but rarely, if ever, their wives) to accompany them. Whenever I went, I felt guilty abandoning the women and insecure about my identity as a non-Muslim. While the men prayed, I often remained outside, where I talked to merchants and others who had gone to the mosque to network and converse about life in Guinea-Bissau and Portugal.

But Kadi, Musu, and Aja did not seem concerned at all about attending Friday prayer, either for themselves or for me, even when I told them that I had neglected to bring a head scarf. "It's not a problem, Fatumata," they assured me as our taxi driver parked across the street from the mosque. Just as I was about to announce that I would wait outside, Musu grabbed my arm and pulled me to the door. An Indian man looked at the women, then at me. Aja stated confidently that I was in their group, and we entered without a problem. I asked a Guinean man inside if I could borrow a head scarf. He handed me one, reminding me to return it after prayer.

Inside, I was surprised to see that Guinean Muslim women dominated the women's quarters. I knew a few of them and recognized others as members of the Sweetness Club. A Mandinga woman dressed in a dazzling white, Saudi-style outfit who had recently made the hajj invited everyone present to attend her buunyaa the next day, location to be announced. One of the points that I have made in this book, that mosques and culture clubs are not mutually exclusive religious spaces but rather overlapping, mutually constitutive ones, emerged more clearly than ever as I observed women from various culture clubs at Friday prayer at Lisbon's central mosque discuss plans to attend a ritual to welcome Aja back from Mecca in customary Mandinga fashion.

Surprised by the different feel of the women's quarters that the Guinean Muslim majority created, I took a careful look beyond my immediate circle as the women performed ablutions, conversed, and arranged their wares—fashionable head coverings, roasted cashew nuts, and boiled cassava—on the wooden benches, hoping to make a few sales before prayer began. There were only a few non-African women there. Turning my attention back to the women with whom I was sitting, I asked, "Where are all the Arabs and Indians?" One woman responded, "They have their own mosques now. We've moved in, and the place is ours." Despite the women's encouragement to join them for prayer, I opted to sit on the couches across from the prayer space, explaining that I wanted to take some pictures for my book, at which point they smiled and told me, "Take our picture and build our names in America, Fatumata." After prayer, I accompanied Kadi, pushing through the lingering crowd of women quickly so that she would have enough time to set up outside the mosque before people exited. After only five minutes, she had sold everything she brought. She turned to me and said, "Fatumata, you brought luck; everything is finished!" Another woman asked to join our group back to Rossio, putting us over the limit for a shared cab. Kadi and I volunteered to take the metro back, which put us back at Rossio well ahead of the others.

Through these and numerous other encounters with my Guinean Muslim interlocutors in Lisbon in 2017, I observed some significant changes. For one, Lisbon's multicultural Muslim community had become more fragmented. As some people put it, "Every group has its own mosque." This was true not only for Arab and Indian Muslims but for Guinean Muslims as well. Rossio was no longer the only ethnic mosque in Lisbon. Others had opened in several of Lisbon's exurbs with significant Guinean Muslim populations, such as Damaia and Queluz. These mosques, people told me, were dominated by Fula peoples from Guinea-Bissau and Senegal. But if the mosques were expanding, so were the culture clubs. The Maternal Kin Club, which had been the dominant Mandinga culture club during my previous fieldwork and of which I myself had been an active member in the late 1990s and early 2000s, was now considerably smaller. Some members had died, some had joined other culture clubs, and others had migrated to other European countries, such as England and Germany. One woman told me that there were now seventeen different culture clubs in Lisbon. Although I received differing responses when I mentioned this number to others (some claimed that it was too high; others claimed that it was too low), the point remains: the number of culture clubs in Lisbon had increased.

In 2017, I also spent much of my time with Aja Fatima's parents, Mansata and Alaaji. During my early fieldwork, Mansata was an active member of the Maternal Kin Club and occasionally attended Friday prayer and Muslim holiday celebrations at Lisbon's central mosque. When I told her that I had seen more Guinean women than ever at Friday prayer, she told me that the environment at the mosque had improved considerably. "The only reason I don't go every Friday is because of my work schedule," she said. She also told me that members of all of Lisbon's culture clubs had recently joined together to hold an especially elaborate Prophet's Birthday celebration (*Gammo*) at the central mosque. She showed me numerous photographs on her phone of the event, which looked spirited and well attended.

During my early fieldwork, Guinean Muslim immigrants were working to carve out a space for themselves in Lisbon and to establish their lives there. In 2017, many shared with me their hopes to migrate to other European countries where they claimed conditions were better for African immigrants. Indeed, some had already managed to leave, including Aja Fatima, who I learned was living in England with her husband and children. "You wouldn't believe how many Guineans there are in England, Fatumata," Mansata told me. When I asked her why England, she responded, "There is more money there, and it's easier to make a life for oneself." Indeed, Mansata told me that Aja Fatima had successfully opened a shop in Bissau, and she traveled there twice a year to stock it with goods she purchased in England. Mansata and Alaaji traveled to London once or twice a year to visit their daughter and grandchildren. As a result of their travels (their other daughter had lived previously in Sweden and was now living in Germany), Alaaji's previously local healing-divining practice had become a booming, transnational one. He showed me WhatsApp contacts for his dozens of clients, who were living all over the world: in Europe, North Africa, and the Middle East. We called Aja Fatima through WhatsApp, and I spoke to her for the first time in years, first in Mandinga, then in Kriolu, and finally in English so that she could show me how well she could speak my native language, which she had always wanted to learn.

Technology had also changed significantly since my early fieldwork. In 1999, I purchased my first mobile phone, which allowed me to stay in contact with community members, who were scattered all over Lisbon and its many exurbs and who relied on mobile phones to stay in touch, using new technologies to constitute community in Lisbon (Johnson 2013). In 2017, smartphones had replaced flip phones, and people communicated predominantly through texting or WhatsApp. At several points when I was completing this book, I used WhatsApp to pose questions to community members, who often responded within minutes. This was especially helpful when I was unsure of my decision to use someone's actual name or a pseudonym or when I felt I needed to revisit the ongoing process of informed consent, checking permission to report certain information or tell a controversial story (for example, Aja Fatima's untimely pilgrimage to Mecca). These evolving technologies have allowed me to stay in close contact with my Guinean Muslim interlocutors in Lisbon, which was impossible or at least much more difficult during my earlier fieldwork periods.

In 2017, the Guinean Muslim women in Lisbon I knew best were reconciling their ethnic and religious identities in two primary ways: through food and fashion. During our time together, we cooked food from the homeland and dressed up in Muslim clothing from North Africa or the Middle East. Technology figured prominently in these experiences. Before eating, we took photographs of the elaborate dishes we prepared, of people serving the rice and sauce in a single bowl with utensils from Guinea-Bissau, and of us poised to eat it. After the meal, we dressed up in outfits from North Africa or the Middle East—literally trying on cosmopolitan Islam—and posed for yet another set of photographs. We then shared these images with other community members through WhatsApp. When I later visited the people who had received them, they commented on the photographs and responded by creating their own parallel experiences—preparing different delectable dishes from home and trying on more fashionable outfits—to photograph and send around again. These activities, I argue, highlight Guinean Muslim women's continued efforts to remake themselves and their faith in a changing diaspora. They underscore the overlapping nature of African custom and cosmopolitan Islam—that it is

Figure E.1. Serving food from the homeland (smoked fish with palm oil and *bajiki*) in Queluz, 2017. Photograph by the author.

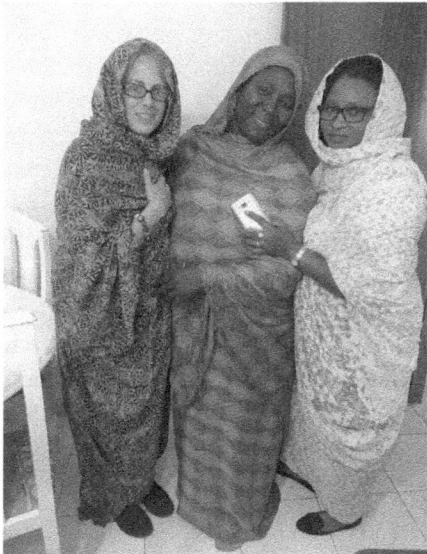

Figure E.2. Trying on Mauritanian clothing and cosmopolitan Islam, 2017. Photographer unknown.

not only possible but even desirable to belong simultaneously to an African ethnic group and to the *umma*, the global Muslim community. The women underscored this point in embodied ways: in preparing, eating, and celebrating food from the homeland, they performed their identity as Africans, as Guineans, and as Mandinga or Fula peoples. By donning clothing styles worn by Muslims beyond Guinea-Bissau and West Africa, they presented themselves to the world as cosmopolitan Muslims.

Finally, ritual practices were as key to the process of remaking Islam for Guinean Muslims in 2017 as they were in 1999, a point that was evident during my first visit with Aminata. Several years after her husband's shocking and untimely death, she married Demba, a Fula man, who owned a shop at Rossio. She showed me a photo album full of enlarged photographs of their "double wedding," which featured the Muslim part—tying the kola nuts—and a European-style banquet and party at their apartment in Queluz. Then Aminata proudly showed me the DVD of their daughter, Fatumata's, name-giving ritual. Unlike most of the life-course rituals I have discussed in this book, which people described as being either Mandinga or Fula, this ritual had a new, distinctively multiethnic character. Mandinga and Fula guests alike had gathered together to witness baby Fatumata receive her name. The focus was not on being Mandinga or being Fula but rather on being Muslim in Lisbon. After the holy man "shaved" Fatumata's head, named and blessed her, and invited her to take up the path that God had set before her, the guests danced and handed money to the traditional praise-singers, who honored their clan names. Even Aminata, who had given birth to Fatumata only one week previously, was dancing in the video. "I was so sick, but the guests wouldn't let me rest," she told me, laughing. Halfway through the dancing, Demba stopped the video, insisting that we watch another video, featuring Sheikh Takdir from Mozambique. In the video, he delivered a sermon in Portuguese about envy, which he considered "the worst of sins."

After we watched and discussed the video, Aminata asked me to accompany her to a postburial sacrifice. The most exciting thing, she told me, was that we would be driving there (even though it was only a few blocks away and was easily walkable). Since my last visit to Lisbon, Aminata had gotten her driver's license, making her the first Guinean Muslim woman I knew in Lisbon to obtain one. As she started the car, she told me that getting her license was actually her husband's idea and that he had even bought her the car. Aminata parked, but before going to the postburial sacrifice, we visited a Muslim healer-diviner I had never met before. He was younger than most healer-diviners I knew in Lisbon (perhaps in his early forties) and wore a white Saudi-style robe. We exchanged greetings in Mandinga, and he told me that he and Aminata were "very close, like family." He explained that he had accompanied Aminata's previous husband back to Guinea-Bissau for treatment for his illness—which was "of the land" and thus could not be successfully treated in Lisbon—how he was at his side when he died, and how he had assisted with the burial. As he recounted the story in Kriolu so that Aminata could understand, I was unable to hold back tears. "Don't cry, Fatumata; suffer it," said Aminata, before asking the healer-diviner to change the subject. He asked Aminata what she needed. She explained she was planning to pursue a business opportunity and needed him to "open her luck." She also sought help for her children to excel in school, especially on their upcoming exams. The healer-diviner told her that he would complete the work and that Aminata could pick it up by the end of the week. As we said goodbye to the healer-diviner and made our way to the postburial sacrifice, it was clear that ritual practices remained the central medium through which Guinean Muslims in Lisbon sorted out, argued about, and attempted to reconcile African custom and cosmopolitan Islam as they continued to remake themselves and their faith, a process that incorporated ideas, images, and experiences across and beyond Lisbon, Mecca, and Bissau.

BIBLIOGRAPHY

Abranches, Maria. 2013a. "Transnational Informal Spaces Connecting Guinea-Bissau and Portugal: Food, Markets and Relationships." *Urban Anthropology and Studies of Cultural Systems and World Economic Development* 42 (3/4): 333–75.

———. 2013b. "When People Stay and Things Make Their Way: Airports, Mobilities and Materialities of a Transnational Landscape." *Mobilities* 8 (4): 506–27.

———. 2014. "Remitting Wealth, Reciprocating Health? The 'Travel' of the Land from Guinea-Bissau to Portugal." *American Ethnologist* 41 (2): 261–75.

Abu-Lughod, Lila. 1991. "Writing against Culture." In *Recapturing Anthropology: Working in the Present*, edited by Richard G. Fox, 137–62. Santa Fe, NM: School of American Research Press.

Amin, Mohammed. 1978. *Pilgrimage to Mecca*. London: Macdonald and Jane's.

Appadurai, Arjun. 1996. *Modernity at Large: Cultural Dimensions of Globalization*. Minneapolis: University of Minnesota Press.

Asad, Talal. 2009. "The Idea of an Anthropology of Islam." *Qui Parle* 17 (2): 1–30.

Auslander, Mark. 1993. "'Open the Wombs!' The Symbolic Politics of Modern Ngoni Witchfinding." In *Modernity and Its Malcontents: Ritual and Power in Postcolonial Africa*, edited by Jean Comaroff and John L. Comaroff, 167–92. Chicago: University of Chicago Press.

Bava, Sophie. 2011. "Migration-Religion Studies in France: Evolving toward a Religious Anthropology of Movement." *Annual Review of Anthropology* 40:493–507.

Becker, Gay. 2002. "Dying Away from Home: Quandaries of Migration for Elders in Two Ethnic Groups." *Journals of Gerontology* 57B (2): S79–S95.

Behar, Ruth. 1996. *The Vulnerable Observer: Anthropology That Breaks Your Heart*. Boston: Beacon Press.

Beidelman, T. O. 1993. *Moral Imagination in Kaguru Modes of Thought*. Washington, DC: Smithsonian Institution Press.

———. 1997. *The Cool Knife: Imagery of Gender, Sexuality, and Moral Education in Kaguru Initiation Ritual*. Washington, DC: Smithsonian Institution Press.

Bellman, Beryl L. 1975. *Village of Curers and Assassins: On the Production of Fala Kpelle Cosmological Categories*. The Hague: Mouton.

Bird, Charles S., and Martha B. Kendall. 1980. "The Mande Hero: Text and Context." In *Exploration of African Systems of Thought*, edited by Ivan Karp and Charles S. Bird, 13–26. Washington, DC: Smithsonian Institution Press.

Bloch, Maurice. 1968. "Astrology and Writing in Madagascar." In *Literacy in Traditional Societies*, edited by Jack Goody, 278–97. Cambridge: Cambridge University Press.

Boddy, Janice. 1988. "Spirits and Selves in Northern Sudan: The Cultural Therapeutics of Possession and Trance." *American Ethnologist* 15 (1): 4–27.

———. 1989. *Wombs and Alien Spirits: Women, Men, and the Zar Cult in Northern Sudan*. Madison: University of Wisconsin Press.

Boone, Sylvia Ardyn. 1986. *Radiance from the Waters: Ideals of Feminine Beauty in Mende Art*. New Haven, CT: Yale University Press.

Bowen, John. 2007. *Why the French Don't Like Headscarves: Islam, the State, and Public Space*. Princeton, NJ: Princeton University Press.

———. 2010. *Can Islam Be French? Pluralism and Pragmatism in a Secularist State*. Princeton, NJ: Princeton University Press.

———. 2012. *A New Anthropology of Islam*. Cambridge: Cambridge University Press.

Brooks, George. 1993. "Historical Perspectives on the Guinea-Bissau Region, Fifteenth to Nineteenth Centuries." In *Mansas, Escravos, Grumetes e Gentio: Cacheu na Encruzilhada de Civilzações*, edited by Carlos Lopes, 27–54. Bissau: Instituto Nacional de Estudos e Pesquisa.

Bruner, Edward M. 1986. "Experience and Its Expressions." In *The Anthropology of Experience*, edited by Victor W. Turner and Edward M. Bruner, 3–30. Urbana: University of Illinois Press.

———. 2005. *Culture on Tour: Ethnographies of Travel*. Chicago: University of Chicago Press.

Carreira, Antonio. 1947. *Mandingas da Guiné Portuguesa*. Lisboa: Sociedade Industrial de Tipografia Limitada.

Carvalho, Clara. 2012. "Guinean Migrants Traditional Healers in the Global Market." In *Medicine, Mobility, and Power in Global Africa: Transnational Health and Healing*, edited by Hanjör Dilger, Abdoulaye Kane, and Stacy A. Langwick, 316–26. Bloomington: Indiana University Press.

Chapin, Bambi. 2014. *Childhood in a Sri Lankan Village: Shaping Hierarchy and Desire*. New Brunswick, NJ: Rutgers University Press.

Clifford, James. 1986. "Introduction: Partial Truths." In *Writing Culture: The Poetics and Politics of Ethnography*, edited by James Clifford and George E. Marcus, 1–26. Berkeley: University of California Press.

Coleman, Simon, and John Eade, eds. 2004. *Reframing Pilgrimage: Cultures in Motion*. London: Routledge.

Comaroff, Jean, and John L. Comaroff, eds. 1993. *Modernity and Its Malcontents: Ritual and Power in Postcolonial Africa*. Chicago: University of Chicago Press.

Combs-Schilling, M. E. 1989. *Sacred Performances: Islam, Sexuality, and Sacrifice*. New York: Columbia University Press.

Conrad, David C., and Barbara E. Frank. 1995. "Introduction: Nyamakalaya: Contradiction and Ambiguity in Mande Society." In *Status and Identity in West Africa: Nyamakalaw of Mande*, edited by David C. Conrad and Barbara E. Frank, 1–23. Bloomington: Indiana University Press.

D'Alisera, JoAnn. 2004. *An Imagined Geography: Sierra Leonean Muslims in America*. Philadelphia: University of Pennsylvania Press.

Daswani, Girish. 2015. *Looking Back, Moving Forward: Transformation and Ethical Practice in the Ghanaian Church of Pentecost*. Toronto: University of Toronto Press.

Davidson, Joanna. 2004. "Wombs and Tombs: Some Symbolic Dimensions of Burial Practices among the Diola of Guinea-Bissau." Paper presented at the American Ethnological Society meetings, Atlanta, GA, April 22–25.

———. 2016. *Sacred Rice: An Ethnography of Identity, Environment, and Development in Rural West Africa*. Oxford: Oxford University Press.

De Jong, Ferdinand. 2007. *Masquerades of Modernity: Power and Secrecy in Casamance, Senegal*. Edinburgh: Edinburgh University Press.

Delaney, Carol. 1990. "The 'Hajj': Sacred and Secular." *American Ethnologist* 17 (3): 513–30.

Dellenborg, Liselott. 2004. "A Reflection on the Cultural Meanings of Female Circumcision: Experiences from Fieldwork in Cassamance, Southern Senegal." In *Re-thinking Sexualities in Africa*, edited by Signe Arnfred, 79–94. Uppsala: Nordic Africa Institute.

Denny, Frederick Mathewson. 1988. "God's Friends: The Sanctity of Persons in Islam." In *Sainthood: Its Manifestations in World Religions*, edited by Richard Kieckhefer and George D. Bond, 69–97. Berkeley: University of California Press.

———. 2016. *An Introduction to Islam*. New York: Routledge.

De Vries, Hent, ed. 2008. *Religion beyond a Concept*. New York: Fordham University Press.

Diouf, Mamadou. 2000. "The Senegalese Murid Trade Diaspora and the Making of a Vernacular Cosmopolitanism." *Public Culture* 12 (3): 679–702.

Douglas, Mary. 1966. *Purity and Danger: An Analysis of the Concepts of Pollution and Taboo*. London: Routledge and Kegan Paul.

Dubisch, Jill, and Michael Winkelman, eds. 2005. "Introduction: The Anthropology of Pilgrimage." In *Pilgrimage and Healing*, edited by Jill Dubisch and Michael Winkelman, ix-xxxvi. Tucson: University of Arizona Press.

Durkheim, Émile. 1965. *The Elementary Forms of the Religious Life*. New York: Free Press.

Ebin, Victoria. 1996. "Making Room versus Creating Space: The Construction of Spatial Categories by Itinerant Mouride Traders." In *Making Muslim Space in North America and Europe*, edited by Barbara Daly Metcalf, 92–109. Berkeley: University of California Press.

Eickelman, Dale F. 1977. "Ideological Change and Regional Cults: Maraboutism and Ties of 'Closeness' in Western Morocco." In *Regional Cults*, edited by R. P. Werbner, 3–28. London: Academic Press.

Eickelman, Dale F., and James Piscatori, eds. 1990. *Muslim Travelers: Pilgrimage, Migration, and the Religious Imagination*. Berkeley: University of California Press.

Einarsdóttir, Jónína. 2004. *Tired of Weeping: Mother Love, Child Death, and Poverty in Guinea-Bissau*. Madison: University of Wisconsin Press.

Ferguson, James. 2006. *Global Shadows: Africa in the Neoliberal World Order*. Durham, NC: Duke University Press.

Ferme, Marianne. 1994. "What 'Alhaji Airplane' Saw in Mecca, and What Happened When He Came Home." In *Syncretism/Anti-syncretism: The Politics of Religious Synthesis*, edited by Charles Stewart and Rosalind Shaw, 27–44. London: Routledge.

Fesenmyer, Leslie. 2016. "'Assistance but Not Support': Pentecostalism and the Reconfiguring of Relatedness between Kenya and the United Kingdom." In *Affective Circuits: African Migrations to Europe and the Pursuit of Social Regeneration*, edited by Jennifer Cole and Christian Groes, 125–45. Chicago: University of Chicago Press.

Fikes, Kesha. 2009. *Managing African Portugal: The Citizen-Migrant Distinction*. Durham, NC: Duke University Press.

Forrest, Joshua. 1992. *Guinea-Bissau: Power, Conflict, and Renewal in a West African Nation*. Boulder, CO: Westview Press.

Gable, Eric. 1995. "The Decolonization of Consciousness: Local Skeptics and the 'Will to Be Modern' in a West African Village." *American Ethnologist* 22 (2): 242–57.

———. 2000. "The Culture Development Club: Youth, Neo-tradition, and the Construction of Society in Guinea-Bissau." *Anthropology Quarterly* 73 (4): 195–203.

———. 2006. "The Funeral and Modernity in Manjaco." *Cultural Anthropology* 21 (3): 385–415.

———. 2011. *Anthropology and Egalitarianism: Ethnographic Encounters from Monticello to Guinea-Bissau*. Bloomington: Indiana University Press.

Geertz, Clifford. 1960. *The Religion of Java*. Chicago: University of Chicago Press.

———. 1968. *Islam Observed: Religious Development in Morocco and Indonesia*. New Haven, CT: Yale University Press.

———. 1973. *The Interpretation of Cultures*. New York: Basic Books.

Gemmeke, Amber. 2009. "Marabout Women in Dakar: Creating Authority in Islamic Knowledge." *Africa* 79 (1): 128–47.

Geschiere, Peter. 1997. *The Modernity of Witchcraft: Politics and the Occult in Postcolonial Africa*. Charlottesville: University Press of Virginia.

———. 2005. "Funerals and Belonging: Different Patterns in South Cameroon." *African Studies Review* 48 (2): 45–64.

Gluckman, Max. 1965. *Politics, Law and Ritual in Tribal Society*. New York: New American Library.

Goody, Jack. 1962. *Death, Property and the Ancestors: A Study of the Mortuary Customs of the LoDagaa of West Africa*. Stanford: Stanford University Press.

———. 1968. "Restricted Literacy in Northern Ghana." In *Literacy in Traditional Society*, edited by Jack Goody, 199–264. Cambridge: Cambridge University Press.

———. 2000. *The Power of the Written Tradition*. Washington, DC: Smithsonian Institution Press.

Gosselin, Claudie. 2000. "Feminism, Anthropology and the Politics of Excision in Mali: Global and Local Debates in a Postcolonial World." *Anthropologica* 42:43–60.

Gottlieb, Alma. 1989. "Witches, Kings, and the Sacrifice of Identity or the Power of Paradox and the Paradox of Power among the Beng of Ivory Coast." In *Creativity of Power*, edited by Ivan Karp and W. Arens, 245–72. Washington, DC: Smithsonian Institution Press.

———. 1992. *Under the Kapok Tree: Identity and Difference in Beng Thought*. Bloomington: Indiana University Press.

———. 2004. *The Afterlife Is Where We Come From: The Culture of Infancy in West Africa*. Chicago: University of Chicago Press.

Granqvist, Hilma. 1975. *Birth and Childhood among the Arabs: Studies in a Muhammadan Village in Palestine*. New York: AMS Press.

Graw, Knut. 2012. "On the Cause of Migration: Being and Nothingness in the African-European Border Zone." In *The Global Horizon: Expectations of Migration in Africa and the Middle East*, edited by Knut Graw and Samuli Schielke, 23–42. Leuven, Belgium: Leuven University Press.

Gruenbaum, Ellen. 2001. *The Female Circumcision Controversy: An Anthropological Perspective*. Philadelphia: University of Pennsylvania Press.

Hastrup, Kirsten, and Karen Fog Olwig. 1997. "Introduction." In *Siting Culture: The Shifting Anthropological Object*, edited by Karen Fog Olwig and Kirsten Hastrup, 1–14. London: Routledge.

Hernlund, Ylva. 2000. "Cutting without Ritual and Ritual without Cutting:
    Female 'Circumcision' and the Re-ritualizaiton of Initiation in the Gambia."
    In *Female "Circumcision" in Africa: Culture, Controversy, and Change*, edited by
    Bettina Shell-Duncan and Ylva Hernlund, 235–52. Boulder, CO: Lynne Rienner.
Hertz, Robert. 1973. "The Pre-eminence of the Right Hand: A Study in Religious
    Polarity." In *Right and Left: Essays on Dual Symbolic Classification*, edited by
    Rodney Needham, 3–31. Chicago: University of Chicago Press.
Hutchinson, Sharon. 1996. *Nuer Dilemmas: Coping with Money, War, and the State.*
    Berkeley: University of California Press.
———. 2000. "Identity and Substance: The Broadening of Bases of Relatedness
    among the Nuer of Southern Sudan." In *Cultures of Relatedness: New Approaches
    to the Study of Kinship*, edited by Janet Carsten, 55–72. Cambridge: Cambridge
    University Press.
Jackson, Michael. 1977. *The Kuranko: Dimensions of Social Reality in a West African
    Society.* London: C. Hurst.
———. 1989. *Paths toward a Clearing: Radical Empiricism and Ethnographic Inquiry.*
    Bloomington: Indiana University Press.
———. 2011. *Life within Limits: Well-Being in a World of Want.* Durham, NC: Duke
    University Press.
Jacobson-Widding, Anita. 1979. *Red-White-Black as a Mode of Thought: A Study of
    Triadic Classification by Colours in the Ritual Symbolism and Cognitive Thought of
    the Peoples of the Lower Congo.* Uppsala: Almqvist and Wiksell International.
Janson, Marloes. 2013. *Islam, Youth and Modernity in the Gambia: The Tablighi
    Jama'at.* Cambridge: Cambridge University Press.
Johnson, Michelle C. 2000. "Becoming a Muslim; Becoming a Person: Female
    'Circumcision,' Religious Identity, and Personhood in Guinea Bissau." In *Female
    "Circumcision" in Africa: Culture, Controversy, and Change*, edited by Bettina
    Shell-Duncan and Ylva Hernlund, 215–33. Boulder, CO: Lynne Rienner.
———. 2006. "The Proof Is on My Palm: Debating Islam and Ritual in a New
    African Diaspora." *Journal of Religion in Africa* 36 (1): 50–77.
———. 2007. "Making Mandinga or Making Muslims? Debating Female
    Circumcision, Ethnicity and Islam in Guinea-Bissau and Portugal." In
    Transcultural Bodies: Female Genital Cutting in Global Context, edited by Bettina
    Shell-Duncan and Ylva Hernlund, 202–23. New Brunswick, NJ: Rutgers
    University Press.
———. 2013. "Culture's Calling: Mobile Phones, Gender, and the Making of an
    African Migrant Village in Lisbon." *Anthropology Quarterly* 86 (1): 163–90.
———. 2016. "'Nothing Is Sweet in My Mouth': Food, Identity, and Religion in
    African Lisbon." *Food and Foodways* 24 (3–4): 234–56.
———. 2017. "'Never Forgot Where You're From': Raising Guinean Muslim Babies
    in Portugal." In *A World of Babies: Imagined Childcare Guides for Eight Societies*,

edited by Alma Gottlieb and Judy DeLoache, 33–70. Cambridge: Cambridge University Press.

———. n.d. "'His Name Is Garbage': Bono Names as Mystical Warfare in Guinea-Bissau." Unpublished manuscript.

Jónsson, Gunvor. 2012. "Migration, Identity and Immobility in a Malian Soninke Village." In *The Global Horizon: Migratory Expectations in Africa and the Middle East*, edited by Knut Graw and Samuli Schielke, 106–20. Leuven, Belgium: Leuven University Press.

Kempny, Marian. 2005. "History of the Manchester 'School' and the Extended-Case Method." *Social Analysis* 49 (3): 144–65.

Kleinman, Julie. 2016. "From Little Brother to Big Somebody: Coming of Age at the Gare du Nord." In *Affective Circuits: African Migrations to Europe and the Pursuit of Social Regeneration*, edited by Jennifer Cole and Christian Groes, 245–68. Chicago: University of Chicago Press.

Kouba, Leonard J., and Judith Muasher. 1985. "Female Circumcision in Africa: An Overview." In *African Studies Review* 28 (1): 95–110.

Kratz, Corrine A. 1994. *Affecting Performance: Meaning, Movement, and Experience in Okiek Women's Initiation*. Washington, DC: Smithsonian Institution Press.

Lamb, Sarah. 2000. *White Saris and Sweet Mangoes: Aging, Gender, and Body in Northern India*. Berkeley: University of California Press.

Lambek, Michael. 1993. *Knowledge and Practice in Mayote: Local Discourses on Islam, Sorcery and Spirit Possession*. Toronto: University of Toronto Press.

Lambek, Michael, and Andrew Strathern, eds. 1998. *Bodies and Persons: Comparative Perspectives from Africa and Melanesia*. Cambridge: Cambridge University Press.

Latham, James E. 1982. *The Religious Symbolism of Salt*. Paris: Éditions Beauchesne.

Launay, Robert. 2004. *Beyond the Stream: Islam and Society in a West African Town*. Long Grove, IL: Waveland Press.

———, ed. 2016. *Islamic Education in Africa: Writing Boards and Blackboards*. Bloomington: Indiana University Press.

Leichtman, Mara A. 2016. *Shi'i Cosmopolitanisms in Africa: Lebanese Migration and Religious Conversion in Senegal*. Bloomington: Indiana University Press.

Levitt, Peggy, and Nina Glick Schiller. 2004. "Conceptualizing Simultaneity: A Transnational Social Field Perspective on Society." *International Migration Review* 38 (3): 1002–39.

Livingstone, E. A., ed. 1997. "Salt." In *The Oxford Dictionary of the Christian Church*, 1447–48. 3rd ed. Oxford: Oxford University Press.

Lopes, Carlos. 1987. *Guinea-Bissau: From Liberation Struggle to Independent Statehood*. Translated by Michael Wolfers. Boulder, CO: Westview Press.

MacCormack, Carol P. 1979. "Sande: The Public Face of a Secret Society." *New Religions of Africa*, edited by Bennetta Jules-Rosette, 27–37. Norwood, NJ: Ablex.

Machado, Fernando Luis. 1998. "Da Guiné-Bissau a Portugal: Luso-Guineenses e Imigrantes." *Sociologia: Problemas e Practicas* 26:9–56. Lisbon: Centro de Investigação de Estudos de Sociologia, ISCTE.

Marcus, Ivan. 1996. *Rituals of Childhood: Jewish Acculturation in Medieval Europe.* New Haven, CT: Yale University Press.

Martin, Richard C. 1987. "Muslim Pilgrimage." In *The Encyclopedia of Religion,* edited by Mircea Eiade, 11:338–46. New York: Macmillan.

Masquelier, Adeline. 2001. *Prayer Has Spoiled Everything: Possession, Power, and Identity in an Islamic Town of Niger.* Durham, NC: Duke University Press.

———. 2009. *Women and Islamic Revival in a West African Town.* Bloomington: Indiana University Press.

McIntosh, Janet. 2009. *The Edge of Islam: Power, Personhood, and Ethnoreligious Boundaries on the Kenya Coast.* Durham, NC: Duke University Press.

McIntyre, J. A. 1996. "A Cultural Given and a Hidden Influence: Koranic Teachers in Kano." In *The Politics of Cultural Performance,* edited by David Parkin, Lionel Caplan, and Humphrey Fisher, 237–74. Providence, RI: Berghan Books.

Mebenga, Luc. 1991. "Les funérailles chez les Ewondo, changements socio-culturels, changements économiques et évaluation de l'esprit de solidarité." Thesis, University of Yaoundé I.

Mendy, Peter Karibe, and Richard Lobban Jr. 2013. *The Historical Dictionary of the Republic of Guinea-Bissau.* 4th ed. Plymouth, UK: Scarecrow Press.

Metcalf, Barbara Daly, ed. 1996. *Making Muslim Space in North America and Europe.* Berkeley: University of California Press.

Metcalf, Peter, and Richard Huntington. 1991. *Celebrations of Death: The Anthropology of Mortuary Ritual.* Cambridge: Cambridge University Press.

Mommersteeg, Geert. 2012. *In the City of the Marabouts: Islamic Culture in West Africa.* Long Grove, IL: Waveland Press.

Morinis, Alan, ed. 1992. *Sacred Journeys: The Anthropology of Pilgrimage.* Westport, CT: Greenwood Press.

Narayan, Kirin. 2012. *Alive in the Writing: Crafting Ethnography in the Company of Chekhov.* Chicago: University of Chicago Press.

Needham, Rodney. 1967. "Percussion and Transition." *Man* 2 (4): 606–14.

———, ed. 1973. *Right and Left: Essays on Dual Symbolic Classification.* Chicago: University of Chicago Press.

Ortner, Sherry B. 1973. "On Key Symbols." *American Anthropologist* 75 (5): 1338–46.

Ottenberg, Simon. 1989. *Boyhood Rituals in an African Society: An Interpretation.* Seattle: University of Washington Press.

Prazak, Miroslava. 2016. *Making the Mark: Gender, Identity, and Genital Cutting.* Athens: Ohio University Press.

Quinn, Charlotte A. 1972. *Mandinga Kingdoms of the Senegambia: Traditionalism, Islam and European Expansion.* Evanston, IL: Northwestern University Press.

Rasmussen, Susan J. 1997. *The Poetics and Politics of Tuareg Aging: Life Course and Personal Destiny in Niger.* Dekalb: Northern Illinois University Press.

———. 2006. *Those Who Touch: Tuareg Medicine Women in Anthropological Perspective.* DeKalb: Northern Illinois University Press.

Riccio, Bruno, and Stefano degli Uberti. 2013. "Senegalese Migrants in Italy: Beyond the Assimilation/Transnationalism Divide." *Urban Anthropology and Studies of Cultural Systems and World Economic Development* 42 (3/4): 207–54.

Richards, Audrey. 1982. *Chisungu: A Girls' Initiation Ceremony among the Bemba of Zambia.* London: Routledge.

Riesman, Paul. 1992. *First Find Yourself a Good Mother: The Construction of Self in Two African Communities.* Edited by David L. Szanton, Lila Abu-Lughod, Sharon Hutchinson, Paul Stoller, and Carol Trosset. New Brunswick, NJ: Rutgers University Press.

———. 1998. *Freedom in Fulani Social Life: An Introspective Ethnography.* Chicago: University of Chicago Press.

Sanneh, Lamin O. 1979. *The Jakhanke: The History of an Islamic Clerical People of the Senegambia.* London: International African Institute.

———. 1997. *The Crown and the Turban: Muslims and West African Pluralism.* Boulder, CO: Westview Press.

Schaffer, Matt, and Christine Cooper. 1987. *Mandinko: The Ethnography of a West African Holy Land.* Prospect Heights, IL: Waveland Press.

Schloss, Mark. 1988. *The Hatchet's Blood: Separation, Power, and Gender in Ehing Social Life.* Tucson: University of Arizona Press.

Schulz, Dorothea. 2012. *Muslims and New Media in West Africa: Pathways to God.* Bloomington: Indiana University Press.

Selby, Jennifer A. 2012. *Questioning French Secularism: Gender Politics and Islam in a Parisian Suburb.* New York: Palgrave Macmillan.

Shell-Duncan, Bettina, and Ylva Hernlund, eds. 2000. *Female "Circumcision" in Africa: Culture, Controversy, and Change.* Boulder, CO: Lynn Rienner.

Simpson, Edward, and Kai Kresse. 2008. "Introduction: Cosmopolitanism Contested: Anthropology and History in the Western Indian Ocean." In *Struggling with History: Islam and Cosmopolitanism in the Western Indian Ocean,* edited by Edward Simpson and Kai Kresse, 1–41. New York: Columbia University Press.

Smith, Daniel Jordan. 2004. "Burials and Belonging in Nigeria: Rural-Urban Relations and Social Inequality in a Contemporary African Ritual." *American Anthropologist* 106 (3): 569–79.

Smith, Jane Idleman, and Yvonne Yazbeck Haddad. 1981. *The Islamic Understanding of Death and Resurrection.* Albany: State University of New York Press.

Soares, Benjamin. 2005. *Islam and the Prayer Economy: History and Authority in a Malian Town.* Ann Arbor: University of Michigan Press.

Stafford, Charles. 2000. *Separation and Reunion in Modern China*. Cambridge: Cambridge University Press.

Stoller, Paul. 1989. *The Taste of Ethnographic Things: The Senses in Anthropology*. Philadelphia: University of Pennsylvania Press.

———. 2002. *Money Has No Smell: The Africanization of New York City*. Chicago: University of Chicago Press.

———. 2014. Yaya's Story: The Quest for Well-Being in the World. Chicago: University of Chicago Press.

Stoller, Paul, and Cheryl Olkes. 1987. *In Sorcery's Shadow: A Memoir of Apprenticeship among the Songhay of Niger*. Chicago: University of Chicago Press.

Thayer, James Steel. 1992. "Pilgrimage and Its Influence on West African Islam." In *Sacred Journeys: The Anthropology of Pilgrimage*, edited by Alan Morinis, 169–87. Westport, CT: Greenwood Press.

Trachtenberg, Joshua. 2004. *Jewish Magic and Superstition: A Study in Folk Religion*. Philadelphia: University of Pennsylvania Press.

Turner, Victor. 1967. *The Forest of Symbols: Aspects of Ndembu Ritual*. Ithaca, NY: Cornell University Press.

———. 1974. *Dramas, Fields, and Metaphors: Symbolic Action in Human Society*. Ithaca, NY: Cornell University Press.

Turner, Victor, and Edith Turner. 1978. *Image and Pilgrimage in Christian Culture: Anthropological Perspectives*. New York: Columbia University Press.

Urdang, Stephanie. 1979. *Fighting Two Colonialisms: Women in Guinea-Bissau*. New York: Monthly Review Press.

Van Dijk, Rijk A. 1997. "From Camp to Encompassment: Discourses of Transsubjectivity in the Ghanaian Pentecostal Diaspora." *Journal of Religion in Africa* 27 (2): 135–59.

Van Gennep, Arnold. 1960. *The Rites of Passage*. Chicago: University of Chicago Press.

Ware, Rudolph T. III. 2014. *The Walking Qur'an: Islamic Education, Embodied Knowledge, and History in West Africa*. Chapel Hill: University of North Carolina Press.

W.E.C. International. 1995. *Mandinka English Dictionary*. Banjul, the Gambia: Adult Literacy Department.

Weiss, Brad. 1992. "Plastic Teeth Extraction: The Iconography of Haya Gastro-Sexual Affliction." *American Ethnologist* 19 (4): 538–52.

———. 1996. *The Making and Unmaking of the Haya Lived World: Consumption, Commoditization, and Everyday Practice*. Durham, NC: Duke University Press.

———. 1997. "Forgetting Your Dead: Alienable and Inalienable Objects in Northwest Tanzania." *Anthropology Quarterly* 70 (4): 164–72.

———. 2009. *Street Dreams and Hip Hop Barbershops*. Bloomington: Indiana University Press.

Werbner, Pnina. 1990. *The Migration Process: Capital, Gifts, and Offerings among British Pakistanis*. New York: Berg.

———. 2008. "Introduction: Toward a New Cosmopolitan Anthropology." In *Anthropology and the New Cosmopolitanism*, edited by Pnina Werber, 1–29. Oxford: Berg.

Werbner, Richard. 2002. "Postcolonial Subjectivities: The Personal, the Political and the Moral." In *Postcolonial Subjectivities in Africa*, edited by Richard Werbner, 1–21. London: Zed Books.

———. 2015. *Divination's Grasp: African Encounters with the Almost Said*. Bloomington: Indiana University Press.

Wieschhoff, Heinz A. 1973. "Concepts of Right and Left in African Cultures." In *Right and Left: Essays on Dual Symbolic Classification*, edited by Rodney Needham, 59–73. Chicago: University of Chicago Press.

Winkel, Eric. 1995. "A Muslim Perspective on Female Circumcision." *Women and Health* 23 (1): 1–7.

INDEX

Page numbers in *italics* indicate photographs.

MICHELLE C. JOHNSON is a cultural anthropologist who specializes in religion and ritual in West Africa and among African immigrants in Europe. She has conducted extensive fieldwork with Muslims in Guinea-Bissau and with Guinean Muslim immigrants in Lisbon, Portugal. She has held grants from the Social Science Research Council, the Department of Education (Fulbright-Hays), and the Woodrow Wilson Foundation and has authored numerous articles and book chapters, including "'Never Forget Where You're From': Raising Guinean Muslim Babies in Portugal" in *A World of Babies: Imagined Childcare Guides for Eight Societies* and "'Nothing Is Sweet in My Mouth': Food, Identity, and Religion in African Portugal." She is Professor of Anthropology in the Department of Sociology and Anthropology at Bucknell University. She was awarded the 2019 Class of 1956 Lectureship for Inspirational Teaching.

www.ingramcontent.com/pod-product-compliance
Lightning Source LLC
Chambersburg PA
CBHW020532270326
41927CB00006B/547